Working With Legal Assistants

A Team Approach for Lawyers and Legal Assistants

Paul G. Ulrich and Robert S. Mucklestone, Editors

Published by the Section of Economics of Law Practice
and the Standing Committee on Legal Assistants
of the American Bar Association

Copyright © 1980 American Bar Association
Produced by the ABA Press
International Standard Book Number: 0-89707-030-5
Library of Congress Catalog Card Number: 80-69532

SUMMARY OF CONTENTS

	Page
Introduction	iii
Table of Contents	vii

1. Organizing, Developing and Managing a Program
   Paul G. Ulrich 1

2. Economic Benefits and Working Relationships
   Donald S. Akins 21

3. The Government Law Office
   Kathryn M. Braeman, Larrine S. Holbrooke and Christine L. Perko 39

4. Creating Your Own Legal Assistant Position
   Karen J. Feyerherm 63

5. Investigation and Fact-Gathering
   Patricia S. Kottner 69

6. Factual Research, Analysis, Discovery and Document Control
   Evelyn E. Rasmussen 93

7. Trial Practice
   Thomas H. Watkins and Cathy Logue 119

8. Insurance Defense Litigation
   Larry L. Gollaher 145

9. Medical-Legal Practice
   Carol J. Morris 157

10. Bankruptcy Practice
    H. Rey Stroube III 185

11. Domestic and Family Law Practice
    Donn C. Fullenweider 209

12. The Corporate Setting
    Melvin S. Merzon 229

13. Appellate Practice
    Paul G. Ulrich 241

Index 257

INTRODUCTION

This book has been sponsored by the American Bar Association's Section of Economics of Law Practice and its Standing Committee on Legal Assistants. It is dedicated to those lawyers, legal administrators, educators and assistants who have worked together to improve the quality of legal services by developing the legal assistant profession. This volume, and a second to follow, are intended to provide a comprehensive source of ideas, guidelines, systems and procedures for working with assistants throughout the practice of law.

Lawyers have always employed assistants. Only in the past decade, however, has a clearly identifiable legal assistant profession emerged. The American Bar Association has been actively involved in encouraging legal assistant education and employment. In 1968, the House of Delegates adopted a resolution calling for a committee, now the Standing Committee on Legal Assistants, to consider the development, encouragement, increased education and employment of non-lawyer assistants to enable lawyers better to discharge their professional responsibilities. Resolutions, 54 A.B.A.J. 1017, 1021-22 (1968). By 1971, this committee had begun to issue reports and proposals concerning a proposed curriculum for law office personnel, and the education and use of legal assistants. See Proposed Curriculum for Training of Law Office Personnel (A.B.A. 1971) and The Training and Use of Legal Assistants: A Status Report (A.B.A. 1974). Similarly, the American Bar Association's former Standing Committee on the Economics of Law Practice and its present Section of Economics of Law Practice also have been concerned with the effective employment of assistants. See, *e.g.*, L. Turner, *Effective Use of Lay Personnel*, in Proceedings of the Third National Conference on Law Office Economics and Management 27 (A.B.A. 1969). That Section has included a committee on legal assistants since its inception. See Legal Economics, Spring 1975, at 37.

During the past few years, much has been written concerning the development and management of law firm legal assistant programs and the effective use of assistants in various categories of law practice. However, these materials have appeared in widely scattered sources, many are not generally available and they often have been written solely with reference to only one state's practice. Several books have recently appeared concerning legal assistant practice and procedures. But many of these are written primarily for assistants — not lawyers and assistants together. This book has been designed to consolidate those scattered efforts, and to focus on the lawyer's role and responsibilities in the employment and use of legal assistants.

This project was begun by the Economics of Law Practice Section's Non-Lawyer Personnel Committee in September, 1979. A steering group representing lawyers, legal assistants, educators, law firm administrators and consultants was formed to solicit chapters, review manuscript drafts and coordinate the book's preparation. Its members are Donald S. Akins, Cathy Logue, Robert S. Mucklestone, Evelyn E. Rasmussen, Paul G. Ulrich and Thomas H. Watkins.

This volume describes some of the many areas of law practice in which legal assistants may be employed effectively. It primarily concerns the management considerations involved in employing assistants, and the use of assistants in civil litigation and appellate practice in private law firms. Its chapters on corporate law departments and government law offices, however, confirm that assistants are employed there as well. The second volume will discuss corporate, labor, real estate, estate planning and probate practice. Chapters are also planned on the use of assistants in criminal practice, in legal service corporations, in state and local governmental agencies, in solo practice or small firms, and in legal research. There will also be a chapter on the professional responsibility considerations in this field.

This book has been written to be a practical and useful guide. Forms, procedure guides and checklists have been included wherever possible. Although substantive law and procedure often vary substantially from state to state, fifty-state surveys of all areas would not be feasible. Authors have therefore often chosen as their examples forms or procedures based upon the law of the state with which they are most familiar. It should be clearly understood that those discussions, forms and procedures are intended only as illustrations. Adaptations will often be required for other jurisdictions.

The chapters in this volume have been prepared by the authors shown for each. They have, however, been edited for consistency of style and to avoid unnecessary duplication. Conscious efforts have been made to combine the benefits of drafting and revision by experienced writers, steering group discussions and suggestions, and intensive editing to produce a book of consistent style and quality. The organization and procedures followed in creating the Arizona Appellate Handbook (State Bar of Arizona, 1978) have been adapted for this purpose. See L. Haire and P. Ulrich, *Writing an Appellate Practice Handbook: A Team Approach to Preparing Continuing Legal Education Texts*, Ariz. B. J., Dec. 1977, at 60, reprinted in ALI-ABA CLE Review, Nos. 1-3, Jan. 1978.

This volume has incorporated and benefited substantially from the many constructive suggestions made by those who reviewed its draft chapters or otherwise assisted in its preparation. The steering group and the various authors, of course, retain responsibility for its quality, accuracy and conclusions. We appreciate the American Bar Association's making this volume's publication possible and thank everyone who provided the necessary editorial and secretarial assistance. Special thanks in these regards go to Christine Spall, our editorial assistant and indexer, and to the Lewis and Roca word processing center staff.

The use of legal assistants has grown, developed and changed steadily during the past ten years. This evolution will undoubtedly continue as more law offices begin to employ assistants and as those already doing so further develop their programs and their assistants' capabilities in additional areas. This volume is current concerning the law and procedures discussed as of September 1, 1980. Any more recent authorities available should also be consulted to ensure that no subsequent changes have affected its discussion in any particular area.

As this book has grown, we have become increasingly aware of the many areas in which legal assistants may be usefully employed. We hope it will provide a useful reference for those lawyers already having a well-developed assistant program, for those whose experience with assistants is more limited, for legal assistant educators

Introduction

and for legal assistants. This book's ultimate value will lie in encouraging lawyers to employ assistants throughout their practice, as well as providing a reference source for assistants. If this occurs, the efforts of all those involved in preparing it will have been well spent.

>American Bar Association
>
>Section of Economics of Law Practice
>Selection, Training and Utilization of Support Staff Committee
>
>Standing Committee on Legal Assistants
>
>Paul G. Ulrich and
>Robert S. Mucklestone, Editors

November, 1980

TABLE OF CONTENTS

1

ORGANIZING, DEVELOPING AND MANAGING A PROGRAM

Paul G. Ulrich

		Page
§ 1.1	This Chapter's Scope	1
§ 1.2	Developing a Systems Approach	1
	§ 1.2.1 Use of Systems Techniques in Developing Law Practice Systems	1
	§ 1.2.2 Using Management by Objectives and Management by Exception Techniques	2
	§ 1.2.3 Application of Systems Management Techniques to Legal Assistants	2
	§ 1.2.3.1 Substantive Law Practice	2
	§ 1.2.3.2 The Legal Assistant Program	3
§ 1.3	Recruiting Legal Assistants	4
§ 1.4	Developing a Professional Approach in Working Relationships	5
	§ 1.4.1 Application to Legal Assistant Programs	5
§ 1.5	Productivity and Profitability Considerations	6
§ 1.6	Establishing a Review and Evaluation Program	7
§ 1.7	Increasing Legal Assistant Responsibilities — The Long-Term Prospects	9
§ 1.8	Summary and Conclusion	9
§ 1.9	Institutions Offering Legal Assistant Education Programs	9
§ 1.10	Selected Bibliography for Legal Assistant Program Managers	18

2

ECONOMIC BENEFITS AND WORKING RELATIONSHIPS

Donald S. Akins

§ 2.1	This Chapter's Scope	21
§ 2.2	The Economics of Using Legal Assistants	21
	§ 2.2.1 The Economic Need	21
	§ 2.2.2 Expense Factors	22
	§ 2.2.2.1 Salary	22
	§ 2.2.2.2 Secretarial Expense	22
	§ 2.2.2.3 Taxes	22
	§ 2.2.2.4 Fringe Benefits	22
	§ 2.2.2.5 Office Rent	22
	§ 2.2.2.6 Dictation Equipment	22

				Page
		§ 2.2.2.7 Furniture		23
	§ 2.2.3	Quotas		23
	§ 2.2.4	Income Production		23
	§ 2.2.5	Immediate Hurdles		23
		§ 2.2.5.1 Client Acceptance		24
		§ 2.2.5.2 Judges' Recognition of Legal Assistants' Billing Rates		24
		§ 2.2.5.3 Acceptance by Opposing Counsel		24
§ 2.3	Continuing Education			24
	§ 2.3.1	Dedication of Lawyers		24
	§ 2.3.2	Office Policies and Procedures		25
	§ 2.3.3	Substantive Education		25
	§ 2.3.4	Legal Assistant Retreats		25
§ 2.4	Working Relationships with Staff			26
	§ 2.4.1	Other Legal Assistants		26
	§ 2.4.2	Secretaries		26
	§ 2.4.3	Bookkeepers		26
	§ 2.4.4	Records Department		26
	§ 2.4.5	Word Processing		26
§ 2.5	The Firm's Office Administrator and the Legal Assistant			27
	§ 2.5.1	The Administrator's Role		27
	§ 2.5.2	Interviewing and Hiring		27
	§ 2.5.3	Education		27
	§ 2.5.4	Evaluation		27
§ 2.6	Access to Support Services			28
	§ 2.6.1	Access to Secretarial/Word Processing Services		28
	§ 2.6.2	Reproduction of Documents		28
§ 2.7	Stress			28
	§ 2.7.1	Deadlines		28
	§ 2.7.2	Unavailable Lawyers		28
	§ 2.7.3	Word Processing		29
	§ 2.7.4	Work Area and Conditions		29
	§ 2.7.5	Unkept Promises		29
	§ 2.7.6	Diversity of Assignments		29
§ 2.8	Use in Firm Administration			29
	§ 2.8.1	Small Firms		29
	§ 2.8.2	Medium to Large Firms		30
	§ 2.8.3	Income Production		30
§ 2.9	Summary and Conclusion			30

FORMS

		Page
2:1	Legal Assistant Projections	31
2:2	Litigation Legal Assistant — Job Description	32
2:3	Position Descriptions	33
2:4	Director of Administration — Job Description	35
2:5	Legal Assistant Evaluation Form	38

Table of Contents

3

THE GOVERNMENT LAW OFFICE

Kathryn M. Braeman, Larrine S. Holbrooke and Christine L. Perko

		Page
§ 3.1	This Chapter's Scope	39
§ 3.2	Incentives to Hiring Paralegals for Government Law Offices	39
§ 3.3	Factors to Consider in Hiring Paralegals for Government Law Offices	40
§ 3.4	The Paralegal and Legal Clerk/Technician Series	41
§ 3.5	Hiring a Paralegal	41
§ 3.6	Effective Use of Paralegals	42
§ 3.7	Organizing Work for Delegation to the Paralegal	43
§ 3.8	The Team Approach to Legal Assignments	44

FORMS

3:1	Some Observations on Preparing a Paralegal Specialist Job Description	45
3:2	Position Descriptions	47
3:3	Managing Litigation for the Federal Government, by Carol Essrick	56
	§ 3A3.1 Introduction	56
	§ 3A3.2 The Team Approach to Litigation	56
	§ 3A3.3 Role of the Paralegal and Other Nonlawyer Support Personnel in Managing Litigation on Behalf of the United States Government	56
	§ 3A3.3.1 The Paralegal's Role	56
	§ 3A3.3.2 Duties Performed by the Paralegal	57
	§ 3A3.3.3 The Legal Technician's Role	57
	§ 3A3.3.4 The Legal Clerk's Role	57
	§ 3A3.4 Discovery	57
	§ 3A3.5 Review of Documents in Preparation of Case-in-Chief	58
	§ 3A3.6 Computers and Litigation	59
	§ 3A3.7 Preparation of the Trial Brief	59
	§ 3A3.8 Preparation of Exhibits	59
	§ 3A3.9 Exhibit Books	59
	§ 3A3.10 Witness Folders	59
	§ 3A3.11 Preparation of Trial Record	60
	§ 3A3.12 Preparation of Witness Testimony	60
3:4	Guidelines for Retaining Paralegals	61

4

CREATING YOUR OWN LEGAL ASSISTANT POSITION

Karen J. Feyerherm

		Page
§ 4.1	This Chapter's Scope	63
§ 4.2	Before You Begin Your Search for Employment	63
§ 4.3	Where to Begin Your Search	64
	§ 4.3.1 Explore the Resources in Your Present Office	64
	§ 4.3.1.1 Promotion Possibilities	64
	§ 4.3.1.2 Lawyers as Resources	64
	§ 4.3.2 Consult Reference Books	64
	§ 4.3.2.1 Law Firms	64
	§ 4.3.2.2 Corporations	64
	§ 4.3.2.3 Government Agencies	64
	§ 4.3.4 Read the Local Newspapers	65
§ 4.4	Arranging for the Interview	65
	§ 4.4.1 Sending a Resume and Letter of Application	65
	§ 4.4.2 Using the Telephone	65
	§ 4.4.3 Distributing Business Cards	65
§ 4.5	Convincing the Lawyer of the Need for a Legal Assistant	66
	§ 4.5.1 Prepare a Portfolio	66
	§ 4.5.2 Check Into Certification Procedures	66
	§ 4.5.3 Make the "Unsuccessful" Interview Worthwhile	66
§ 4.6	Creating the Position	66
	§ 4.6.1 Define Your Responsibilities	66
	§ 4.6.2 Know Your Limits in Accepting Assignments	67
§ 4.7	Developing a System	67
§ 4.8	Conclusion	67

5

INVESTIGATION AND FACT-GATHERING

Patricia S. Kottner

§ 5.1	This Chapter's Scope	69
§ 5.2	Establishing the Lawyer-Legal Assistant Roles	69
§ 5.3	The Investigative Process: Initial Stages	69
	§ 5.3.1 Client Interview or Initial Conference with Lawyer	69
	§ 5.3.2 The Case's Background	70
	§ 5.3.3 Objectives and Reporting	70
	§ 5.3.4 Checklists	70
	§ 5.3.5 File Organization	70
§ 5.4	Skip-Tracing: Location of Witnesses	70
	§ 5.4.1 Telephone and Other Directories	71

Table of Contents

			Page
	§ 5.4.2	Post Office Check	71
	§ 5.4.3	Registrar of Voters	71
	§ 5.4.4	Motor Vehicle Department	71
	§ 5.4.5	Credit Bureau	71
	§ 5.4.6	Other Investigative Sources	72
§ 5.5	Agencies as Sources of Information		72
	§ 5.5.1	Court Property and Records	72
	§ 5.5.2	General Sources	73
§ 5.6	Interviewing Witnesses		73
	§ 5.6.1	General Considerations	73
	§ 5.6.2	Taking a Written Statement	74
	§ 5.6.3	Expert Witnesses	75
§ 5.7	Summary and Conclusion		75

FORMS

5:1	Client Interview Sheet	76
5:2	Personal Injury Investigation Checklist	81
5:3	Incorporation Checklist	83
5:4	File Control Sheet	85
5:5	Investigative Checklist	87
5:6	Voter Registration Affidavit	88
5:7	Arizona MVD Title Search Report	89
5:8	Witness Questionnaire	90

6

FACTUAL RESEARCH, ANALYSIS, DISCOVERY AND DOCUMENT CONTROL

Evelyn E. Rasmussen

§ 6.1	This Chapter's Scope			93
§ 6.2	Research and Analysis Based on Informal Investigation			93
	§ 6.2.1	Publicity Research and Analysis		93
	§ 6.2.2	Historical Research and Analysis		93
		§ 6.2.2.1	Research of Territorial, Water and Mineral Rights	94
		§ 6.2.2.2	Research of Governmental Agency Jurisdiction	94
		§ 6.2.2.3	Historical Research of Business Entities and Enterprises	95
	§ 6.2.3	Statistical Research and Analysis		95
	§ 6.2.4	Research in Other Substantive Law Areas		95
§ 6.3	Research and Analysis Based on Formal Discovery			96
	§ 6.3.1	Systems for Coordinating Discovery		96
		§ 6.3.1.1	Drafting Interrogatories	96
		§ 6.3.1.2	Drafting Requests for Admissions	97

				Page
		§ 6.3.1.3	Drafting Requests for Production of Documents or Things	98
		§ 6.3.1.4	Summarizing Answers to Interrogatories and Requests for Admissions	99
	§ 6.3.2	Digesting Depositions		99
		§ 6.3.2.1	Preliminary Considerations	99
		§ 6.3.2.2	Language Techniques	100
		§ 6.3.2.3	Format	101
		§ 6.3.2.4	Information in the Digest	101
	§ 6.3.3	Summarizing a Deposition		102
	§ 6.3.4	Digesting the Trial Transcript or Trial Notes		102
§ 6.4	Document Management in Complex Cases: Discovery			102
	§ 6.4.1	System for Depositions and Exhibits to Depositions		103
		§ 6.4.1.1	The Court Reporter	103
		§ 6.4.1.2	Marking and Indexing Exhibits to Depositions	103
	§ 6.4.2	Systems for Handling Productions of Documents		104
		§ 6.4.2.1	The Court Reporter	104
		§ 6.4.2.2	Marking and Indexing Documents Produced	104
§ 6.5	Manual Systems for Control and Retrieval in Complex Cases: The Legal Assistant's Role Throughout the Case			104
	§ 6.5.1	The Role of the Legal Assistant in Relation to Other Support Personnel		104
	§ 6.5.2	Considerations and Guidelines for Control and Retrieval Systems		105
		§ 6.5.2.1	The System Should Be Simple	105
		§ 6.5.2.2	Legal Documents	106
		§ 6.5.2.3	Legal Research and Investigation	106
		§ 6.5.2.4	Documents Produced	106
§ 6.6	Summary and Conclusion			107

FORMS

6:1	Form Sub-Interrogatories	108
6:2	Checklist and Form Interrogatories	109
6:3	Deposition Digest: Sequential	111
6:4	Deposition Digest: Subject Matter	112
6:5	Master Index of Depositions	113
6:6	Index of Documents Produced: Sequential	114
6:7	Index of Documents Produced: Chronological	115
6:8	Master File Index	116
6:9	Master File Index	118

Table of Contents

7

TRIAL PRACTICE

Thomas H. Watkins and Cathy Logue

		Page
§ 7.1	This Chapter's Scope	119
§ 7.2	The Trial Book	119
§ 7.3	Jury and Argument	119
§ 7.4	Exhibit System	120
	§ 7.4.1 Requirements	120
	§ 7.4.1.1 Index	120
	§ 7.4.1.2 Cross Reference	120
	§ 7.4.1.3 Reconstructable	120
	§ 7.4.2 Preparation of Exhibits	120
	§ 7.4.3 Number of Exhibits	121
	§ 7.4.4 Use of Exhibits During Trial	121
	§ 7.4.5 Maintaining the Exhibit System During Trial	121
§ 7.5	Depositions	122
	§ 7.5.1 Indexing the Deposition	122
	§ 7.5.2 The Lawyer's Use of Depositions	122
	§ 7.5.3 Witness's Use of Depositions	122
	§ 7.5.4 Use of Depositions in Trial	122
	§ 7.5.4.1 For Cross-Examination	122
	§ 7.5.4.2 In Cross-Examination of Own Witness	123
	§ 7.5.4.3 To Present Testimony	123
§ 7.6	Witness List	123
	§ 7.6.1 Individual Witness Statements	123
§ 7.7	Legal Authorities and Case Decisions	123
	§ 7.7.1 Use of a Trial Brief	123
	§ 7.7.2 Use of Major Cases	124
	§ 7.7.3 Use of Other Authorities	124
§ 7.8	Instructions	124
	§ 7.8.1 Preparation of Instructions	124
	§ 7.8.2 Instructions and Other Sections of Trial Book	124
	§ 7.8.3 Presentation of Instructions	125
§ 7.9	Trial Notes	125
	§ 7.9.1 The Date and Hour	125
	§ 7.9.2 The Witness and Examining Lawyer	125
	§ 7.9.3 Exhibits	125
	§ 7.9.4 Objections and Rulings	125
	§ 7.9.5 Stylistic Considerations	125
§ 7.10	Relationships with Court Personnel	126
	§ 7.10.1 Clerks	126
	§ 7.10.2 Court Reporters	126
	§ 7.10.3 Bailiffs	126
	§ 7.10.4 Constables, Sheriffs and Other Process Servers	126
§ 7.11	Relationships with Lawyers	127

		Page
§ 7.12	Summary and Conclusion	127

FORMS

7:1	Trial Book Outline	128
7:2	Docket Control Entries	129
7:3	The Trial Book	131
7:4	Procedures for Preparing the Trial Book	132
7:5	Master Trial Checklist	133
7:6	Exhibit List	134
7:7	Deposition Analysis	135
7:8	Requested Special Issue	137
7:9	Trial Manual Discovery Section	138

8

INSURANCE DEFENSE LITIGATION

Larry L. Gollaher

§ 8.1	This Chapter's Scope	145
§ 8.2	Introduction	145
§ 8.3	The Legal Assistant File	145
§ 8.4	The Litigation Assistant's Checklist	145
§ 8.5	The Legal Assistant Reference Directions	146
§ 8.6	The Litigation Assistant's Responsibilities	146
§ 8.7	The File Summary Memorandum	146
§ 8.8	Preparing Pleadings	147
§ 8.9	Preparing Correspondence	147
§ 8.10	Interrogatories	147
§ 8.11	Depositions	148
§ 8.12	Investigation	149
§ 8.13	Final Trial Coordination	149
§ 8.14	Settlements and Satisfaction of Judgments	149
§ 8.15	Monthly Report by Legal Assistant	150
§ 8.16	Summary and Conclusion	150

FORMS

8:1	Initial Defense Checklist	151
8:2	Discovery Checklist	152
8:3	Trial Checklist	154
8:4	Legal Assistant Reference Directions	155
8:5	Active Case Status List	156

9

MEDICAL-LEGAL PRACTICE

Carol J. Morris

		Page
§ 9.1	This Chapter's Scope	157
§ 9.2	Selection of Employees	157
	§ 9.2.1 Education Requirements	157
	§ 9.2.2 Special Medical Knowledge Necessary	157
	§ 9.2.3 Education by the Firm	157
	§ 9.2.4 Continuing Education Programs	158
§ 9.3	Analyzing the Need for Legal Assistants	158
§ 9.4	General Suggestions	158
	§ 9.4.1 Obtaining Authorization Forms	158
	§ 9.4.2 Ownership of Medical Records; Subpoenas	158
	§ 9.4.3 Obtaining Hospital Information	158
	§ 9.4.4 Obtaining Information from Physicians	158
§ 9.5	Systems Development	159
	§ 9.5.1 Use of Word Processing and Forms	159
§ 9.6	Task Analysis	159
	§ 9.6.1 Recordkeeping Functions	159
	§ 9.6.1.1 Suggested Methods of Organizing Files — Medical Reports Storage and Indexing: The Medical Portion of the Personal Injury File	159
	§ 9.6.1.2 Special Damages, Wage Loss Computation and Settlement Notes	159
	§ 9.6.1.2.1 Details in Recording Medical Expenses and Special Damages	160
	§ 9.6.1.2.2 Items of Special Damages	160
	§ 9.6.1.3 Preparing the Summary	160
	§ 9.6.1.4 Recording Office Costs and the Legal Assistant Expense Account	160
	§ 9.6.1.5 Calendar Monitoring and Followup	160
	§ 9.6.1.6 Medical Library Maintenance Functions	160
	§ 9.6.2 Interviewing	160
	§ 9.6.2.1 Preliminary Interview	161
	§ 9.6.2.2 Documenting Pain, Suffering and Disability	161
	§ 9.6.2.3 Witness Interviews	161
	§ 9.6.2.4 Interviewing Medical Agencies	161
	§ 9.6.2.5 Authorization to Release Medical Information	161
	§ 9.6.3 Interpretation of Medical Reports	161
	§ 9.6.3.1 Further Research	161
	§ 9.6.3.2 Audiovisual Graphs, Charts, and Trial Aids	161

			Page
	§ 9.6.4	Investigation, Research and Communication with Outside Medical Facility Personnel	161
	§ 9.6.5	Litigation Documents	162
	§ 9.6.6	Assistance at Hearings and Trials	162
	§ 9.6.7	Continuing Education and Systems Development	162
		§ 9.6.7.1 Further References for Form Development	162
§ 9.7	Worker's Compensation		162
§ 9.8	Suggested Additional Forms		162
§ 9.9	Bibliography		162

FORMS

9:1	Checklist of Legal Assistant Duties in Medical Litigation	164
9:2	Training Courses and Texts	165
9:3	Personal Injury Flow Chart	166
9:4	Labor Cases Flow Chart	168
9:5	Loss of Wages and Profits Summary	170
9:6	Special Damages Summary Sheet	172
9:7	Preliminary Client Data Sheet	174
9:8	Pain, Suffering and Disability Chart	178
9:9	Form Letter to Physicians	183
9:10	Authorization for Release of Medical Information	184

10

BANKRUPTCY PRACTICE

H. Rey Stroube III

§ 10.1	This Chapter's Scope		185
§ 10.2	The Legal Assistant's Role in Bankruptcy Practice		185
§ 10.3	Debtor Relief Under the Bankruptcy Code		185
	§ 10.3.1	Initial Client Conference	185
	§ 10.3.2	Gathering and Assimilating the Facts	186
		§ 10.3.2.1 Completing the Bankruptcy Information Form	186
		§ 10.3.2.2 Reviewing and Verifying the Client's Answers	186
		§ 10.3.2.3 Preparing the Schedule of Liabilities	187
		§ 10.3.2.4 Listing Claims for Exempt Property	187
		§ 10.3.2.5 Preparing the Formal Petition, Statement and Schedule of Assets and Liabilities	187
	§ 10.3.3	Creditor Contacts	188
	§ 10.3.4	First Meeting of Creditors	188
	§ 10.3.5	Post-Filing Matters	189
	§ 10.3.6	Chapter 13 Plans	189
	§ 10.3.7	Discharge	190
	§ 10.3.8	Discharge Hearing	190

Table of Contents

		Page
§ 10.4	The Trustee in Bankruptcy	191
	§ 10.4.1 The Trustee's Responsibilities	191
	§ 10.4.2 Avoiding Transfers of Property	191
	§ 10.4.3 Liquidating Property	191
	§ 10.4.4 Preparing Accountings	192
	§ 10.4.5 Paying Creditors' Claims	192
	§ 10.4.6 Opposing Discharges	192
	§ 10.4.7 Handling Contested Matters and Adversary Proceedings	192
§ 10.5	Creditor Representation	193
	§ 10.5.1 Preparing Creditors' Claims	193
	§ 10.5.2 Secured Creditors	193
§ 10.6	Summary and Conclusion	194

FORM

10:1	Bankruptcy Information Form	195

11

DOMESTIC AND FAMILY LAW PRACTICE

Donn C. Fullenweider

§ 11.1	The Unique Problems in Family Law Practice	209
§ 11.2	Locating the Appropriate Legal Assistant	209
§ 11.3	Stages of the Developing Family Law Case and the Legal Assistant's Role	210
§ 11.4	The Decision Stage	210
§ 11.5	The Status Quo Stage	211
§ 11.6	Discovery	212
§ 11.7	Evaluation	213
§ 11.8	The Concluding Stages	213
§ 11.9	The Custody Case	214
§ 11.10	General Responsibilities	214
§ 11.11	Summary and Conclusion	214

FORMS

11:1	Potential Client Telephone Interview Form	215
11:2	Client Information Form	216
11:3	Financial Information Form	219
11:4	Financial Spread Sheets	222
11:5	Family Law Property Pathfinder	226

12

THE CORPORATE SETTING

Melvin S. Merzon

		Page
§ 12.1	This Chapter's Scope	229
§ 12.2	Introduction	229
§ 12.3	The Litigation Assistant Discovery Specialist	230
	§ 12.3.1 Reviewing and Responding to Claims	230
	§ 12.3.2 Working with Local Counsel	230
	§ 12.3.3 Investigating Claims and Obtaining Background Information	230
	§ 12.3.4 Indexing Information for Future Reference	231
	§ 12.3.5 Preparing and Responding to Interrogatories and Requests for Production	231
	§ 12.3.6 Depositions	232
	§ 12.3.7 File Maintenance and Control	232
§ 12.4	The Labor Relations Legal Assistant	233
	§ 12.4.1 Employment Claims	233
	§ 12.4.2 Fair Employment Practices	233
	§ 12.4.3 Worker's Disability Cases	233
§ 12.5	Creditors' Rights Matters	234
§ 12.6	Residential Real Estate Transactions	234
§ 12.7	Property Taxes	234
§ 12.8	Transportation	235
§ 12.9	Document Reviewer/Analyst	235
§ 12.10	Patents	236
§ 12.11	Antitrust	237
§ 12.12	Legislative Assistant	237
§ 12.13	Office Manager/Administrative Assistant	238
§ 12.14	Summary and Conclusion	238

13

APPELLATE PRACTICE

Paul G. Ulrich

§ 13.1	This Chapter's Scope	241
§ 13.2	The Importance, Need and Benefits of Managing Litigation and Appellate Practice	241
§ 13.3	Use of Legal Assistants in the Appellate Process	241
	§ 13.3.1 Preparing Findings of Fact, Conclusions of Law and Judgments	241
	§ 13.3.2 Organizing the Record for Appeal	242
	§ 13.3.3 Preparing Briefs	242

Table of Contents

		Page
	§ 13.3.4 Participation in Oral Argument	243
	§ 13.3.5 Preparation of Motions for Rehearing, Responses or Applications for Further Review	243
	§ 13.3.6 Summary and Conclusion	243
§ 13.4	Use of Legal Assistants in Managing an Appellate Practice	244
	§ 13.4.1 Basic Roles	244
	§ 13.4.2 The Appellate Assistant's Responsibilities	245
	§ 13.4.3 Elements of an Appellate Management System	245
	§ 13.4.4 Docketing and Routing Systems	246
	§ 13.4.5 Other Appellate Responsibilities	247
	§ 13.4.6 Summary and Conclusion	248
§ 13.5	Bibliography	248

FORMS

13:1	Outline of Procedural Steps and Time Limits	250
13:2	Appellate Status Sheet	253
13:3	Appellate Docket File Card	254
13:4	Appeals Calendar	255
13:5	Appeals Status Report	256

INDEX

Subject Matter Index	257
Table of Citations	273

1

ORGANIZING, DEVELOPING AND MANAGING A PROGRAM

Paul G. Ulrich*

§ 1.1 This Chapter's Scope. This chapter discusses the management concerns involved in organizing, developing and managing a law firm's employment of legal assistants. "Law firm" as defined throughout this book also includes such law offices as government agencies, corporate law departments and legal aid organizations. Other chapters suggest specific areas of law practice in which assistants can be employed effectively. Before this can occur, however, the goals, objectives, management structure and framework for the program's development and growth should be carefully defined. This chapter suggests elements of planning, systems development and management that should be implemented to make the assistant program most effective.

§ 1.2 Developing a Systems Approach.

§ 1.2.1 Use of Systems Techniques in Developing Law Practice Systems. Developing a legal assistant program is simply one aspect of a more general systems approach to law firm practice and management. A law firm is a network of interrelated systems involving personnel, work flow, finances, information and operating procedures. Too often, lawyers are so caught up in the immediate pressures of their practice that they fail to allow time for reflective, creative thought about how the quality of their practice and their firm's internal operations might be improved. This sort of thought process, however, is most important in achieving those results.

The starting point for developing law practice systems is for the individual lawyer to analyze his or her practice critically and then to identify the portions that could be standardized and delegated to legal assistants or other non-lawyer personnel. A good reference is R. Ramo, ed., How to Create-A-System for the Law Office (A.B.A. 1975). Most lawyers deal at least in part with somewhat standard, recurring situations. Many, however, have not sufficiently delegated those responsibilities to free their time for more challenging, creative, professionally satisfying tasks.

Lawyers should develop the habit of reviewing each task's requirements to decide whether some or all of them could be delegated to a qualified assistant. The necessary procedures should then be developed and education provided to make such delegation a reality on a continuing basis. For example, in appellate practice, the status and progress of each of the firm's appeals should be continuously monitored throughout the appellate process. Trial court records and transcripts need to be organized, summarized and reviewed. Briefs must be researched, drafted and edited.

---

*Partner, Lewis and Roca, Phoenix, Arizona. Copyright © 1980 by Paul G. Ulrich. All rights reserved.

Many of these tasks can be delegated effectively to legal assistants. See generally the discussion at chapter 13.

Forms should be designed to facilitate gathering and presenting the information necessary for any particular task. For example, structured interview forms can ensure that all necessary information is obtained from clients in such situations as will drafting, estate planning, formation of business organizations and personal injury litigation. Procedural guides can be devised to state the sequence and content of each type of recurring situation and to define the assistant's role and responsibilities in each. As each project progresses, recurring forms of pleadings, correspondence or other documents should be developed, retained, improved and used whenever possible. Devising and using checklists, task descriptions, forms and procedural guides in as many areas of practice as possible encourages and facilitates delegation of responsibility to assistants. Assistants can prepare these materials for the lawyer's review and approval. Adapting the examples contained in this volume to a particular state's practice and developing additional, similar materials should be an ongoing, cooperative process between lawyers and assistants as additional specific areas of the firm's practice are identified as suitable for such treatment.

§ 1.2.2 Using Management by Objectives and Management by Exception Techniques. Management by objectives ("MBO") and management by exception ("MBE") principles provide powerful tools for managing both substantive law practice and a firm's internal operations. For discussions of the theory and practice of MBO and MBE techniques see, *e.g.*, P. Drucker, The Practice of Management (Harper and Row, 1954); P. Mali, Managing by Objectives (Wiley-Interscience 1972); D. Mackintosh, Management By Exception: A Handbook With Forms (Prentice-Hall, Inc. 1978). Articles describing the theory and application of MBO and MBE techniques to law firms and legal assistant programs include P. Ulrich, *Managing a Law Practice "By Objectives and Self-Control,"* 20 LOEM 183 (1979); P. Ulrich and C. Multhauf, *Law Firm Working Relationships: Developing a Long-Term Legal Assistant Program*, 20 LOEM 289 (1979). Use of MBO and MBE techniques should permit substantial amounts of a law firm's work to be delegated to legal assistants. Such assignments can thereafter simply be reviewed on completion or whenever any unusual situations occur, to be certain that the project plan is being completed as intended. The following sections suggest how this can be accomplished.

§ 1.2.3 Application of Systems Management Techniques to Legal Assistants.

§ 1.2.3.1 Substantive Law Practice. MBO and MBE techniques can be applied both to substantive law practice involving legal assistants and to the program's management itself. As to substantive law practice, the first step is to identify specific situations, types of practice or continuing working relationships in which tasks can often be routinely delegated. Project teams or task groups can then be formed for each such situation. Lawyers, secretaries, assistants and any other necessary support personnel can become members of such groups as might be required. Any particular person might be a member of several such groups simultaneously.

Management by objectives assumes that each member of a project team will participate in planning how its responsibilities will be performed. There should be conferences to discuss the situation, the plan and the means for achieving it. One of the lawyers on the project team should be its "project manager." This person may, but need not, also be the team's senior lawyer. Substantial portions of the more routine administrative tasks involved in achieving the project plan might thereafter become the responsibility of a legal assistant working under the team leader's or project manager's general supervision.

The project manager's responsibilities include (a) verifying the plan, (b) defining, planning and scheduling the sequence and relationship of each member's contributions, and then (c) supervising and monitoring each person's performance as the plan progresses so that all activities are completed as required. These responsibilities are a continuing process. Any changes required in the plan or the task to be performed should be made easily whenever necessary in light of changing circumstances. By periodically reviewing and revising the plan in relation to the general situation and the project's overall objectives, the most efficient progress possible should be made toward their achievement. For this to occur effectively, however, each member of the project team should participate in the planning and review processes and be aware of how the tasks for which he or she is responsible relate to the larger effort.

§ 1.2.3.2 The Legal Assistant Program. The concepts discussed above are also applicable to managing the legal assistant program itself. Procedures should be developed for analyzing the firm's practice on a continuing basis to determine whether and where additional assistants might be required. There should also be an ongoing process of more clearly defining, systematizing and delegating to assistants as much of the firm's routine practice in as many areas as possible. An affirmative strategy should be developed for encouraging the firm's lawyers to increase their delegation of work to assistants and for employing a sufficient number of qualified assistants so that such delegation can in fact more easily occur.

Every legal assistant should be given a basic initial orientation to the firm. The orientation should introduce the firm's personnel, policies, procedures and working relationships with which the assistant will be directly involved. See the discussion at § 2.3.2. Standard procedures, checklists and information packets should be developed to ensure that all necessary orientation is completed efficiently and that all necessary written materials are provided for future reference. Each assistant should then be assigned to a supervising lawyer directly responsible for his or her continued orientation, education, work assignments and performance. The number of lawyers from whom each assistant receives assignments should also be kept to a minimum, so that each lawyer is encouraged to improve the organization of his or her practice and to delegate more responsibility on a continuing basis.

The program should be reviewed periodically to determine whether its specific objectives and goals are being met. Included in this review process should be the determination whether the firm has a sufficient number of legal assistants, whether and in what directions further growth or development is desired, whether the firm's continuing education program for assistants is satisfactory, and whether each assistant is performing and progressing satisfactorily both toward meeting the firm's requirements and achieving his or her own personal objectives.

Finally, objective criteria should be established for measuring legal assistants' financial contributions and their cost to the firm. These should include such matters as anticipated and actual annual chargeable hours, standard average hourly billing rates where appropriate, overhead expense factors, and periodic salary adjustments based on quality of performance and contributions to the firm. See the discussion at § 2.2. Other factors, more difficult to measure, must also be considered. These include more lawyer time made available, faster completion for many tasks, and reduced risks of malpractice by maintaining schedules, checklists and standardized procedures. Implementing such criteria should result in more extensive, productive employment of assistants throughout the firm.

§ 1.3 Recruiting Legal Assistants. Legal assistants can be recruited from many sources. The sources chosen and the kinds of people the firm employs will substantially affect the nature and quality of the firm's program. Another important factor will be the firm's attitude toward encouraging specialized, continuing on-the-job education, and advancement once the assistant is employed.

One recommended approach is that the program be as professionally oriented as possible. This would involve, for example, hiring legal assistants who have completed specialized courses. This approach may be very successful for a larger firm or a firm in a community having access to such graduates. The larger firm can employ assistants with more narrowly specialized, highly developed skills in each of the firm's sections or departments.

There are an increasing number of legal assistant programs throughout the country. A list of such programs appears at § 1.9. Some are two-year community college programs. Others offer a legal assistant major in a four-year college curriculum. Proprietary, private schools also offer courses of widely varying length, content and quality. Firms should consider but carefully screen available applicants having completed such courses.

The applicant may well have a good record and have diligently completed the prescribed course of study. There may not, however, be any direct relationship between many of those courses and the assistant's responsibilities once he or she is employed by the firm. The firm should not assume that the assistant necessarily has previously mastered every conceivable legal situation. Instead, the firm should develop its own continuing, on-the-job education program for its assistants both as to each area of its practice and as to its more general administrative policies and procedures.

Other major potential sources of legal assistants include persons working in related fields, such as title researchers, real estate agents, escrow agents, trust officers, claims adjusters, private investigators or court personnel. Although it might be assumed that such persons have some familiarity with certain kinds of law practice, the exact extent of each such applicant's knowledge and initial responsibilities will have to be defined carefully. Their initial skills may then thereafter be improved and expanded by a systematic on-the-job continuing education program or by attending college courses or continuing legal education seminars on subjects relating to their employment.

The firm's own legal secretaries may also be a good source of applicants for legal assistant positions. The firm should consider posting notices of openings for assistants on an employee bulletin board so that interested secretaries may also apply. Successful, experienced secretaries are already familiar with the firm's procedures, clients and working relationships. They are also familiar with many of the recurring situations in the areas of the firm in which they have been employed. Many experienced secretaries may already be performing legal assistant responsibilities, at least in part, because of their demonstrated ability and lawyers' resulting willingness to delegate responsibility to them.

Secretaries should be assigned to full-time legal assistant positions only with considerable thought, care and attention to the resulting changes in their responsibilities. For example, some secretaries seem reluctant to part with their typewriters.

For greatest efficiency, however, legal assistants should use dictation equipment to prepare the written work for which they are responsible and delegate the typing. The former secretary should understand that time will be much more productive if he or she does not have to type the materials being prepared. Similarly, some secretaries seem to prefer detailed directions and repetitious, highly structured assignments. Such persons may feel insecure or uncomfortable if they are required to assume more affirmative, unstructured, open-ended responsibilities. A secretary unable to make an effective transition to a legal assistant position may also not be able to return to the former secretarial position without admitting failure. As the result, the firm may lose a capable person entirely. Conflicts may also arise between other legal assistants and "promoted" secretaries, as well as in situations where other secretaries apply for but are not "promoted" to assistant positions.

Firms may also recruit as legal assistants either inexperienced liberal arts college graduates or graduate students, those in other careers such as teaching who are looking for a change or unemployed spouses returning to the job market. Employing persons in any of these categories clearly requires the firm to have continuing on-the-job education programs. The firm must recognize that part of the cost involved in obtaining the additional income from assistants and being able to delegate work to them effectively includes continuing education, orientation and review to ensure that they understand their responsibilities and that their work is being performed properly. In this regard, providing clear definitions, standard forms and checklists for as many recurring tasks as possible is most beneficial. This effort should be given continuing high priority as additional categories of work that can be delegated to assistants are identified.

There is no single most desirable personality profile for assistants. If any generalizations could be made, however, they might include such characteristics as good written and oral communication skills, general facility with language, careful attention to detail, willingness to accept some unstructured responsibility, good work habits, and proven accomplishments in either prior education or work experience. Because of the professional nature of their work, assistants should have intelligence and legal aptitude comparable to beginning law students. Otherwise, lawyers may not have sufficient confidence to delegate substantial responsibility without reservation.

§ 1.4 Developing a Professional Approach in Working Relationships.

To be most successful, a legal assistant program should be based on positive motivation and management. The firm should seek to develop assistants with long-term career potential to increase both their value to the firm as well as their own personal and professional satisfaction with their responsibilities.

Much has been written about the importance of motivation in relation to understanding and improving the quality of working relationships. Abraham H. Maslow, Douglas McGregor and Frederick Herzberg, among others, have provided varied insights concerning understanding positive motivation and the factors affecting work satisfaction. For references, see the bibliography at § 1.10.

§ 1.4.1 Application to Legal Assistant Programs.

General motivation theory suggests that the firm should strive to establish positively motivated working relationships throughout its operations. As applied to legal assistants, one important aspect of such relationships is for each assistant to be responsible to a supervising lawyer. The supervising lawyer should (a) provide, screen and review work assignments; (b) orient the assistant both to the particular categories of work involved and to the firm and its procedures generally; and (c) develop and expand the assistant's skills and the kinds of tasks assigned. The supervising lawyer also should serve as a buffer between the assistant and others in the firm who might otherwise impose conflicting or excessive work requirements.

The legal assistant program should be supervised by a lawyer or committee of lawyers whose concerns include organizing, defining and expanding the program; identifying needs or opportunities for additional assistants; establishing and reviewing the individual supervising lawyer-assistant relationships; encouraging lawyers to increase their use of assistants; and providing necessary continuing or more specialized education. Although the firm's office administrator might also be a member of the committee, lawyers should be responsible for the program.

Maslow's "hierarchy of needs" concept holds that when one's basic physical, safety, belonging and relating needs are satisfied, further motivation results from satisfaction of the needs to receive respect, admiration, recognition and status from others, and thereafter from working toward expressing one's own individuality. McGregor asserts that most people are capable of a high degree of imagination, ingenuity and creativity in solving problems; that most people under proper conditions not only accept but seek responsibility; and that under normal conditions the average person's intellectual potential is only partially used. These theories suggest that assistants can perform high quality professional work, given adequate instruction and motivation. As suggested at § 1.2, lawyers should evaluate their practice to see what might be systematized, taught and delegated to assistants with proper supervision. If this is done and an MBO approach taken to planning work assignments, the result should be a much greater delegation of responsibility, much greater satisfaction for assistants and high quality professional work.

For best efficiency, legal assistants should not type their own work. Dictation substantially increases productivity, since words can be spoken much more quickly than they can be typed. Assistants therefore should be provided secretarial and typing assistance so that their more routine, clerical work can be further delegated. Assistants should also have equal access to the firm's word processing systems. Often, as the result of systematizing an area of law practice, the assistant's task will include preparing documents based on standard forms stored in word processing equipment. Assistants may also generate more paperwork than lawyers because of the delegation to them of that responsibility. The firm must understand that with this delegation must come adequate provision for secretarial, clerical and word processing assistance.

Developing professional working relationships with assistants should not interfere with more traditional lawyer-secretary working relationships or working relationships among the firm's personnel generally. There need not be jealousies or jurisdictional disputes over legal secretary and legal assistant responsibilities. Instead, everyone involved should be made to understand that assistants, as well as other firm personnel, are valued members of a legal services team to which each member contributes particular talents or skills. Everyone in the firm should be motivated to meet those responsibilities professionally and efficiently. Positive reinforcement will encourage such continued performance.

§ 1.5 Productivity and Profitability Considerations. If a proper motivation system exists and lawyers are encouraged and able to delegate effectively, legal assistants should be productive and profitable to the firm. Supervising lawyers and those responsible for the program's general administration should, however, review each assistant's assignments, responsibilities, working relationships and chargeable hours regularly to ensure that previously established objectives are being met. A plan should be developed with each assistant concerning such matters as the expected number of chargeable hours per month, the types of tasks to be performed and objective criteria for determining whether responsibilities have been met successfully.

Since assistants are, for the most part, doing work that would otherwise be done by lawyers and since their work is supervised and reviewed by lawyers, the firm should record and bill for their time. Accordingly, assistants must record their time. Standard hourly billing rates should be assigned each assistant reflecting ability, experience and value in performing the tasks. Assuming those hours are able to be billed and paid for on the same basis as lawyer billings, an income budget can be developed both for each assistant and for the program generally. An expense budget can also be prepared, including such items as direct and indirect salary and fringe benefit expense, office and equipment expense, and the cost of secretaries, other support personnel and facilities to which assistants have access. The difference between these budgets will be the program's net income contribution to the firm. For examples, see Form 2:1. These budgets should be developed and thereafter monitored, reviewed and verified against actual experience to determine whether objectives are being met and to identify any variances to be corrected.

Employing an income-expense budgeting process over a period of time should confirm that assistants can provide a substantial net income contribution. This occurs as the result both of billing for their chargeable hours and of freeing lawyers to assume more demanding responsibilities for which higher hourly rates are justified. The firm thus benefits as well from greater lawyer income contribution based on the higher average quality of the lawyer's time.

One basis for making decisions concerning increased salaries for assistants is their income contributions and profitability to the firm. As assistants become more experienced, consideration should be given to increasing their standard hourly billing rates because of their greater responsibility and efficiency. Performing work of greater responsibility should thus increase that assistant's income contribution to the firm. Increased responsibility should also result in periodic salary increases justified at least in part by that income contribution.

It is possible that an experienced legal assistant may make a greater income contribution to the firm than a beginning lawyer. Given career employees and appropriate supporting data, there is no reason why assistants' salaries should be held artificially below those of beginning lawyers. Instead, the firm should honestly attempt to evaluate both assistants' and lawyers' economic value to the firm and compensate fairly in relation to performance.

§ 1.6 Establishing a Review and Evaluation Program. Another important aspect in any effective legal assistant program is creating a meaningful review and evaluation system. As has been previously suggested, a program functions best when managed by positive motivation and MBO techniques. A review and evaluation system is necessary to determine whether objectives are being accomplished and, more generally, whether the program is responding satisfactorily to the firm's requirements.

Review and evaluation should interact with continuous planning and development of future objectives. This process should occur both as to each assistant's own performance and development and whether the program generally is meeting its stated objectives. The review process should establish specific objectives to be verified in subsequent reviews. The legal assistant committee should coordinate and direct the reviews.

One suggested format for these reviews is conferences at six-month intervals among each assistant, supervising lawyer, any other lawyers for whom the assistant does substantial work and the legal assistant committee. At least a portion of each assistant's conference should occur without the supervising lawyer being present. Written evaluations following a standard format should be obtained from all lawyers for whom the assistant has worked. These conferences should be positive and constructive. Such conferences should recognize each assistant's successes, discuss areas where improvement is required, solve any particular problems encountered by the assistant and, where necessary, redefine the assistant's responsibilities or working relationships. Consideration should also be given to salary adjustments as the result of increased responsibilities or successful performance. Review conferences should also provide a meaningful opportunity for each assistant to discuss his or her work situation or any necessary changes or improvements in working responsibilities or relationships.

In addition to these periodic, more formal review conferences, there should be ongoing, informal conferences between each legal assistant and his or her supervising lawyer and other lawyers for whom work is being performed concerning specific projects as they are completed. There should also be an affirmative program of continuing on-the-job education to increase each assistant's skill in the areas of practice in which he or she is employed. In addition to reviewing the assistant's work, each assigning lawyer should be available to answer questions or solve specific problems as they arise before time, money and energy are wasted performing useless tasks. These discussions should also consider whether each project in which the assistant is involved is progressing satisfactorily toward completion or whether any adjustments are required in the project plan to accommodate changed circumstances or unanticipated problems.

Review and evaluation should also occur at other levels throughout the firm. For example, the legal assistant committee should meet periodically to define its objectives and determine whether they are being met. Discussions within each section of the firm should include considering whether the assistants working in each area are performing satisfactorily in relation to the section's requirements. Assistants should be encouraged to participate in section meetings whenever possible. In addition, there should be periodic general meetings of assistants and the legal assistant committee. Such meetings should include continuing education in legal subjects of general interest; discussion of the firm's policies and procedures that affect assistants; and discussion of firm operations, objectives and plans when appropriate so that assistants are kept informed. These meetings should also provide an opportunity for assistants to discuss their current activities or concerns.

Assistants should not be isolated from the rest of the firm or excluded from the general discussion process as to its future development and growth. Cooperation and teamwork among assistants should also be encouraged, so that they are better able to shift responsibilities among themselves. The details of the conferences and programs discussed in this section obviously will vary according to the firm's size, the number of its assistants and the kinds of law practice in which the firm is involved.

Even a small firm, however, should provide its assistants with opportunities for review, evaluation, education and participation in the ongoing dialogue concerning the firm's future development and growth.

§ 1.7 Increasing Legal Assistant Responsibilities — The Long-Term Prospects. If the program is properly managed and developed, assistants can be given steadily increasing responsibility. Their employment should be viewed as a satisfying lifetime career opportunity. Achieving this objective, however, requires continuing effort by all concerned. Given the diversity in assistants' qualifications and backgrounds, the firm should be careful not to assume too much based on prior education and experience. Instead, each assistant should be carefully evaluated in terms of his or her background, experience, education and potential, and then given responsibilities consistent with those considerations to the greatest practical extent. A corollary of this process is that each assistant requires continuing education, evaluation and review under the direction of the supervising lawyer and legal assistant committee.

Once such a program has been established, continued delegation and increased responsibility should be encouraged. Each assistant should be encouraged to extend his or her competency into related fields on the basis of successful completion of prior responsibilities. Each supervising lawyer and assistant should together devise a continuing program for the assistant's development. They should also together prepare any necessary standard instructions, procedure checklists and forms as each area of responsibility has been defined. The availability of such materials also permits other assistants to perform those tasks successfully with a minimum of additional instruction.

No exact definition can be given concerning the extent to which assistants can be delegated increased responsibilities. So long as the assistant's work is carefully structured, supervised and reviewed, and no legal advice is given or court appearances made, an assistant should be able to perform substantial, complex factual investigation, document preparation or legal research as well or better than many lawyers. This is by no means to suggest that assistants should take over the practice of law. But as lawyers continue to delegate increasingly complex responsibilities to assistants able to perform them satisfactorily, assistants may well accomplish projects many lawyers originally would not have thought possible.

§ 1.8 Summary and Conclusion. The keys to success in developing legal assistant capabilities are carefully organizing and systematizing the lawyer's practice, identifying and delegating specific tasks and procedures wherever appropriate with proper regard for the education necessarily required, and thereafter reviewing and evaluating the assistant's performance and encouraging assumption of greater professional responsibility based on past success. The result is clearly worth the effort. The firm's lawyers, however, must be willing to make the necessary educational investment and to select and manage their assistants on a positive basis to accomplish that goal.

§ 1.9 Institutions Offering Legal Assistant Education Programs.
(As of September, 1980)

As a result of the growing interest in the legal assistant field and the substantial number of inquiries, the following list of legal assistant education programs has been developed. Although every effort has been made to include all schools currently offering training programs, it is highly probable that some schools have been overlooked due to the rapid growth of formal training programs in this field. As the need for program evaluation became apparent, the American Bar Association established appropriate guidelines for institutions to follow when considering establishing a legal assistant program. Thereafter, procedures for obtaining ABA approval of legal assistant programs were developed. Seeking approval of a legal assistant education program from the American Bar Association is a voluntary effort initiated by the institution offering the program. Therefore, non-approval does not necessarily mean that the program being offered is not of good quality and reputable. This list is for informational purposes only and should not be construed to be approval, endorsement or accreditation by the American Bar Association or the Standing Committee on Legal Assistants unless otherwise indicated by: *ABA final approval or **ABA provisional approval.

ALABAMA

Auburn University at
  Montgomery
Legal Assistant Education
Department of Justice and
  Public Safety
Montgomery, AL 36193
Darrell L. Schlotterback
George S. Schrader

*Samford University
Division of Paralegal Studies
Birmingham, AL 35209
Margaret D. Sizemore

Southern Institute
2015 Highland Avenue
Birmingham, AL 35205
Bibbie McLaughlin

Spring Hill College
Legal Studies Program
Mobile, AL 36608
Ricki C. LeFave

University of South Alabama
Div. of C.E. & Evening Studies
307 University Blvd.
Mobile, AL 36688
Laura A. Lambert

ALASKA

University of Alaska-Anchorage
Anchorage Community College
Law Science Program
2533 Providence Avenue
Anchorage, AK 99501
Robert E. Congdon

ARIZONA

Arizona State University
Paralegal Program
Department of Administrative
  Services
College of Business
  Administration
Tempe, AZ 85281
Marianne Moody Jennings

*Northern Arizona University
Legal Assistant Program
Box 15044
Flagstaff, AZ 86011
C. Dudley Brandom

Paralegal Institute (The)
Ste. 104, 5350 North 16th Street
Phoenix, AZ 85016
Charles Lehan

Phoenix College
Department of Business
1202 West Thomas Road
Phoeniz, AZ 85013
Theodore Borek — John Goff

Scottsdale Community College
9000 East Chapparral
Scottsdale, AZ 85253
Gloria Little

Sterling School (The)
1010 East Indian School Road
Phoenix, AZ 85014
Ruby Sterling

CALIFORNIA

American College of
  Paramedical Arts and Sciences
1800 N. Broadway
Santa Ana, CA 92706
William J. Anthony

American Legal Services
  Institute
c/o 2719 Canada Blvd.
Glendale, CA 91208
Gary James Joslin

American River College
4700 College Oak Drive
Sacramento, CA 95841

California College of Paralegal
  Studies
6832 Van Nuys Boulevard
Van Nuys, CA 91405
Roy Schneider
Larry Ulman

California State College — San
  Bernardino
Paralegal Studies
Department of Political Science
550 State College Parkway
San Bernardino, CA 92407
Brij. B. Khare

California State University,
  Chico
Chico, CA 95929
Edward J. Bronson

California State University,
  Dominguez Hills
Public Paralegal Certificate
  Program
School of Social & Behavioral
  Sciences
Carson, CA 90747
Marilyn Garber

*California State University at
  Los Angeles
Certification Program for the
  Legal Assistant
5151 State University Drive
Los Angeles, CA 90032
Peter Madsen

Canada College
4200 Farm Hill Boulevard
Redwood City, CA 94061
Arthur J. Katz

Cerritos College
11110 East Alondra Boulevard
Norwalk, CA 90650

*City College of San Francisco
A.A. Legal Assisting Program
  and
Legal Assisting Certificate
  Program I
50 Phelan Avenue
San Francisco, CA 94112
Jack H. Aldridge

Coastline Community College
10231 Slater Avenue
Fountain Valley, CA 92708
Dr. Ardoline

Organizing, Developing and Managing a Program § 1.9

Dominican College of San Rafael
San Rafael, CA 94901
Henry Aigner

Fresno City College
1101 E. University Avenue
Fresno, CA 93741
G. A. Eckenrod

Humphreys College
6650 Inglewood Drive
Stockton, CA 92507
Gladys Humphreys

Imperial Valley College
P.O. Box 158
Imperial, CA 92251
Wm. D. Rudolph

Lake Tahoe Community College
Legal Assistant Certificate
2659 Lake Tahoe Blvd.
P.O. Box 14445
South Lake Tahoe, CA 95702
Roger Welt

Los Angeles City College
855 N. Vermont Avenue
Los Angeles, CA 90029
John Weaver

Los Angeles Southwest College
Legal Assistant Program
1600 West Imperial Highway
Los Angeles, CA 90047
Carl M. Ross

Merritt College
12500 Campus Drive
Oakland, CA 94619
Jean M. Chapman

Orange Coast College
2701 Fairview Road
Costa Mesa, CA 92626
Frances M. Potter

Pasadena City College
Business Department
1570 E. Colorado Boulevard
Pasadena, CA 91106
L. Edmond Kellogg

Pepperdine University
Legal Studies Program
8035 Vermont Avenue
Los Angeles, CA 90044
Stephen Nelvin

Rio Hondo College
Paralegal Program
3600 Workman Mill Road
Whittier, CA 90608
Judy A. Long

**St. Mary's College
Legal Assistant Certificate
  Program A
P.O. Box 52
Moraga, CA 94575
Mary Ann Mason

San Bernardino Valley College
Legal Administration Program
701 South Mt. Vernon Avenue
San Bernardino, CA 92403
Dorothy Bumiller

San Francisco State University
Continuing Education/
  Extension
Paralegal Studies Program
1600 Holloway Avenue
San Francisco, CA 94132
Lee Gallery

San Jose State University
Legal Assistant Studies
Continuing Education
San Jose, CA 95192
Jerome S. Burstein

Santa Ana College
Seventeenth at Bristol
Santa Ana, CA 92706
Anthony Mazzone

Sawyer College of Business
6832 Van Nuys Boulevard
Van Nuys, CA 91405

Skyline College
Paralegal Program
3300 College Drive
San Bruno, CA 94066
Douglas Oliver

South Bay Community Law
  Center
387 Third Avenue
Chula Vista, CA 92010
Robert Burns

*UCLA, University Extension
Attorney Assistant Training
  Pgm.
10995 LeConte Avenue, Suite
  214
Los Angeles, CA 90024
Janet Kaiser

University of California at
  Irvine
Certificate Program in Legal
  Asst.
Irvine, CA 92717
Carol Booth Olson

University of LaVerne
1950 Third Street
LaVerne, CA 91750
Alan Spears

*University of San Diego
Lawyer's Assistant Program
Room 318, Serra Hall
Alcala Park
San Diego, CA 92110
Sue Sullivan

University of Santa Clara
Institute for Paralegal
  Education
Bannan Hall, Room 261
Santa Clara, CA 95053
Emalie M. Ortega

*University of Southern
  California
Program for Legal
  Paraprofessionals
Law Center
University Park
Los Angeles, CA 90007
Elizabeth Horowitz

*University of West Los Angeles
School of Paralegal Studies
10811 Washington Boulevard
Culver City, CA 90230
Therese A. Cannon

Valley College of Paralegal
  Studies
10911 Riverside Drive
North Hollywood, CA 91602
Edward Fierstadt

West Valley College
1400 Fruitvale Avenue
Saratoga, CA 95070
Lois Kittle

COLORADO

*Arapahoe Community College
Assoc. Degree Legal Asst.
  Program
5900 S. Santa Fe Drive
Littleton, CO 80120
Joan R. Schliebner

Community College of Denver
Auraria Campus
Service Occupations Division
Room CA-313
1111 West Colfax
Denver, CO 80204
Robert W. Battey

*Denver Paralegal Institute
General Practice Legal Assistant
  Program
Suite 908
1108 - 15th Street
Denver, CO 80202
Richard C. Hopkins

El Paso Community College
2200 Bott Street
Colorado Springs, CO 80904
D. Morgan Dilling

Metropolitan State College
Legal Assistant Program
1006 Eleventh Street
Denver, CO 80204

Paralegal Training Center
Suite 215
8000 East Girard Avenue
Denver, CO 80231
Robert Natelson

Southern Colorado State College
Behavioral & Social Sciences
900 W. Ormon
Pueblo, CO 81001
W. R. Stealey

University of Denver
College of Law
Pgm. of Adv. Prof. Development
200 W. 14th Avenue
Denver, CO 80204
Charles Turner

CONNECTICUT

Hartford College
Counseling Center for Women
1283 Asylum Avenue
Hartford, CT 06105
Betty Bidwell

Manchester Community College
Legal Assistant Program
P.O. Box 1046
Manchester, CT 06040
Fred A. Ramey, Jr.

Mattatuck Community College
Legal Assistant Program
640 Chase Parkway
Waterbury, CT 06708
Wm. R. Liedlich

Norwalk Community College
333 Wilson Avenue
Route 136
Norwalk, CT 06854
Maurice Godin

Post College
Legal Assistant Program
800 Country Club Road
Waterbury, CT 06708
Robert I. Kirkwood

Quinnipiac College
Legal Assistant Program
Mount Carmel Avenue
Hamden, CT 06518
Shalom Endleman

*Sacred Heart University
P.O. Box 6460
Bridgeport, CT 06606
Muriel Small

DELAWARE

Delaware Technical and
  Community College
Southern Campus
Legal Assistant Technology
Georgetown, DE 19947
William Q. Clements

Goldey Beacom College
P.O. Box 5047
Wilmington, DE 19808
Margaret H. Juhl

University of Delaware
Legal Assistant Education
  Program
2800 Pennsylvania Avenue
Wilmington, DE 19806
Matthew M. Shipp

Wesley College
Paralegal Program
Dover, DE 19901
William Thomas Barrett

DISTRICT OF COLUMBIA

Antioch School of Law
Legal Technician Program
1624 Crescent Pl., N.W.
Washington, D.C. 20009
John Wernet

*Georgetown University
  School for Summer & Ctng.
    Edtn.
  Legal Assistant Program
Washington, D.C. 20057
Steve Clark

*George Washington University
  CEW Ctr.-College of General
    Studies
2130 H Street, N.W.
Library, Suite 621
Washington, D.C. 20052
Ruth F. Dearden

Southeastern University
501 Eye Street, S.W.
Washington, DC 20024
Margaret Goodman

FLORIDA

Barry College
11300 N.E. Second Avenue
Miami, FL 33161

Florida Atlantic University
Institute for Legal Assistants
Center for Management &
  Professional Development
Boca Raton, FL 33431
Jane Sonnenburg

Hillsborough Community
  College
P.O. Box 22127
Tampa, FL 33622
Edward R. Mattson

Langley Paralegal Institute
315 Hyde Park Avenue
Tampa, FL 33606
Steven H. Engler

Manatee Junior College
Legal Assistant Program
P.O. Box 1849
Bradenton, FL 33507
Peter G. Choulas

Miami Dade Community College
Legal Assistant Program
300 N.E. 2nd Avenue
Miami, FL 33312
Harry Hoffman

*Santa Fe Community College
P.O. Box 1530
3000 N.W. 83rd Street
Gainesville, FL 32601
J. Pope Cheney

Southern Career Institute
1580 N.W. 2nd Avenue
Boca Raton, FL 33432
R.W. Beaver

St. Petersburg Junior College
Legal Assistant Program
P.O. Box 13489
St. Petersburg, FL 33733
Barbara M. Whitney

University of Central Florida
Allied Legal Services Program
P.O. Box 25000
Orlando, FL 32816
Ransford C. Pyle

University of Miami
Institute for Paralegal Studies
P.O. Box 248005
Coral Gables, FL 33124
Patrick Michaud

University of West Florida
Faculty of Political Science
Pensacola, FL 32504
Robert L. Anderson

Valencia Community College
East Campus
P.O. Box 3028
Orlando, FL 32802
Marian Baker

GEORGIA

Gainesville Junior College
Legal Assistant Program
Mundy Mill Road
Gainesville, GA 30501
Louise Holcomb
David Sargent

*National Center for Paralegal
    Training
  Lawyer's Assistant Program
Suite 430
3376 Peachtree Road, N.E.
Atlanta, GA 30326
Sandra Jennings

HAWAII

*Kapiolani Community College
Legal Assistant Program
620 Pensacola Street
Honolulu, HI 96814
Robert J. LeClair

ILLINOIS

Illinois State University
Legal Studies Program
Department of Political Science
Schroeder 306
Normal, IL 61761
Thomas Eimermann

MacCormac Junior College
327 S. LaSalle Street
Chicago, IL 60604
Kathleen Polk

*Mallinckrodt College
Legal Assistant Program
1041 Ridge Road
Wilmette, IL 60091
Frank Keating

McKendree College
Paralegal Studies of
  Administration of Justice
College Road
Lebanon, IL 62254
Mr. Arnesson

Midstate College
Paralegal Services
244 S.W. Jefferson, Box 148
Peoria, IL 61602
Arline H. Bunch

National College of Education
Legal Assistant Program
2840 Sheridan Road
Evanston, IL 60201
Robert Shuford

The National Council of Black
  Lawyers Community College
  of Law and International
  Diplomacy
Paralegal Studies
4545 S. Drexel Blvd.
Chicago, IL 60653

*Roosevelt University
Lawyer's Assistant Program
430 S. Michigan Avenue
Chicago, IL 60605
Laura Brussell

Sangamon State University
Center for Legal Studies
Shepherd Road
Springfield, IL 62708
Patricia A. Langley

*William Rainey Harper College
Legal Technology Program
Algonquin and Roselle Roads
Palatine, IL 60067
Sharrie Hildebrandt

INDIANA

Ball State University
Legal Assistance and Legal
  Admin.
Muncie, IN 47306
Sally Jo Vasicko

Butler University
Legal Assistant Program
4600 Sunset
Indianapolis, IN 46208
George M. Waller

Indiana Central University
1400 E. Hanna Avenue
Indianapolis, IN 46227
Stephen M. Maple

*University of Evansville
Legal Paraprofessional
  Programs
P.O. Box 329
Evansville, IN 47702
Roger Sublett

Vincennes University
Paralegal Program
1002 North 1st Street
Vincennes, IN 47591
Jack Wilson

IOWA

Des Moines Area Cmty. College
2006 Ankeny Boulevard
Ankeny, IA 50021
Cary A. Israel

Iowa Lakes Community College
826 N. 13th Street
Estherville, IA 51334
Randy J. Abbott

Kirkwood Community College
6301 Kirkwood Boulevard, S.W.
P.O. Box 2068
Cedar Rapids, IA 52406
Michael R. LaFrance

Marycrest College
1607 W. 12th Street
Davenport, IA 52804
John McAndrews

KANSAS

Barton County Community
  College
Legal Assisting
Great Bend, KS 67530
Delores Meyer

Hutchinson Community Junior
  College
Legal Assistant Program
1300 North Plum
Hutchinson, KS 67501
Vern Hoglund

*Johnson County Cmty. College
Paralegal Program
College Boulevard at Quivera
  Road
Overland Park, KS 66210
Michael A. Pener

*Wichita State University
Legal Assistant Program
College of Business
  Administration
Wichita, KS 67208
Curtis D. Terflinger

KENTUCKY

*Eastern Kentucky University
Legal Assistance Education
  Program
Lancaster Avenue
Richmond, KY 40475
James W. H. McCord

Midway College
Paralegal Program
Midway, KY 40347
Maureen Carman

LOUISIANA

Louisiana State University
8515 Youree Drive
Shreveport, LA 71115
John B. Powell

Nicholls State University
Legal Assistant Studies
P.O. Box 2024, N.S.U.
Thibodaux, LA 70301
David M. Landry

Tulane University
University College
New Orleans, LA 70118
Sarah Sang

MAINE

Beal College
Paralegal Program
629 Main Street
Bangor, ME 04401

University of Southern Maine
Department of Conferences &
  Special Programs
96 Falmouth Street
Portland, ME 04103
Joanne Spear

MARYLAND

Cmty. College of Baltimore
2901 Liberty Heights Avenue
Baltimore, MD 21215
Frederick S. Lee

Dundalk Cmty. College
7200 Sollers Point Road
Baltimore, MD 21222
Arnold M. Zerwitz

Harford Community College
401 Thomas Run Road
Bel Air, MD 21014
Bert Cooperstein

University of Maryland
University College
College Park Campus
College Park, MD 20742
Elvira White

*Villa Julie College
Legal Assistant Program
Greenspring Valley Road
Stevenson, MD 21153
Francis X. Pugh

MASSACHUSETTS

Anna Maria College
Paralegal Program
Paxton, MA 01612
George R. Griffin

Bay Path Junior College
Legal Assistant Program
588 Longmeadow Street
Longmeadow, MA 01106
James Barden

Becker Junior College
Paralegal Assistant
61 Sever Street
Worcester, MA 01609
Florence Harrison

*Bentley College
Institute of Paralegal Studies
Beaver & Forest Streets
Waltham, MA 02154
Patricia A. Segerson

Boston State College
Paralegal Program
625 Huntington Avenue
Boston, MA 02115
Herman W. Hemingway

Hampshire College
Amherst, MA 01002
Oliver Fowlkes — David Kerr

Middlesex Cmty. College
Division of C.E.
Springs Road
Bedford, MA 01730
Ralph G. Soderberg
Kathleen Crooks

Mount Ida Junior College
Legal Assistant Program
Evening Division
777 Dedham Street
Newton, MA 02159
Rodney Barker

Newbury Junior College
Paralegal Program
921 Boylston Street
Boston, MA 02115
Willard P. Warwick

Northeastern University
Paralegal Program
7 Water Street
Boston, MA 02109
Shelley G. Widoff

Regis College
Legal Studies Program
235 Wellesley Street
Weston, MA 02193
Elizabeth C. Barrington

University of Massachusetts
Division of C.E.
Legal Assistant Training
  Program
Amherst, MA 01002
Frederick Robinson

University of Massachusetts-
  Boston
Center for Legal Education
  Services
100 Arlington Street
Boston, MA 02116
David E. Matz

MICHIGAN

Baker Junior College of
  Business
1110 Eldon Baker Drive
Flint, MI 48507
Sandra Kunard

*Ferris State College
Legal Assistant Program
Big Rapids, MI 49307
Laura Bazell
R. Dale Hobart

Grand Valley State Colleges
School of Public Service
College Landing
467 Mackinac Hall
Allendale, MI 49401
Ricardo Meana

Henry Ford Community College
5101 Evergreen Road
Dearborn, MI 48125
Thaddeus C. Matley

Hillsdale College
33 College Street
Hillsdale, MI 49242
Robert Blackstock

Kellogg Community College
Legal Assistant Program
450 North Avenue
Battle Creek, MI 49016
Thomas R. Blaising

Lansing Community College
Accounting & Office Programs
  Department
419 N. Capitol Avenue
P.O. Box 40010
Lansing, MI 48901
Ronald K. Edwards

Macomb County Cmty. College
South Campus
14500 Twelve Mile Road
Warren, MI 48093
Margaret Rose

Madonna College
26600 Schoolcraft Road
Livonia, MI 48150
Dennis Bozyk

Mercy College of Detroit
Legal Assistant Program
Center for the Administration of
  Justice
8200 W. Outer Drive
Detroit, MI 48219
Sheldon A. Silver

Michigan Paraprofessional
  Training Institute, Inc.
21700 Northwestern Highway,
  Ste. 515
Southfield, MI 48075

Mott Community College
1401 E. Court Street
Flint, MI 48503
Peter K. Petro

Muskegon Business College
Paralegal Program
141 Hartford Street
Muskegon, MI 49442
Roger A. Miller

*Oakland University
Diploma Program for Legal
  Assts.
Division of C.E.
Rochester, MI 48063
Priscilla Hildum

MINNESOTA

*Inver Hills Community College
Legal Assistant Program
8445 College Trail
Inver Grove Heights, MN 55075
Gordon W. Shumaker

*North Hennepin Community
  College
Legal Assistant Program
7411 85th Avenue North
Minneapolis, MN 55445
John Hinsverk — Darel
  Swenson

*University of Minnesota
General College
Legal Assistant Program
106 Nicholson Hall
Minneapolis, MN 55455
Denise Templeton

*Winona State University
Paralegal Program
4330 W-7
Winona, MN 55987
Roderick Henry

MISSISSIPPI

Mississippi University for
  Women
Paralegal Program
Department of Social Sciences
Columbus, MS 39701
Billy Pounds

Northwest Mississippi Jr.
  College
300 North Panola Street
Senatobia, MS 38668
Carl Horn

University of Mississippi
Paralegal Studies Program
Universities Center, Ste. 116
Jackson, MS 39211
Bruce J. Bellande

University of Southern
  Mississippi
Paralegal Studies
P.O. Box 5267, Southern Station
Hattiesburg, MS 39401
Ronald G. Marquardt

MISSOURI

Avila College
11901 Wornall Road
Kansas City, MO 64145
Kathryn Kelm

Columbia College
Legal Assistant Program
Columbia, MO 64201
Diana Berry

Marysville College
13550 Conway Road
St. Louis, MO 63110
James E. McKee

Missouri Western State College
4525 Downs Drive
St. Joseph, MO 64507
David Dye

Penn Valley Community College
Legal Technology Program
3201 S.W. Tfwy.
Kansas City, MO 64111
John K. Enenbach

Rockhurst College
Evening Division
5225 Troost Avenue
Kansas City, MO 64110
Ellen C. Iseman

St. Louis Community College at
  Florissant Valley
3400 Perhall Road
St. Louis, MO 63135
J.A. Miller

St. Louis Community College at
  Forrest Park
5600 Oakland Avenue
St. Louis, MO 63110

St. Louis Community College at
  Meramec
11333 Big Bend
St. Louis, MO 63122
George Wang

Southeast Missouri State
  University
Cape Girardeau, MO 63701
Carolyn Mae Rainey

*William Woods College
Paralegal Studies Program
Fulton, MO 65251
Granville E. Collins

NEBRASKA

*Lincoln School of Commerce
1821 K Street
P.O. Box 82826
Lincoln, NB 68501
Dale C. Holmes

University of Nebraska
Omaha, NB 68132

NEVADA

Reno Junior College of Business
Wells & Wonder
Reno, NV 89502
Don S. Thompson

NEW HAMPSHIRE

McIntosh College
23 Cataract Avenue
Dover, NH 03820

*Rivier College
Baccalaureate & Certificate
  Paralegal Studies Programs
Nashua, NH 03060
Angelo T. Andriopoulos

NEW JERSEY

Brookdale Community College
Paralegal Technology
Newman Springs Road
Lincroft, NJ 07738
Charlotte Engelman

*Burlington County College
CA 267
Pemberton-Browns Mills Road
Pemberton, NJ 08068
Jack Tapper

*Cumberland County College
Legal Technology Program
P.O. Box 517
Vineland, NJ 08360
Thomas H. Brown

First School of Secretarial &
  Paralegal Studies
333 Rt. 46 West
Fairfield, NJ 07006
Jerrold Kaminsky

First School of Secretarial &
  Paralegal Studies
516 Main Street
East Orange, NJ 07018
Jerrold Kaminsky

Institute for Legal Assistant &
  Paralegal Training
61 North Maple Avenue
Ridgewood, NJ 07450
Julie M. Clark

*Mercer County Community
  College
Legal Assistant Program
P.O. Box B
Trenton, NJ 08690
James F. Rowe

Middlesex County College
Legal Assistant Program
9 Ennis Drive
Hazlet, NJ 07730
Charlotte A. Engleman

Montclair State College
Paralegal Studies Program
Upper Montclair, NJ 07043
Marilyn Frankenthaler

Ocean County College
A.A.S. Legal Assistant
Toms River, NJ 08753
C. E. Strain

Plaza School
Garden State Plaza
Rt. 17 & Rt. 4
Paramus, NJ 07652
Charles B. Knower

South Jersey Paralegal School
302 Sherry Way
Cherry Hill, NJ 08034
Leonard J. Talarico

Sutton Paralegal School
1 Sutton Terrace
Collingswood, NJ 08107

Upsala College
Paralegal Program
Office of C.E. Beck 205
East Orange, NJ 07019
Diane C. Borman

NEW MEXICO

University of Albuquerque
St. Joseph's Place
Albuquerque, NM 87140
Walt Niederberger

Navajo Community College
Legal Advocates Training
  Program
P.O. Box 580
Shiprock, NM 87420
Robin Duboe Seigle

NEW YORK

*Adelphi University
University College
Division of Special Programs
Lawyer's Assistant Program
Garden City, L.I., NY 11530
Ruth Goldsmith

Broome Community College
Paralegal Assistant Program
P.O. Box 1017
Binghamton, NY 13902
Matthew A. Vitanza

College for Human Services
201 Varick Street
New York, NY 10014

Corning Community College
Paralegal Assistant Program
Spencer Hill Road
Corning, NY 14830
Pauline Leveen

Elizabeth Seton College
Legal Assistant Program
1061 North Broadway
Yonkers, NY 10701
Jane G. Kaplan

Herkimer County Cmty. College
Herkimer, NY 13350
Linda B. Vincent

*Hilbert College
Legal Assistant Program
5200 South Park Avenue
Hamburg, NY 14075
Roger E. Stone

Hunter College
Paralegal Program
Center for Lifelong Learning
466 Lexington Avenue
New York, NY 10017
Martha Zelman

Junior College of Albany
140 New Scotland Avenue
Albany, NY 12208
Michael J. Smith

*Long Island University
Paralegal Studies Program
University Plaza
Room M500
Brooklyn, NY 11201
Terrence Fogarty

Manhattanville College
Continuing Education
Purchase, NY 10577
Janet Gutterman

Marist College
North Road
Poughkeepsie, NY 12601
Carolyn C. Landau

*Mercy College
White Plains Extension Center
Paralegal Studies Program
White Plains, NY 10601
Anthony Libertella
Rachel Berkey

§ 1.9 Working With Legal Assistants

Nassau Community College
Paralegal Assistant Program
Stewart Avenue
Garden City, NY 11530
Elliot Kleinman

New York University
Institute of Paralegal Studies
School of C.E. in Law &
 Taxation
11 W. 42d Street
New York, NY 10036
Nicolas Liakas
Kathleen Kroitor

Paralegal Institute
132 Nassau Street
New York, NY 10038
Carl E. Person

St. John's University
Legal Assistant Program
Grand Central and Utopia
 Parkway
Jamaica, Queens, NY 11439
George Ansalone

Schenectady County Cmty.
 College
Washington Avenue
Schenectady, NY 12305
Robert D. Larson

Suffolk County Cmty. College
A.A.S. Paralegal Studies
533 College Road
Selden, NY 11784
John Edward Coen, Jr.

Sullivan County Cmty. College
Para-Legal Assistant Program
Loch Sheldrake, NY 12759
John F. Gallagher, Jr.

Syracuse University/University
 College
610 East Fayette Street
Syracuse, NY 13202
Helen Buck

NORTH CAROLINA

Central Carolina Technical
 Institute
Department of Community
 Colleges
1105 Kelly Drive
Sanford, NC 27330
Carolyn L. Register

Davidson Cty. Community
 College
P.O. Box 1287
Intersection of Old Greensboro
 Road & Interstate 40
Lexington, NC 27292
Lilona Schiro

*Fayetteville Technical Institute
P.O. Box 5236
Fayetteville, NC 28303
Melvin Hartley

Greensboro College
Department of Business
 Administration, Legal
 Administration & Sociology
Greensboro, NC 27420
Laws Parks

Meredith College
Legal Assistant Program
Dept. of Continuing Education
P.O. Box E-144
Raleigh, NC 27611
Emily P. Johnson

Pitt Technical Institute
Paralegal Program
P.O. Drawer 7007
Greenville, NC 27834
Lloyd Huggins

Southwestern Technical
 Institute
P.O. Box 95
Sylva, NC 28779
Charles Hipps

OHIO

Academy of Paralegal Studies,
 Paralegal Institute of the
 Western Reserve
Suite 201, Silver Building
Public Square
Wooster, OH 44691
Mark W. Altier

Capital University
2199 E. Main Street
Columbus, OH 43209
John W. McCormac

Clark Technical College
Legal Assisting
570 East Leffels Lane
P.O. Box 570
Springfield, OH 45501
J. Thomas Fourman

*Dyke College
Paralegal Education Programs
1375 E. 6th Street
Cleveland, OH 44114
Sharon Siders

Hammel Actual College
59 East Market Street
Akron, OH 44308

Ohio Paralegal Institute
1001 Euclid Avenue
Suite 404
Cleveland, OH 44115
Salvatore L. Volpe

Sinclair Community College
444 West Third Street
Dayton, OH 45402
Garnett McDonough

University of Cincinnati
Paralegal Program
University College, Mail
 Location #168
Cincinnati, OH 45221
Ruth McCalla Edwards

University of Toledo
Paralegal Program
Scott Park Campus
2501 Bancroft
Toledo, OH 43606
Nancy Robon

OKLAHOMA

*Oscar Rose Junior College
Business Division
6420 Southeast 15th
Midwest City, OK 73110
Judy Shaw

Tulsa Junior College
Business Service Division
909 South Boston
Tulsa, OK 74119
Bobbie Reed

*University of Oklahoma
C. L. E. Law Center
Paralegal Program
300 Timberdell, Rm. 314
Norman, OK 73019
Annette H. Prince

OREGON

Clackamas Community College
Business Education Department
19600 South Molalla Avenue
Oregon City, OR 97045
Mel Hostager

Lane Community College
Business Department
4000 E. 30th Avenue
Eugene, OR 97405
John W. Kreitz
Sharon Moore

Mt. Hood Community College
26000 S. E. Stark Street
Gresham, OR 97030
John Dier

Oregon State Department of
 Education
942 Lancaster Drive, N. E.
Salem, OR 97310
John W. Havery

*Portland Community College
Legal Assistant Program
Department of Government
 Services
12000 Southwest 49th Avenue
Portland, OR 97219
John M. Koroloff

PENNSYLVANIA

Allegheny Community College
808 Ridge Avenue
Pittsburgh, PA 15212

*Cedar Crest College
Legal Assistant Program
Allentown, PA 18104
Richard L. Kolbe

*Central Pennsylvania Business
School
College Hill Road
Summerdale, PA 17093
Amy Hershner

Gannon College
Perry Square
Erie, PA 16501
Ted G. Miller

Harrisburg Area Cmty. College
3300 Cameron Street Road
Harrisburg, PA 17110
William R. Ferencz

Indiana University of
 Pennsylvania
Paralegal Program
School of Business
Indiana, PA 15705

*Institute for Paralegal Training
 (The)
235 S. 17th Street
Philadelphia, PA 19103
Molly Lunkenheimer

King's College
Legal Assistant Program
Department of Criminal Justice
Wilkes Barre, PA 18711
Thomas J. Glenn, Jr.

Main Line Paralegal Institute
121 N. Wayne Avenue
Wayne, PA 19087
Rusch O. Dees
Frances M. Guth

Marywood College
Legal Assistant Program
Scranton, PA 18509
John W. Barrett

Northampton County Area
 Community College
Legal Assistant Certificate
 Program
3835 Green Pond Road
Bethlehem, PA 18017
Alice Dornish
Frank Ensminger

Pennsylvania State University,
 Allentown Campus
Continuing Education
Paralegal Certificate Program
Allentown Campus, Academic
 Building
Fogelsville, PA 18051
Kenneth A. McGeary

Pennsylvania State University,
 Fayette Campus
Paralegal Education Program
Continuing Education
 Department
University Drive
P.O. Box 519
Uniontown, PA 15401
D. J. Nurkiewicz

Pennsylvania State University,
 Main Campus
Paralegal Program
College of Business
 Administration
201 Old Main
University Park, PA 16802

Pennsylvania State University,
 McKeesport Campus
Paralegal Certificate Program
Continuing Education
University Drive
McKeesport, PA 15132
Frances Jordan

Pennsylvania State University,
 York Campus
Paralegal Certificate Program
1031 Edgecomb Avenue
York, PA 17403
James F. Campbell

Robert Morris College
Legal Assistant Certificate
 Program
610 Fifth Avenue
Pittsburgh, PA 15219
Ronald Cammarata

*Widener University
Delaware County
Chester, PA 19013
Martin Goldstein

RHODE ISLAND

Roger Williams College
Paralegal Studies
Old Ferry Road
Bristol, RI 02809
John P. Pozzi
Thomas E. Wright

Salve Regina — The Newport
 College
Legal Assistant Program
Newport, RI 02840
Charles W. Cooke

SOUTH CAROLINA

Greenville Technical College
P.O. Box 5616 Station B
Greenville, SC 29606
R. S. Fisher

Midlands Technical College
Drawer Q
Columbia, SC 29250
Joseph J. Mallini, Jr.

SOUTH DAKOTA

Yankton College
Legal Assistance Program
12th and Douglas
Yankton, SD 57078
John Nies

TENNESSEE

*Cleveland State Cmty. College
Legal Assistant Program
P.O. Box 1205
Cleveland, TN 37311
John E. Cook

Memphis State University
School of Law
Memphis, TN 38152
G. Robert Alsobrook

University of Tennessee
Paralegal Training Program
Stokely Management Center
 (SMC) 608
Knoxville, TN 37916
Mary A. Herr

TEXAS

*Del Mar College
Legal Assistant Program
Baldwin & Ayers
Corpus Christi, TX 78404
Stonewall Van Wie, III

El Centro College
Main and Lamar
Admissions Office
Dallas, TX 75202
Sharman Beasley

El Paso Community College
Legal Assistant Program
6601 Dyer Street
El Paso, TX 79904
Ted Martinez

Houston Community College
 System
Legal Assistant Program
4310 Dunlavy Avenue
Houston, TX 77006
John E. Sharp

Lamar University
Continuing Education
P.O. Box 10008
Beaumont, TX 77710
James D. Spencer

St. Edwards University
Legal Assistance Program
Austin, TX 78704
Cliff Roberson

San Antonio College
Legal Assistant Program
1300 San Pedro Avenue
San Antonio, TX 78284
Program Coordinator

Southwest Texas State
 University
Lawyer's Assistant Program
Department of Political Science
San Marcos, TX 78666

*Southwestern Paralegal
  Institute
Basic Legal Assistant Studies
  Program
5512 Chaucer Drive
Houston, TX 77005
Janet R. Covington

Texas Para-Legal School —
  Dallas
810 Main Street, Suite 203
Dallas, TX 75202
James D. Hinman

Texas Para-Legal School —
  Houston
608 Fannin, Ste. 1903
Houston, TX 77002
Lee S. Kooistra

Texas Woman's University
Legal Assistant Program
Department of History and
  Government
P.O. Box 23974
Denton, TX 76204
Martha Swain

University of Texas at Arlington
Paralegal Program
Dept. of Political Science
Arlington, TX 76019
Charles W. Van Cleve

West Texas State University
School of Business
Department of Business
  Education & Office Education
Canyon, TX 79016
Willie J. McCall

UTAH

Utah Technical College at Provo
Legal Assistant Program
Box 1009
Provo, UT 84601
Maxine K. Christensen

VERMONT

Champlain College
232 S. Willard Street
Burlington, VT 05401
R. Austin Skiff

VIRGINIA

Central Virginia Community
  College
Legal Assistant Program
Lynchburg, VA 24502

Ferrum College
Ferrum, VA 24088
Ralph Rhodes
Bruce Welch

James Madison University
Paralegal Studies Program
Department of Political Science
Harrisonburg, VA 22807
William R. Nelson

J. Sargeant Reynolds Cmty.
  College
Parham Road Campus
P.O. Box 12084
Richmond, VA 23241
Susan E. Holleman

Northern Virginia Community
  College,
  Alexandria Campus
Legal Assistant Technology
3001 North Beauregard Street
Alexandria, VA 22311
William T. Shannon

Para-Legal Institute
Suite 300
6801 Whittier Avenue
McLean, VA 22101
Kenneth Eaton

Thomas Nelson Community
  College
Legal Assistant Program
P.O. Box 9407
Hampton, VA 23670
Marie D. Tyler

Tidewater Community College
Legal Assistant Program
1700 College Crescent
Virginia Beach, VA 23456
Eric H. Steentofte

University of Richmond
University College Evening
  School
University of Richmond, VA
  23173
Jean H. Proffitt

Virginia Western Cmty. College
3095 Colonial Avenue, S.W.
Roanoke, VA 24015
Martha B. Brown

WASHINGTON

Bellevue Community College
Bellevue, WA 98007
Daniel J. LaFond

Central Washington University
Program in Law & Justice
Ellensburg, WA 98926
Robert Jacobs

City College
403-405 Lyon Building
Seattle, WA 98104
Kathleen M. Milne-Banks

*Edmonds Community College
20000 68th Avenue West
Lynnwood, WA 98036
Michael Fitch

Fort Steilacoom Cmty. College
9401 Farwest Drive SW
Tacoma, WA 98498
Jan Halverson

*Highline Community College
Legal Assistant Program
Community College District 9
Midway, WA 98031
Davidson Dodd

Lower Columbia College
Legal Assistant Program
1600 Maple
Longview, WA 98632
Jerry Zimmerman

Spokane Community College
Legal Assistant Program
North 1810 Greene Street
Spokane, WA 99207
Jonnie L. Owens
James S. McLean

WEST VIRGINIA

Fairmont State College
Legal Assistant Program
Division of Social Science
Fairmont, WV 26554
Patricia P. Ryan

Marshall University
Community College
Legal Assistant Program
Huntington, WV 25701
Dan O'Hanlon — J. Robert
  Amos

WISCONSIN

*Lakeshore Technical Institute
1290 North Avenue
Cleveland, WI 53015
John B. Knight

Milwaukee Area Technical
  College
1015 North 6th Street
Milwaukee, WI 53203
William Breese

District #1 Vocation Technical
  Adult Education
620 W. Clairmont Avenue
Eau Claire, WI 54701
Joanne Dowe

§ 1.10 Selected Bibliography For Legal Assistant Program Managers.

A.B.A., People in the Law Office, Eighth National Conference on Law Office Economics and Management (1978).

M. Altman and R. Weil, How to Manage Your Law Office (Matthew Bender, 1976).
E. Berne, The Structure and Dynamics of Organizations and Groups (J.B. Lippincott Co., 1963).
R. Bolton, People Skills (Prentice-Hall, Inc. 1979).
J. Brill, *How Planning Your Practice Will Produce Pleasure and Profitability!*, Legal Economics, Spring 1978, at 11.
C. Bruno, Paralegal's Litigation Handbook (Institute for Business Planning, Inc. 1980).
W. Cobb, Planning Workbook for Law Firm Management (A.B.A. 1978).
E. Dale, Management Theory and Practice (McGraw-Hill, 2d ed. 1969).
P. Drucker, The Effective Executive (Harper & Row, 1966).
P. Drucker, The Practice of Management (Harper & Row, 1954).
J. Gardner, *How to Prevent Organizational Dry Rot*, Harper's Magazine, Oct. 1965, at 21.
J. Gardner, Self-Renewal (Perennial Lib. ed., 1971).
G. Gilhool, *Working Together: Professional and Paraprofessional*, Trial, Feb. 1978, at 54.
F. Herzberg, *One More Time: How Do You Motivate Employees?*, Harv. Bus. Rev., Jan.-Feb. 1968, at 53.
F. Herzberg, Work and the Nature of Man (World Pub. Co. 1966).
A. Lakein, How to Get Control of Your Time and Your Life (Signet, 1973).
D. Larbalestrier, Paralegal Practice and Procedure (Prentice-Hall, Inc. 1977).
Law Office Economics and Management Manual (Callaghan & Co. 1970).
R. Mackenzie, The Time Trap (McGraw-Hill, 1972).
D. Mackintosh, Management by Exception: A Handbook With Forms (Prentice-Hall, Inc., 1978).
P. Mali, Management by Objectives (Wiley-Interscience, 1972).
Manual for Managing the Law Office (Prentice-Hall, Inc., 1970).
A. Maslow, Motivation and Personality (Harper & Row, 2d ed. 1970).
D. McGregor, The Human Side of Enterprise (McGraw-Hill, 1960).
D. McGregor, The Professional Manager (McGraw-Hill, 1967).
R. Murdick and J. Ross, Information Systems for Modern Management (Prentice-Hall, Inc., 2d ed. 1975).
J. Newman, Release Your Brakes! (Charles B. Stack, Inc. 1977).
W. Oncken, Jr. and D. Wass, *Management Time: Who's Got the Monkey?*, Harv. Bus. Rev., Oct.-Nov. 1974, at 95.
L. Peter, The Peter Prescription (Morrow, 1972).
R. Ramo, ed., How to Create-A-System for the Law Office (A.B.A., 1975).
J. Ross, Managing Productivity (Reston Publishing Co., Inc. 1977).
J. Ross, Modern Management and Information Systems (Reston Publishing Co., Inc., 1977).
W. Statsky, *The Education of Legal Paraprofessionals: Myths, Realities and Opportunities*, 24 Vand. L. Rev. 1083 (1971).
W. Statsky, Introduction to Paralegalism (West Pub. Co., 1974).

W. Statsky, *Techniques for Supervising Paralegals*, 22 Practical Lawyer No. 4, at 81 (1976).

G. Steiner, ed., The Creative Organization (University of Chicago, 1965).

D. Thomas, *Strategy Is Different in Service Businesses*, Harv. Bus. Rev., July-Aug. 1978, at 158.

J. Thomas and W. Bennis, eds., Management of Change and Conflict (Penguin Books, 1972).

R. Townsend, Up the Organization (Fawcett Crest Book, 1970).

L. Tracy, *Postscript to the Peter Principle*, Harv. Bus. Rev., July-Aug., 1972, at 65.

P. Ulrich, *Managing a Law Practice "By Objectives and Self-Control,"* 20 LOEM 183 (1979).

P. Ulrich, *Managing an Effective Legal Assistant Program*, Ariz. B.J., Aug. 1978, at 42, *reprinted in* Legal Economics, Jan.-Feb. 1979, at 35.

P. Ulrich and S. Clarke, *Building Your Firm's Legal Assistant Program*, Ariz. B.J., Oct. 1976, at 20, *reprinted in* 19 LOEM 117 (1978).

P. Ulrich and C. Multhauf, *Law Firm Working Relationships: Developing a Long-Term Legal Assistant Program*, 20 LOEM 289 (1979).

J. VanFleet, How to Use the Dynamics of Motivation (Parker Pub. Co., 1967).

G. Zaltman and R. Duncan, Strategies for Planned Change (Wiley-Interscience, 1977).

2

ECONOMIC BENEFITS AND WORKING RELATIONSHIPS

Donald S. Akins*

§ 2.1 This Chapter's Scope. This chapter discusses the legal assistant's working relationships with lawyers and members of the law firm's staff. It also highlights the economic benefits derived from effective use of assistants. This includes the economic impact assistants have on a firm and the commitment required of lawyers to make the program efficient and profitable. The author's opinions are based on his experience as a law firm administrator and management consultant. Experiences of firms around the country are also incorporated to illustrate successful approaches to a legal assistant program.

§ 2.2 The Economics of Using Legal Assistants.

§ 2.2.1 The Economic Need. In the last few years, some firms have experienced a decrease in either gross fees, net income per lawyer or both. This has caused many lawyers to realize that their methods for delivering legal services must be carefully examined if they are to continue their practices successfully. Since a lawyer's time is limited, systems and procedures must be implemented to improve the return on each invested hour. In short, lawyers must practice "smarter law."

For years, the legal profession has been criticized for its failure to offer legal services to middle and lower income families at prices they can afford. With a shrinking net profit, such services could decline and, in fact, could almost disappear. The profession cannot permit this to happen. Lawyers must decide how to expand the availability of legal services to this large segment of the population, despite the adverse economic forces.

Another major problem facing the legal profession is the public's view of attorneys' fees. Many people believe these fees are excessive for the service received. At the same time, most lawyers believe that hourly rates must continue to increase to keep up with inflation. These forces have now met head on. The legal profession must explore ways to solve the problem other than by simply increasing billing rates.

Many firms believe that effective use of legal assistants is one of their major options. Most are now employing one or more legal assistants. Other firms have thought about such a program but have given only "lip service" to implementation; still others do not believe such a program will work and have decided not to explore it any further. With all due respect, these latter two viewpoints are shortsighted. There are many ways to practice "smarter law." Proper use of legal assistants is one of the better ones. The following sections will illustrate how valuable such assistants can be to the firm's delivery of legal services.

---

*Vice-president and manager of Dallas, Texas office, Bradford W. Hildebrandt & Company.

§ 2.2.2 Expense Factors. Like other people-oriented activities, legal assistants will be costly unless there is a commitment to the program and sufficient time is devoted to its implementation. Simply employing assistants and assuming they will be productive and self-sustaining is wishful thinking. Many firms have concluded that assistants cannot function effectively for them because of this approach. An interesting comparison can be made to the hiring of associate lawyers. Lawyers just completing law school are employed with the general understanding that they may not be productive and profitable until their second or third year of practice. Yet most firms expect legal assistants to be productive immediately. Except on rare occasions, this is not possible.

Legal assistants are now receiving substantial salaries. They should therefore not be employed unless the firm is committed to making its program a success. Unless the assistant is properly motivated, he or she will in all likelihood go to another firm or find another career offering greater job enrichment. Such departures create a dual problem of both economics and turnover. The cost of turnover is staggering — each firm should conduct an analysis of what it costs when an assistant resigns. Economically, it is much cheaper to do without assistants than to employ them inefficiently. The expense factors to be considered are shown at Form 2:1. Even though the form tends to portray profitability, this is not its only purpose. The firm should realize that encouraging the assistant to become a motivated employee is the first priority.

§ 2.2.2.1 Salary. Legal assistants should receive proper compensation based upon market conditions, experience, education and position evaluation. In certain cities proper compensation is not a reality. Some cities have a high rate of use of assistants, with average to above average salaries. Others have a poor rate of use, with less than acceptable salaries. It is not uncommon to find this wide variance within firms in the same city. The major difference is that too many firms have made no attempt to pay an adequate salary in relation to the position's requirements. As the result, salaries may be less than acceptable.

§ 2.2.2.2 Secretarial Expense. The legal assistant must have access to secretarial and word processing support. Legal assistants, on the average, each require at least one-third of the time of a secretary/word processor, and sometimes more. This need is discussed at § 2.6 and shown as an expense on Form 2:1.

§ 2.2.2.3 Taxes. This expense includes all of the various taxes relating to payroll and unemployment.

§ 2.2.2.4 Fringe Benefits. This area has shown vast improvement in the past two years, primarily as a result of competition and the beginning of position evaluation by some firms. Some of the more common benefits are bonuses, health and life insurance coverage for the legal assistant and dependents, retirement, firm-paid attendance at continuing education seminars and parking.

§ 2.2.2.5 Office Rent. The legal assistant's work area should be at least 10' x 10'. Using a square foot cost of $9.00 per year, this would equal $900.00.

§ 2.2.2.6 Dictation Equipment. This is a capital expenditure; annual depreciation is the yearly expense. The $400.00 is included in Form 2:1 to indicate a cash outlay the first year. In order to determine profitability, the annual depreciation would be used and not the entire $400.00.

§ 2.2.2.7 Furniture. The legal assistant requires a desk, an executive chair, one or more side chairs, a credenza or work table, a filing cabinet or shelves, and other miscellaneous items. The firm should establish an allowance for furnishing legal assistant offices of at least $1,000.00.

§ 2.2.3 Quotas. Billing and collection quotas for legal assistants should be handled carefully. Even though many firms have minimum requirements for evaluation purposes, publicized quotas are not popular with assistants. Since assistants have no control over the firm's billing and collection practices, it is unfair to reward one with high numbers who had the good fortune of working with a lawyer having excellent billing practices and penalize another with less than acceptable numbers who had the misfortune of working with a lawyer having poor billing practices. In this example, the fault does not necessarily lie with the assistant. If assistants have assigned quotas which are used for evaluation, the result may well prove damaging and possibly cause the loss of a good employee.

Another consideration relating to quotas is the amount of work available for each legal assistant. Some are given too much to do, others not enough. Someone in the firm — a lawyer, administrator or another assistant — must be responsible for coordinating each assistant's work to maintain some control of assignments. An assistant with minimal firm administrative responsibilities should be able to spend from 75% to 80% of his or her time on client matters.

It is important for the firm to know how each legal assistant spends his or her time. The firm's time analysis reports should include the assistants. A production report including hours worked, billable hours, billed hours, inventory of hours and collections should be prepared monthly for each assistant and reviewed to identify any large accumulations of time, write-offs and write-downs, and nonbillable time. These reviews are excellent aids in improving the billing practices of certain lawyers and for evaluation sessions with the assistants.

§ 2.2.4 Income Production. An example of direct and indirect fee income production by a legal assistant is also shown on Form 2:1. Although the figures shown are attainable, the philosophy of each firm must be considered before establishing them. Quotas or formulas measuring profitability as the basis for a program's success may become self-defeating. One formula approach is the "rule of three," which holds that an assistant's fee income should be allocated in equal thirds to salary, overhead and profit. This approach assumes that the assistant's time is being fully employed in income-producing matters. Many assistants, however, have responsibilities other than client matters. Quotas should therefore be used carefully, especially as to those assistants with other duties requiring substantial amounts of nonchargeable time.

The contribution to fee income caused by saving additional lawyers' time should be large. This return is also illustrated on Form 2:1. Two other major contributions in this area should also be noted. Some of the work previously the responsibility of a lawyer may not have been billed because the lawyer thought his or her billing rates were too high or simply never got around to performing those tasks. The legal assistant will solve both these problems and the client will be better served. In addition, lawyers' standard billing rates may well increase because of the higher concentration of responsibility, decision-making and supervision per chargeable hour.

§ 2.2.5 Immediate Hurdles. There are a number of external considerations affecting the use of legal assistants that should also be considered.

§ 2.2.5.1 Client Acceptance. Client acceptance of legal assistants generally has been good. In some instances, the client initially may be reluctant to talk with anyone other than "my attorney." This attitude will not generally persist if the lawyer explains to the client the value of dealing with the assistant and the assistant's ready availability for gathering and supplying information. After this explanation, a client often asks for the assistant unless the lawyer must in fact be consulted. Most lawyers could save additional time if they would encourage clients to ask for their assistants instead.

The assistant should be introduced to the client during the first visit or asked to join the interview for introduction and fact-gathering. If a lawyer shows confidence in the assistant, usually the client will also. If a lawyer does not show confidence, neither will the client. Involvement is the answer.

§ 2.2.5.2 Judges' Recognition of Legal Assistants' Billing Rates. Some judges have taken the position that fees for legal assistants will be allowed only to the extent of salary and overhead, and that billing rates in excess of those figures will be disallowed. A few allow no charges for assistants at all. Fortunately, these positions are not the majority view. It is the lawyer's and organized bar's responsibility to present to the courts evidence of the value of assistants' time in delivering legal services to clients. When arguing legal fees before the court, the lawyer should understand the value of the service performed by the assistant and attempt to persuade the court of that value, if a portion of the fee is based on the assistant's time.

§ 2.2.5.3 Acceptance by Opposing Counsel. Some lawyers are unwilling to deal with a legal assistant in another firm. However, as with client acceptance, great strides have been made on this problem. The lawyer asking opposing counsel to deal with an assistant should encourage this communication with an understanding that the assistant will only gather and supply information. Although there has been some concern over the unauthorized practice of law by legal assistants, adequate training and supervision should solve or at least minimize this problem.

It is critical to the development of the legal assistant program that clients, judges and opposing counsel be educated to the value of these employees as well as to the belief that one major way to practice "smarter law" and deliver quality legal services at a reasonable cost is the effective use of assistants.

§ 2.3 Continuing Education. Regardless of prior education, training or experience, every legal assistant needs the benefits of an organized continuing education program to become efficient and productive. The purposes of such a program should include qualifying the assistant to meet applicable job requirements. For an example of a litigation legal assistant job description see Form 2:2.

§ 2.3.1 Dedication of Lawyers. The key to the success of the firm's legal assistant program is the dedication of its lawyers. This dedication must be more than talk. It must include action. The program must be planned, organized, implemented, evaluated and changed by the lawyers as required. See the discussion of these matters in chapter 1. Responsibility for each facet of the program varies by firm. In some, the department head is responsible for the assistants; in others the assistants are assigned to supervising lawyers. In yet others a lawyer or committee of one or more lawyers from each section using assistants is responsible for the program. Each of these approaches has been successful. The one approach that has not worked is when the assistant is hired and then left alone to sink or swim to success. Unfortunately, the latter approach is only too common, causing many programs to fail to achieve the results desired. This failure is costly. The criticism coming from such firms hinders the overall program.

§ 2.3.2 Office Policies and Procedures.
It is important for the legal assistant to understand office policies and procedures. A formal orientation program should be established. If the firm has an administrator whose job description is similar to that shown at Form 2:4, this orientation should be the administrator's responsibility. If not, the managing partner, another lawyer dedicated to the program or possibly other assistants should conduct these meetings. The orientation should include all aspects of the firm's operations, with emphasis on timekeeping, billing, file control, word processing, copying, telephone usage, docket control, information retrieval, accounting and the responsibilities of the supervisors of the various administrative activities. Some of these supervisors should participate in the orientation. These orientation meetings should be held before the assistant is given any assignments. A great deal of time is wasted by assistants because they are unaware of how to perform certain tasks, whom to ask or where to find needed material.

Legal assistants should also be asked for their suggestions as to proposed changes in the firm's systems with which they are involved. The best ideas usually come from those doing the work. Training sessions should always be held before new systems are begun, not after. On some occasions, additional sessions will be needed because of complexity or complications. In any event, the system should be examined carefully by all concerned before being imposed on the assistants.

§ 2.3.3 Substantive Education.
Prior education and experience, whether at a legal assistant school or another firm, will not replace the need for additional continuing education by the firm itself. "How we do it" is very important. Substantive educational sessions should be initiated as quickly as possible after a new assistant arrives, or when there have been major changes in the firm's procedures or in the substantive law relating to a particular area of practice. Some firms have scheduled a definite time each week or month for these sessions. Others conduct sessions for specific purposes from time to time. Still others provide no such education other than sending memos "for your information."

The first policy is the most effective. A few firms conduct these meetings in the evening or on Saturday and have found that many employees in addition to the assistants were interested in attending. Some furnish dinner at the evening sessions.

In litigation, it has proven helpful for assistants to understand all aspects of a lawsuit. Some attend trials, others do not. However, litigation assistants should participate in a trial at least periodically to understand better how the process works and to see how a case on which they have worked unfolds.

An understanding of the library is very important. One or more educational sessions should be devoted to the library. Although some assistants do more legal research than others, a general understanding of what is in the library and how to find and use it is essential.

§ 2.3.4 Legal Assistant Retreats.
Another good setting for training is a retreat. Some firms have conducted legal assistant retreats, usually over a weekend, with expenses paid by the firm. This includes at least one and possibly one-and-one-half days of training sessions, with organized social events in the evening. Although care must be taken in the organization of such meetings, some firms believe this is the best approach. Whatever approach is taken, the firm must realize that these

training sessions are necessary in order to obtain satisfactory results from a legal assistant program. Again, lawyer dedication is the key.

§ 2.4 Working Relationships with Staff. It is very important for legal assistants to have good working relationships with other members of the office staff. Every staff member should understand the assistants' roles, how their work is to be done and who are responsible for supervising them.

§ 2.4.1 Other Legal Assistants. Although a little competition never hurt anyone, the firm must develop a program that will encourage cooperation, not competition, among its legal assistants. Internal competition among lawyers has caused the destruction of some law firms. The same can be true for the legal assistant program. Assistants must be encouraged to help each other without worrying about what such help does to their chargeable hours or income production figures. Although the supervising lawyers should control the work loads, occasionally assistants must help each other through an immediate crisis. Open communication must exist between assistants. They should feel free to share ideas.

§ 2.4.2 Secretaries. Legal assistants need the secretaries' support and encouragement. This relationship has been the most strained of all; the reasons are obvious. When some firms announced the decision to employ assistants, often no discussion or announcement was made prior to their arrival as to how they would function in relation to the traditional, established, lawyer-secretary relationships. This approach creates all kinds of problems, usually justified. Although jurisdictional disputes and personality conflicts can never be fully eliminated, those firms that have fostered the team approach have taken a giant step toward doing so.

Secretaries may sometimes feel threatened, and rightly so, if there is lack of proper communication. In those firms where secretaries are kept informed as to what is happening, the requirements for becoming an assistant and the firm's position on being reassigned from secretarial to assistant responsibilities, minimal problems have arisen. The key is respect for each person's position with an understanding of the role played by each member of the team.

§ 2.4.3 Bookkeepers. Legal assistants' relationships with the firm's bookkeeping staff are also important. A great deal of contact is required in requesting financial information about certain matters, the status of the trust account for advanced costs, and all aspects of timekeeping and billing. When time sheets are late or inaccurate, the bookkeeper is responsible for obtaining the information to keep the matters current for billing purposes, as well as to answer inquiries from clients about statements sent by the firm.

§ 2.4.4. Records Department. The records department is usually responsible for the files, their location and their retrieval. All or a portion of daily filing will be done by these employees. In many firms the copying responsibility also rests with them. The personnel performing these duties are very important to the assistant. Assistants should strive to have a good relationship with them. When a crisis occurs, the records department personnel can be a lifesaver.

§ 2.4.5 Word Processing. This may be the most important of all of the staff relationships. Legal assistants are often given very short deadlines for their projects. Yet word processing employees work for everyone, and the assistant must determine how best to request priority for certain projects. The word processing supervisor is probably responsible for making priority assignments. The assistant should therefore get to know the supervisor and follow the applicable guidelines for requesting priority work. The quality of instructions given to word processing is also important. With deadlines to be met all around, the assistant must have a good relationship with the word processing center.

§ 2.5 The Firm's Office Administrator and the Legal Assistant.
The legal assistant's relationship with the firm's office administrator varies a great deal in each firm. This is a very important relationship, both for those firms with an administrator and those contemplating the employment of one.

§ 2.5.1 The Administrator's Role.
It is important that the legal assistant understand the administrator's role in the firm, including his or her job description, position in the firm's structure and authority. Form 2:3 shows various position descriptions developed for survey purposes by the Association of Legal Administrators. The responsibilities and authority are shown for each position. Form 2:4 is a sample job description for a director of administration. The following discussion assumes that the administrator's qualifications and responsibilities meet those descriptions.

§ 2.5.2 Interviewing and Hiring.
The administrator's role in interviewing and hiring legal assistants varies a great deal by firm. Some administrators conduct the interviews and do the actual hiring; some interview and make recommendations; others do not participate at all in this activity. The most common method is the second. Legal assistant applicants are first interviewed by the administrator or a personnel director who works for the administrator. Only those applicants recommended by the administrator are interviewed by the responsible lawyers. Once the interviews are completed, the administrator and responsible lawyers make the hiring decision. The administrator should be heavily involved in this process because of his or her personnel management expertise, including interview techniques. This gives the firm a dual benefit — personality evaluation by the administrator and substantive evaluation by the lawyer. Both of these considerations are necessary to project accurately the applicant's probability of success.

Another successful interview technique is the group interview. For a description, see B. Turner, *Finding People to Help Us*, in People in the Law Office (A.B.A. 1978). If properly used, the group interview may be an excellent tool in selecting legal assistants. With the applicant's competitors listening to responses, the interview process helps determine which applicants respond effectively under pressure. This procedure also saves time for the interviewer. The leader, however, must be capable of handling group interviews. The administrator may be more likely to possess this talent than any other member of the firm.

§ 2.5.3 Education.
The administrator plays an important role in the education of legal assistants if he or she is responsible for their orientation, the explanation of system changes, and the organization and leadership of staff meetings. The overall understanding of internal procedures by the assistant should be the administrator's responsibility.

§ 2.5.4 Evaluation.
The administrator also may play a vital role in the evaluation process for legal assistants. This does not include how assistants handle client matters or their use of time, but does include their attitude, and their willingness and desire to follow internal procedures. The administrator should also be responsible for follow-up to ensure that proper procedures are being followed.

Evaluation is a very important aspect of developing legal assistants. However, a word of caution is needed here. Evaluations should be a training tool and not a disciplinary tool unless absolutely necessary. A great deal of harm can be done by an evaluating lawyer for whom the assistant has done very little or whom the lawyer dislikes for personal reasons. Evaluations should serve a useful purpose or not be done at all. A sample evaluation form for assistants is shown at Form 2:5.

§ 2.6 Access to Support Services.

§ 2.6.1 Access to Secretarial/Word Processing Services. The failure of some legal assistant programs has been the result of the assistants' inability to secure support services from a secretary or word processor or the unavailability of these services. Although inability may be the result of a poor working relationship or lack of understanding the firm's internal procedures, unavailability is the hardest to explain. If legal assistants are given numerous assignments, many requiring priority word processing support, adequate services must be made available to get the work done. One approach used by many firms is for the legal assistant to use the secretary of the lawyer making the assignment. This has proven somewhat successful, except when that secretary has an excessive amount of work. The one condition that should never exist is for the assistant to have to spend time looking for someone to do the work. Instead, assistants should be assigned sufficient secretarial and clerical assistance on a clearly defined basis so that their work can be completed efficiently.

§ 2.6.2 Reproduction of Documents. Large copying jobs are very common for legal assistants. In some firms, assistants have to make their own copies. In others, their copies are given low priority behind those for lawyers and secretaries. Both procedures are unacceptable. Again, legal assistants should be given as much priority as anyone else. They should not spend excessive time trying to find someone to make copies for them or making the copies themselves.

§ 2.7 Stress. The legal profession may be the most stress-ridden of all professions. The characteristics of the practice of law, combined with lawyers' personality traits, tend to produce a great deal of stress. The firm's support services, office space and working conditions all significantly affect the stress under which many legal assistants work.

§ 2.7.1 Deadlines. Everything in the legal profession has a deadline, either imposed by law or self-inflicted. Although the deadlines established as matters of law are usually known in advance and often inflexible, procrastination by lawyers often has a tendency to turn them into a time of crisis. Self-inflicted deadlines, particularly those that could be better controlled, create more tension than the former, simply because of spur-of-the-moment commitments by lawyers to clients for completion of documents or research. Lawyers should be more aware of personnel and equipment availability when making commitments for completing client matters. In many instances, one or two more hours would make the difference between frustration, coupled with client dissatisfaction, and organization, with total client satisfaction.

§ 2.7.2 Unavailable Lawyers. Lawyers must be available to answer legal assistants' questions and to offer guidance. With numerous short deadlines, unavailable lawyers make it very difficult for the assistant to meet deadlines. One common problem is for a lawyer to give an assignment with a specified time for an answer. When the assistant completes the assignment and finds the lawyer gone for the day, he or she properly may question the deadline and develop a great deal of anxiety.

Supervising lawyers should establish procedures for guaranteeing that assistants will have access to lawyers when they have questions.

§ 2.7.3 Word Processing. This topic has been covered at § 2.6. Lack of sufficient word processing support causes a great deal of stress, since the legal assistant as the result faces the probability of not meeting a deadline and having to reorganize the day's planned activities.

§ 2.7.4 Work Area and Conditions. Legal assistants need a private work area with adequate working facilities. Only one assistant should be in an office, a telephone should be available, dictation equipment should be furnished, and adequate lighting and ventilation should be provided. Poor working facilities cause production to go down, stress to build up and some legal assistants to resign. Most firms make all of these conveniences available to each legal assistant. Those firms that fail to do so usually experience a high, costly turnover.

§ 2.7.5 Unkept Promises. Another factor that causes stress is unkept promises. If a legal assistant is told that a salary review will be made in 90 days, then one should be made in 90 days. If assistants were promised more privacy when the remodeling or move was completed, they should receive it. There are many aspects about the practice of law that cannot be controlled, but promises do not fall into this category.

§ 2.7.6 Diversity of Assignments. Like lawyers, legal assistants will not remain motivated unless they are given a variety of assignments. Supervising lawyers should ensure that each assistant has the opportunity to work on as many different matters and for as many of the lawyers in a particular section of the firm as possible. Some stress is healthy, but too much affects the human body's ability to function effectively. The result may be emotional instability causing frustration, disorganization, absenteeism, missed deadlines and possibly resignation. With a little more concern and evaluation of firm procedures, a great deal of the stress can be eliminated.

§ 2.8 Use in Firm Administration. Some administrative activities usually are included in each legal assistant position. This section discusses the assistant's role in handling or supervising the firm's administration.

§ 2.8.1 Small Firms. In some small firms, a legal assistant is also the administrator. In most of these firms, administration does not require all of the assistant's time, thereby allowing certain other activities to be included in the job description. Such employees may carry the title of administrator, legal assistant or both. This has been a workable arrangement in a few firms. Except in the smallest firms, however, wearing two hats may well be next to impossible. The main problem is priority setting, since certain activities in each category may at times result in conflicting priorities. Although it may provide variety, constantly changing roles does not always promote efficiency.

The role of administrative assistant varies by firm. As to administration, some have a system whereby the administrator/legal assistant simply researches and implements ideas with the decision-making being handled by the lawyers. Some give the assistant the authority to implement certain changes without approval from the lawyers. As the firm grows, a decision should be made concerning a full-time administrator. In some firms, the assistant is offered the position. Other firms go into the marketplace to find the administrator.

§ **2.8.2 Medium to Large Firms.** In some of the larger firms legal assistants perform specified administrative functions. Some of the more common are docket control, information retrieval and library. See, *e.g.*, the discussions in chapters 8 and 13. These assignments usually require the assistant to take responsibility for the procedures used by the firm. They may therefore require a great deal of research, training and follow-up in order to guarantee success.

§ **2.8.3 Income Production.** If a legal assistant has substantial administrative responsibility, billable hours will of course be lower than for the assistant with minimal administrative duties. These activities must be identified and taken into consideration in evaluating the assistant's contribution to the firm. The assistant should be encouraged to keep accurate time records concerning administrative responsibilities. If profitability is the underlying theme of the legal assistant program, care must be taken not to penalize those with other responsibilities.

§ **2.9 Summary and Conclusion.** There are many economic benefits to be derived from the proper employment and use of legal assistants. Unless the program is well organized, however, it will become very costly and will possibly fail to achieve the desired results. Although assistants can make money for the firm, profitability should not be the program's only purpose. Other professional considerations are equally important.

All legal assistants require continuing education to remain current in any particular area of practice and concerning the firm's internal policies and procedures. Assistants should be encouraged to attend continuing education seminars at firm expense on topics relating to their employment and to participate in all aspects of the continuing education provided by the firm.

Good working relationships must be developed with all other members of the firm. It is important that legal assistants understand the role of every employee, especially the administrator. These relationships will be very helpful when requesting support from the various administrative departments.

Working conditions in most firms and the characteristics of the practice of law create a great deal of stress. The legal assistant must realize that numerous short deadlines will be imposed, lawyers will occasionally be unavailable and evaluation may be irregular. Even under these conditions, however, the legal assistant position offers a tremendous challenge with many personal rewards.

Form 2:1 — Legal Assistant Projections.

Text — § 2.2.2.

CASH OUTLAY FOR FIRST YEAR
DIRECT COSTS:
Salary ($1,300 per mo.)		$15,600	
Secretary (⅓ of $13,000)		4,335	
Taxes		1,500	
Fringe Benefits:			
Bonus (one mo. salary)	$1,300		
Insurance	1,000		
Retirement	1,100		
Seminars	750		
Parking	600	4,750	
Office Rent		900	$27,085

INDIRECT COSTS:
10% of Salary		1,560

CAPITAL EXPENDITURES:
Equipment		500	
Furniture		1,000	1,500
FIRST YEAR CASH OUTLAY			$30,145
			(Round to $30,100)

PROFITABILITY PROJECTIONS
1000 Hours at $20 per hour	$20,000
First Year Outlay	30,100
FIRST YEAR CASH LOSS	(10,100)
NOTE: Cash Position, Not Profit Position	
1500 Hours at $20 per hour	$30,000
First Year Outlay	30,100
FIRST YEAR CASH LOSS	(100)
1500 Hours at $25 per hour	$37,500
First Year Outlay	30,100
FIRST YEAR CASH GAIN	$ 7,400
1500 Hours at $30 per hour	$45,000
First Year Outlay	30,100
FIRST YEAR CASH GAIN	$14,900

ADDITIONAL RETURN — ATTORNEY TIME SAVED
ONE HOUR PER DAY FOR 48 WEEKS at $75 PER HOUR (240 × 75)
Attorney's Increased Billable	$18,000
From Legal Assistant	7,400
Increased Cash Position	$25,400

TWO HOURS PER DAY FOR 48 WEEKS at $75 PER HOUR (480 × 75)
Attorney's Increased Billable	$36,000
From Legal Assistant	7,400
Increased Cash Position	$43,400

Form 2:2 — Litigation Legal Assistant Job Description.
Text — § 2.8.2.

1. Assistance in drafting complaints;
2. Answering complaints;
3. Drafting interrogatories;
4. Answering interrogatories;
5. Drafting requests for production of documents;
6. Responding to requests for production of documents;
7. Attendance at document productions;
8. Attending depositions and summarizing them there rather than waiting for the transcript;
9. Summarizing depositions from the transcript when unable to attend the deposition;
10. Organizing and refining files;
11. Summarizing, analyzing and organizing exhibits and documents in general;
12. Investigation of factual aspects of a case;
13. Construct factual chronologies;
14. Assistance in legal research;
15. Trial preparation and organization;
16. Attendance and assistance at trial;
17. Post trial/post settlement follow-up.

Form 2:3 — Position Descriptions.*

Text — § 2.5.1.

01 Director of Administration

Directs the administration of the affairs of an organization of lawyers such as a private law firm, governmental legal body, or corporate legal or patent department. The Director of Administration is at the partner level in the organization, reports to the operating head or senior committee of the organization. Directs the formalization of policy in the areas of finance, personnel and general administration. Participates in recruiting of lawyers and directs non-legal personnel recruiting. Participates in the orientation, training and evaluation of associates; directs the preparation of income and expense budgets, financial plans and forecasts of capital expenditures and cash flow. Maintains supervision of control and follow-up systems concerned with management data and special management reports. Has custody, control and supervision of partnership financial books, payrolls and records; responsibility for firm's timely submittal of all local, state and federal tax reports; responsible for firm banking relationships and investment policy; approves all firm-related physical facilities. Is an ex officio member of all committees and attends all executive, management and partnership committee meetings. Responsible for communication of partnership actions to partners not in attendance at partnership meetings.

02 Administrative Manager

Administers the affairs of an organization of lawyers, such as a private law firm, governmental legal body, or corporate legal or patent department. Reports directly to the operating head or senior committee of the organization. Meets regularly with an existing policy-making body (such as senior partners' committee or its equivalent). Formulates annual budget proposals, prepares and interprets management reports, expends allocated budgets for non-professional personnel, equipment and supplies, supervises all accounting and non-professional personnel functions and systems, negotiates for office space, maintains firm insurance, and has final responsibility and authority in non-professional personnel matters, including hiring, training, salary advancement, discipline and discharge.

An Administrative Manager may supervise other administrative employees, such as supervisors, services supervisors, accountants, librarians, head file clerks and the like.

03 Office Manager

Administers the affairs of an organization of lawyers for a private firm, governmental legal body, or corporate legal or patent department, and reports to a managing lawyer or committee. Generally supervises or conducts the accounting function and exercises direct, day-to-day supervision over the clerical and other support functions of the organization. May assist the managing lawyer in the preparation of budgets and may make recommendations with regard to changes in systems, major purchases, personnel benefits and the like. This position differs from Administrative Manager (01) largely in degree.

---

* Used with permission of the Association of Legal Administrators.

Form 2:3 *Continued*

04 Personnel Supervisor

Supervises the secretarial, stenographic, filing, clerical and typing services to attorneys as a primary duty. Generally conducts or assists in employment recruiting and interviewing, trains new employees, allocates and assigns work, maintains benefits and personnel records, and may have additional duties in such matters as purchasing supplies or reception-switchboard. May report to an administrative manager or to a managing lawyer.

Form 2:4 — Director of Administration — Job Description.

Text — § 2.5.1.

Administration

1. **Personnel-Staff.**
   1.1 Interview, screen and hire applicants for office staff positions.
   1.2 Evaluate office staff at least annually.
   1.3 Counsel employees who are not meeting firm standards and tell them how to improve.
   1.4 Take disciplinary action against employees, including dismissal.
   1.5 Speak for support staff in dealing with the attorneys.
   1.6 Receive and consider problems of the office staff.
   1.7 Establish office staff compensation plans, including raises and fringe benefits.
   1.8 Maintain personnel records for each employee.
   1.9 Train all support staff.
   1.10 Regulate work flow within the office and work load of individual members of the office staff.
2. **Financial.**
   2.1 Prepare and review financial plan including budgets.
   2.2 Monitor cash flow.
   2.3 Approve the payment of all accounts payable.
   2.4 Establish the procedural aspects of the billing process.
   2.5 Responsible for the layout and information accumulation for management reports.
   2.6 Prepare analysis of accounts receivable. Cooperate with the billing attorneys in the collection effort.
3. **Physical Facilities.**
   3.1 Handle the management and expansion of firm's physical facilities.
   3.2 Make recommendations for future needs of the firm.
   3.3 Work directly with the architect in drawing layout for use of facilities.
   3.4 Handle cost projections.
   3.5 Responsible for general appearance of the office.
4. **Office Equipment and Supplies.**
   4.1 Become familiar with new developments and equipment through regular contact with sales representatives, attending business shows, and subscribing to professional and trade publications.
   4.2 Set up maintenance for all equipment.
   4.3 Prepare cost studies comparing various equipment alternatives.
   4.4 Purchase, lease or rent necessary equipment.
   4.5 Approve quality of and purchase office supplies.
5. **Files.**
   5.1 Set up, control and maintain a filing system for active and dormant files.
   5.2 Set up and control the internal and external routing systems.
   5.3 Purchase or lease equipment as needed.

Form 2:4 *Continued*

6. **Insurance.**
   6.1 Administer the existing insurance program for the firm.
   6.2 Analyze new insurance programs from time to time.
7. **Mail.**
   7.1 Responsibility for procedure used in handling both incoming and outgoing mail.
8. **Telephone.**
   8.1 Purchase or lease telephone equipment.
   8.2 Responsible for proper utilization of telephone system.
   8.3 Responsible for receptionist and relief switchboard operators.
9. **Library.**
   9.1 Responsible for general supervision of the library.
10. **Forms.**
    10.1 Responsible for purchase and indexing of printed forms.
    10.2 Responsible for upkeep of sample forms once established by the attorneys.
11. **Timekeeping.**
    11.1 Set up and control timekeeping system.
    11.1 Monitor timekeeping practices and keep system current.
    11.1 Recommend better ways to improve timekeeping.
12. **Retrieval System.**
    12.1 Set up and manage the firm's retrieval system.
    12.1 Encourage utilization of the system.
13. **Docket Control.**
    13.1 Set up and manage the docket control system.
14. **Office Manual.**
    14.1 Prepare and keep current an office manual of all administrative procedures used in the firm.
    14.2 Expand the manual as needed.

Management

1. **Associate Attorneys.**
   1.1 *Recruiting.*
       a. Member of the recruiting team.
       b. Set up the firm's recruiting plan.
   1.2 *Training.*
       a. Set up the administrative training procedures.
   1.3 *Evaluation.*
2. **Marketing.**
   2.1 *Business Development.* Direct the business development program established by the shareholders or partners.
   2.2 *Relations with Existing Clients.* Meet and visit with as many of the firm's clients as possible.
   2.3 *Outside Activities.* Become active in civic affairs.

Form 2:4 *Continued*

3. **Long-Range Planning.**
    3.1 *Size of the Firm.* Project growth and cost for the future.
    3.2 *Specialties.* Project costs for new specialties.
    3.3 *New Clients.* Maintain client lists and accumulate potential client lists.
    3.4 *Billing Rates.* Keep the shareholders or partners informed as to the financial requirements which will control billing rates.
    3.5 *Cost of Operation.* Prepare a 3-year and 5-year budget projection.
4. **Continuing Legal Education.**
    4.1 Monitor cost of firm's C.L.E. participation.
5. **Meetings.**
    5.1 *Shareholder or Partner Meetings.*
        a. Attend all shareholder or partner meetings.
        b. Gather information as required.
        c. Put together and distribute agendas.
    5.2 *Firm Meetings.*
        a. Attend all firm meetings.
        b. Prepare information as requested.
    5.3 *Firm Retreat.* Set up and coordinate the firm's retreats.
6. **Compensation and Profit Distribution.**
    6.1 Keep adequate records of all aspects of the profit distribution system.
    6.2 Continually monitor the system for fallacies and make appropriate recommendations.
7. **Committees.**
    7.1 *Management Committee.*
        a. Attend all management committee meetings.
        b. Prepare agenda for meetings.
        c. Make recommendations for procedures including alternatives.
        d. Prepare reports for board of directors or management committee meetings.
    7.2 *Recruiting Committee.*
        a. Responsible for all administrative duties relating to recruiting.
        b. Set up interviews at law schools.
        c. Set up interviews with graduates who are invited to visit the firm.
    7.3 *Other Committees.*
        a. Set up meetings.
        b. Keep minutes of the meeting.
        c. Other activities as required by chairman.

Form 2:5 — Legal Assistant Evaluation Form.

Text — § 2.5.4.

LEGAL ASSISTANT'S NAME: _____ DATE: _____

INSTRUCTIONS: As one who has worked with this legal assistant, you are asked to evaluate his or her various attributes. Please consider each factor separately. In considering each factor, think over the legal assistant's performance during the entire year or since date of employment (if a new employee).

	Item	Out-standing	Above Average	Average	Below Average
1.	PRODUCTION: Speed of work; consider all functions.				
2.	QUALITY OF WORK.				
3.	PROMPT COMPLETION OF ASSIGNMENTS				
4.	ACCEPTING RESPONSIBILITY: Does he or she accept responsibility and keep attorneys informed?				
5.	COOPERATION: Is this legal assistant easy to work with? Does he or she cooperate with others and maintain a smooth working relationship among the legal and support staff?				
6.	APPEARANCE AND PERSONAL HABITS: Is he or she neat?				
7.	RESPECT: Does he or she command the respect of the firm and you?				
8.	OVERALL EVALUATION:				

COMMENTS:

Signature of Evaluator_____

3

THE GOVERNMENT LAW OFFICE

Kathryn M. Braeman,*
Larrine S. Holbrooke**
and Christine L. Perko***

§ 3.1 This Chapter's Scope. This chapter concerns the use of paralegals in federal government law offices. Although the American Bar Association generally uses the term "legal assistant," the federal government uses the term "paralegal specialist." Accordingly, this chapter will use "paralegal" in describing government practice. It discusses similarities between government legal practice and private practice, and how the former presents the same advantages for working with legal assistants. It also discusses opportunities and problems in using paralegals unique to government practice.

§ 3.2 Incentives to Hiring Paralegals for Government Law Offices. Creative lawyers who first designed positions for legal assistants discovered how to structure their practice to take advantage of the highly skilled talent of the college educated. By analyzing their work and by careful planning, they learned how to delegate extensive responsibility for narrow areas of the law. They found that the use of assistants expanded their effectiveness as lawyers. For example, litigators were able to increase the number of cases they could handle because assistants had responsibility for certain aspects of them. Lawyers involved primarily in office practice were also able to delegate much of the responsibility for fact-gathering and document preparation.

The incentives for adding paralegals to government law offices are similar. As workloads explode in the government, many offices find it essential to assign the more predictable legal work to paralegals. Without paralegals in a government law office, experienced lawyers often become frustrated at not having adequate resources to make them effective. They often are bogged down and unable to expand their responsibilities to match their legal expertise. By adding paralegals to the legal team, lawyers are freed for more complex or unusual responsibilities.

There are short-term financial advantages similar to those in private law firms for the government law office employing paralegals. For example, the beginning paralegal specialist usually starts at a GS-5 ($11,249), while the beginning lawyer level is normally a GS-9 ($17,035) or GS-11 ($20,611). Thus, there is an immediate budgetary advantage. Some agencies with many lawyers also find that adding low-graded employees decreases their agency grade average, a concern of the Office of Management and Budget ("OMB").

---

* Deputy Director, Office of Information Law and Policy, United States Department of Justice, Washington, D. C.
** Associate, Gibson, Dunn & Crutcher, Washington, D.C.; formerly with the Federal Trade Commission.
*** Paralegal Intern, Office of Information Law and Policy, United States Department of Justice, Washington, D. C.

Further long-range advantages become clearer as the paralegal fits into the law office team. When the paralegal takes over many of the preliminary tasks on a case, the lawyer has more time for complex strategy issues and long-range planning. The lawyer also has more time to organize and prepare the case thoroughly when a paralegal can assist in organizing the documents and analyzing the facts.

§ 3.3 Factors to Consider in Hiring Paralegals for Government Law Offices. Government law offices have often not had support staff comparable to that of private law firms or corporate law departments. According to Survey of Law Firm Economics (Altman & Weil, Inc., 1980), private law firms have 1.15 support personnel per lawyer — secretaries, clerks, office managers, librarians and paralegals. Government law offices generally do not have as high a ratio of support personnel. Many factors have contributed to this different balance. First, the manner in which "ceiling spaces" *i.e.*, the maximum number of positions allowed an agency each year by OMB, are counted creates an absolute limit on the number of people in an agency. Congressional policy limiting the growth of the federal civilian work force has been continued as § 311 of the Civil Service Reform Act of 1978. This limitation in turn affects each agency through the number of permanent personnel positions OMB allots each agency each year. In allocating personnel positions, except for special situations outlined in the Part-Time Act, each person counts equally. With limited numbers, a federal lawyer-manager may have to choose between hiring one lawyer or one paralegal. On the other hand, a managing partner in a private law firm, having more flexibility, can decide to hire one lawyer at $30,000 or two paralegals at $15,000 because budget figures — not personnel ceilings — provide the constraint. A government lawyer-manager may also decide to hire a lawyer instead of a paralegal to have more depth to deal with an uncertain future workload.

A second factor is that lawyers at the federal level can be hired with greater ease than paralegals since they are in the "excepted" service. Federal lawyers have been placed in Schedule A of the Excepted Service, 5 C.F.R. § 213.3102(d), which includes those positions for which it is "not practicable to examine." It is "not practicable to examine" for lawyer positions because Congress has enacted every year since 1945 a rider to the appropriation acts of the Civil Service Commission (now the Office of Personnel Management ("OPM")) prohibiting the central examination of lawyers. Each agency establishes its specific qualification standards within the general OPM requirement that a federal lawyer must be a member of a state bar. OPM does regulate the classification of lawyers after they are hired. These classification standards — now under review — connect the complexity of the work to the lawyer's grade.

Hiring paralegals or legal clerk/technicians who are in the "competitive" service is a more complex matter. Generally, a person may be appointed to a position in the competitive service only if he or she has passed an appropriate examination. 5 U.S.C. § 3304. Governing statutes also require that certain procedures be followed in conducting such examinations and in making appointments from among those who pass. These include requiring that lists (called "registers") of eligible persons be kept, and making appointments from among the top three on any given list. *See, e.g.*, 5 U.S.C. § 33. This competitive examination requirement distinguishes the competitive service appointment process from the excepted service.

The principal hallmarks of the competitive service are career mobility and tenure. After having completed an initial "probationary period" of one year, 5 U.S.C.

§ 3321; 5 C.F.R. § 315.801 *et seq.*, an employee in the competitive service acquires "competitive status" making the person eligible to be assigned by promotion or transfer to any other position in the competitive service for which he or she is otherwise qualified, without having to compete in an open examination. The employee also becomes entitled to an elaborate array of procedural and substantive protections against "adverse action" (removal, suspension, or reduction in rank or pay) by the employing agency. Because lawyers are not in the competitive service, those in the federal service without veterans' preferences generally do not have the tenure protections held by persons in the competitive service.

Appointing authorities in each agency have discretion to fill a vacancy in the competitive service either (a) "non-competitively," by selecting a person with such "status," or (b) "competitively," by appointing a person from the list of "eligibles" who have passed the appropriate civil service examination. 5 C.F.R. § 7.1. A federal lawyer-manager thus may find a built-in incentive to add more lawyers instead of mastering the complex personnel rules necessary to hire paralegals. Despite these obstacles, many lawyer-managers who want to manage their work more effectively and to employ their human resources more fully are hiring paralegals for specialized responsibilities in government law offices.

§ 3.4 The Paralegal and Legal Clerk/Technician Series. The paralegal and the legal clerk/technician series were defined by the United States Civil Service Commission in its Standards Bulletin 930-17, published August 11, 1975. Instead of using the single term "legal assistant," the federal government chose a two-tier description of the position, GS-950 "paralegal specialist," a professional level series, and GS-986 "legal clerk/technician," a "bridge" series for clerical or technical personnel. The paralegal series favors the four-year college graduate who may not have any specialized paralegal training but who scores well on the Professional and Administrative Career Examination (PACE). A secretary with no specialized paralegal training but having specialized law office knowledge thus may be able to bridge into the legal clerk/technician series or the paralegal series.

Persons in other specialized employment series also requiring some knowledge of the law may be considered for paralegal-type positions, *e.g.*, research analysts, equal employment specialists or procurement specialists. Such persons may either fit in an existing specialized series or may be in a general administrative series with specialized duties.

Many federal government agencies employ "paralegals" under these different and varying titles. To ensure uniformity among agencies, efforts are being made to establish classification standards. These "classification standards" are still in draft form. At OPM, some believe that a vague or overly restrictive definition might limit the growing profession. Because these standards may be used as a model for both private and public practice, they should be reviewed when they are made available for comment from the Office of Personnel Management, Standards Development Center, Washington, D.C. 20415.

§ 3.5 Hiring a Paralegal. Planning is essential in hiring a paralegal. The lawyer-manager must consider the budget cycle so that positions and budgets are approved for paralegals. The lawyer-manager deciding to hire a paralegal must also study the agency's personnel rules, as well as OPM's published qualifications standards. Implementing these rules also requires a close working relationship with the agency's personnel office.

The lawyer-manager must first define the duties the legal clerk or paralegal will perform and outline those responsibilities in the job description. Sample job descriptions and related materials are shown at Form 3:2. At the federal level, a job notice must be published. Then a panel reviews the qualifications of applicants who have submitted a Standard Form 171 employment application or an appropriate internal personnel form. Because paralegals and legal clerks are in the competitive service, they must be on the central OPM register of qualified people or must already be in federal government in a "competitive" position. The top candidates are selected and referred to the hiring official for further review and decision-making.

When making a hiring decision, the lawyer-manager should examine the particular jobs involved in the law office and evaluate the applicants' backgrounds to determine whether their credentials are "job-related." *See Adoption of Employee Selection Procedures*, 43 Fed. Reg. 38,290 (Aug. 25, 1978). If the lawyer plans to provide on-the-job education, previous experience or schooling may be less important. A candidate who has completed a paralegal program with a government specialization should require less on-the-job training and may make a better candidate because of his or her knowledge of the federal system. On the other hand, a candidate with a specialized knowledge of the agency who may have less formal education might make a good candidate because of that knowledge.

Since the paralegal profession is relatively new, it is difficult to generalize about paralegal training programs at universities, junior colleges or proprietary schools. For a list of such schools see § 1.9. The government lawyer-manager needs to evaluate the relevance of each candidate's paralegal training for the position, as well as the relevance and quality of each applicant's experience and education. For example, testing at the Department of Justice showed that previous educational background is not necessarily the only indicator of success. Many high school graduates performed as well as college graduates when given the same paralegal training.

After a hiring decision is made, the lawyer-manager should take the time to brief the paralegal on his or her responsibilities. The paralegal needs to know that the supervisor's door is always open for questions, either to clarify the assignment or to provide the necessary substantive or procedural background. Many lawyer-managers institute regular seminars or staff lunches with lawyers to focus on particular legal problems. When communication lines are kept open, issues or questions can be answered at an early stage.

If the paralegal has previously been a secretary, the lawyer-manager must permit the paralegal to establish a "new identity," work harmoniously with the secretaries and obtain the proper support. If all concerned feel an important part of the team, this integration is much easier.

§ 3.6 Effective Use of Paralegals. Effective use of paralegals in government practice is generally no different from that in a private or corporate law office. The suggestions made elsewhere throughout this volume apply to the government law office as well.

To employ paralegals effectively, the lawyer-manager should develop a "systems" approach to legal work so that it is clear what work may be delegated to the legal clerk or paralegal, what tasks must be supervised by the lawyer and what tasks must be performed exclusively by the lawyer. See generally § 1.2. Because there are few incentives for government lawyer-managers to take the extensive time required to develop these systems, there is often inadequate planning of the most efficient way to handle legal responsibilities. Without proper planning, both lawyers and paralegals may be under-employed. Lawyers and paralegals may be photocopying to meet a deadline while secretaries are taxed with unnecessary retyping of legal documents. For guidelines concerning effective use of paralegals, see Form 3:4.

As with private law firms, government agencies vary in their organizational structure. In most agencies, the legal team is located within the Office of the General Counsel. Some organizations are more complex than others and have variations based on legal needs as well as on such factors as organizational size, structure and power bases. The needs of agencies for paralegals also vary with these other factors.

The Department of Interior is one example of an agency that has looked to paralegals as a means for better control over its delivery of legal services. It is a department with many subgroups within the system where competition for relevant legal work among the lawyers is a problem. Since the administrators did not want lawyers competing with each other within the department, they held the number of lawyers and clerks within each subsystem to a minimum. Consequently, paralegals became the answer to the needs of legal services in that department, since they could successfully fit between these two groups and fulfill the department's legal requirements.

In government, the many offices with specialized practices are ideal for employment of paralegals who can master a certain area of the law and perform the work under a lawyer's general supervision. When a lawyer-manager plans and organizes the work, paralegals who become responsible for the more predictable legal work can unburden the lawyers. For example, in the federal government, many paralegals work as Freedom of Information Act specialists. This area of the law can give the paralegal an opportunity to specialize and become an expert in a new legal field.

In another cabinet-level department, one lawyer spends approximately 90% of his time on reviewing Financial Disclosure Reports, which are part of the requirements of the government's Ethics Act. This report is a simple form which must be completed to allow evaluations of the financial holdings of agency personnel for conflicts of interest. Because this department does not have a personnel position for a paralegal, the lawyer is spending time on a job that could be done more efficiently by a paralegal. In summary, hiring paralegals in many agencies creates better delegation of responsibilities and allows for much more consistent and efficient work flow within the department.

§ 3.7 Organizing Work for Delegation to the Paralegal. In order to employ a paralegal effectively, the lawyer-manager should organize the work so that it will match the paralegal's needs and abilities. Generally, legal clerks or technicians are assigned document control duties, paralegals do the factual analysis and lawyers concentrate on legal analysis.

With appropriate instructions and lawyer review, many tasks formerly performed by lawyers can effectively be delegated to paralegals. For example, such duties might include but are not limited to reviewing and summarizing documents; indexing and analyzing legislative bills; investigating complaints; interviewing witnesses or clients; preparing digests and indexes; doing legal research; and reading, briefing and analyzing cases. The list is limited only by the lawyer-manager's imagination. The opportunities for paralegals suggested in this chapter may be used as a guideline for developing similar tasks in specific offices. The specific duties and the system for delegation and supervision may vary from agency to agency.

§ 3.8   Working With Legal Assistants

At the higher grade levels, the paralegal with greater experience and expertise requires less and less lawyer supervision. One agency devised a progression in the type of work a paralegal does at various levels and then defined the quality and quantity of supervision. OPM standards do not require that paralegals be supervised by a lawyer. However, ethical standards generally require an attorney to supervise legal work. To delegate effectively, some government offices are now using substantive systems modeled on R. Ramo, ed., How to Create-A-System for the Law Office (A.B.A. 1975). A lawyer may spend more time initially in giving a paralegal detailed explanations concerning work that may take a lawyer half the time to do. However, in the long run, assigning the task to a paralegal will ultimately result in less time as the paralegal masters the specialized legal work.

§ 3.8 The Team Approach to Legal Assignments. Because it is not always easy to delegate individual segments of an office's legal work, the team approach often works best. Lawyers and paralegals working on a project together can analyze the work as it progresses. As the paralegals prove their competence, they can be assigned more complex tasks. In some federal agencies, the lawyer delegates work directly to the paralegal. This technique enhances the team atmosphere and creates a smooth work flow. For a description of a team approach to litigation, see Form 3:3.

In a structured agency with a hierarchical system such as the Internal Revenue Service, work is usually delegated to paralegals from branch chiefs. Even in that system, however, lawyers may periodically make direct assignments to paralegals for special projects. In addition, in the IRS, small Tax Court cases, designated "S" cases, are often assigned directly to experienced paralegals to allow them to handle the entire preparation of the case right up to court time. Some agencies, such as the Securities and Exchange Commission, are much more unstructured and decentralized in their use of paralegals. Work is delegated by a lawyer on more of a case-by-case system with fairly close supervision.

A team approach has advantages and allows for more consistency in the day-to-day administration of a case. Such an arrangement allows the senior lawyer to reassign personnel easily since each individual on the team is fully aware of what is happening to the case. By having a cohesive unit, each team member can build up an expertise in matters arising within his or her skills area.

Paralegals in the government are professionals. They should be included in key strategy sessions and key meetings so that they have full background on the subject. Lawyers must be encouraged to keep paralegals informed. The lawyer-paralegal relationship is a partnership that is advantageous to all involved, and one that produces an effective and efficiently run government law office.

Form 3:1 — Some Observations on Preparing a Paralegal Specialist Job Description.

Text — § 3.5.

Most job descriptions should contain the following information:

I. Position Summary, which should *briefly* state the following:
1. in which division or branch the position is located;
2. the purpose of the position, *i.e.*, what this position is expected to accomplish;
3. the duties that the person selected will be expected to perform; and
4. a brief statement of how this task will be accomplished.

II. Major Duties and Responsibilities

This paragraph should explain exactly and in detail what the duties and responsibilities of the job will be. It should also explain the steps necessary to accomplish the job. This means you must explain how and what you will be doing. This section should also mention any other division, branch, regional counterparts or any other group that you will be responsible for dealing with, either public or private.

III. Supervision and Guidance Received

State who will be your supervisor, in which division and/or branch. Define the scope of such supervision and guidance, *i.e.*, incumbent will receive minimal supervision on all aspects of work *or* incumbent is responsible for planning own time and accomplishing the workload independently.

If this is a trainee position, be sure to state that the trainee will perform specific assignments and follow detailed instructions and that the finished work will be reviewed for adherence to instructions and established policy and procedures. You should also state that supervision and guidance received by trainee are for the purpose of developing the abilities of the trainee. Further, state that trainee assignments will become progressively more difficult and will ultimately include the performance of duties at the next grade level.

IV. Knowledge, Skills and Abilities Required

This is a very important section. This is where you must be sure to include all the "magic" words italicized below that describe the GS-950 Paralegal Specialist. It should contain the following:

1. ability to *evaluate* and *analyze* pertinent facts and evidence;
2. must be able to *communicate effectively,* either orally or in writing, by *using own judgment;*
3. ability to do *legal research* and to *understand* and *analyze* the *significance* of such research;
4. possess and demonstrate a good background in English composition, proper vocabulary, grammar and spelling, and good writing ability;
5. ability to deal with *tact* and *discretion* with others on a person-to-person basis;

Form 3:1 *Continued*

6. ability to be a *mediator* and *coordinate* with other offices, both legal and administrative; and
7. ability to *recognize, interpret, understand* and *apply* the applicable titles and sections, etc. of the laws and regulations with which your agency will be dealing.

The Government Law Office — Forms

Form 3:2 — Position Descriptions.
Text — § 3.2.

POSITION DESCRIPTION *(Please Read Instructions on the Back)*

1. Agency Position No.: **58485E**
2. Reason for Submission: [X] Other (Explanation: GS-950-7 No. 58485E of 10/9/77)
3. Service: [X] Dept'l
4. Employing Office Location: **Washington, DC**
7. Fair Labor Standards Act: [X] Exempt
9. Subject to IA Action: [X] Yes
10. Position Status: [X] Competitive
14. Agency Use: **Second Edition**

15. Classified/Graded by	Official Title of Position	Pay Plan	Occupational Code	Grade	Initials	Date
a. Civil Service Commission						
b. Department, Agency, or Establishment						
c. Bureau	Paralegal Specialist	GS	950	7	JHH	
d. Field Office						
e. Recommended by Supervisor or Initiating Office						

16. Organizational Title of Position: **Paralegal Specialist**

18. Department, Agency, or Establishment: **Treasury Department**
  a. First Subdivision: **Internal Revenue Service**
  b. Second Subdivision: **Office of the Chief Counsel**
  c. Third Subdivision: **Office of the Deputy Chief Counsel (Gen.)**
  d. Fourth Subdivision: **General Legal Services Division**
  e. Fifth Subdivision:

19. Employee Review — This is an accurate description of the major duties and responsibilities of my position

20. Supervisory Certification. I certify that this is an accurate statement of the major duties and responsibilities of this position and its organizational relationships, and that the position is necessary to carry out Government functions for which I am responsible. This certification is made with the knowledge that this information is to be used for statutory purposes relating to appointment and payment of public funds, and that false or misleading statements may constitute violations of such statutes or their implementing regulations.

21. Classification/Job Grading Certification. I certify that this position has been classified/graded as required by Title 5 U.S. Code, in conformance with standards published by the Civil Service Commission or, if no published standards apply directly, consistently with the most applicable published standards.

22. Standards Used in Classifying/Grading Position

Information for Employees. The standards, and information on their application, are available in the personnel office. The classification of the position may be reviewed and corrected by the agency or the Civil Service Commission. Information on classification/job grading appeals, and complaints on exemption from FLSA, is available from the personnel office or the Commission.

23. Position Review
  a. Employee (optional)
  b. Supervisor
  c. Classifier

24. Remarks

25. Description of Major Duties and Responsibilities *(see attached)*

Optional Form 8 (Revised 8-77)
U.S. Civil Service Commission, FPM Chap. 295

Form 3:2 *Continued*

I. Introduction

The incumbent assists attorneys of the General Legal Services Division in the handling and disposition of cases concerning labor management relations, personnel litigation, tort claims and suits brought against the United States and/or employees in their official or individual capacities, fiscal and budgetary matters, Inspection Service matters, enforcement of civil remedies against tax return preparers, employee liability in disclosure matters, and other matters involving non-tax legal work of the Office.

II. Principal Duties and Responsibilities

The incumbent performs preliminary legal research and analysis. He/she digests the work product of the General Legal Services function and assists in maintaining a nationwide retrieval system for the function. The incumbent prepares correspondence to arbitrators, civil service appeals officers, and administrative law judges concerning administrative matters. The incumbent prepares correspondence concerning minor Claims Collection Act matters and letters to claimants advising them of the disposition of their administrative tort claims. The incumbent assists in the preparation of affidavits to be used in civil litigation or in a quasi-judicial proceeding such as an unfair labor practice, an adverse action, a contract arbitration, an EEO, or Director of Practice case. Also, in connection with these cases he/she will aid in the preparation of exhibits, pertinent administrative files, and will make arrangements and assist in interviewing of prospective witnesses. The incumbent will make necessary searches of Division files and records pursuant to requests made under the FOIA and Privacy Act. Performs other duties of a legal or quasi-legal nature, as assigned.

III. Supervision and Guidance Received

The incumbent is under the general supervision of a Branch Chief and the direct supervision of the attorney that the incumbent is assisting. Initially, detailed instructions are given at the time an assignment is made. The incumbent's research, legal analysis, prepared comments, and other work products are fully reviewed at the completion of the assignment by the attorney (and where appropriate, by supervisory personnel) for content, compliance with office format, and legal sufficiency. Latitude for independent judgment is enlarged in proportion to the degree of continuing development of expertise. As the employee becomes more proficient, detailed instructions are not given on fairly routine assignments.

IV. Other Significant Factors

Assignments serve in part to develop the technical skills, knowledge, and abilities required for the performance of more difficult assignments or the assuming of a greater degree of responsibility. Progress is regularly monitored by attorney and supervisory personnel. The incumbent may be required to attend seminars or receive formal classroom training in subjects related to present assignments or to projected future assignments. The incumbent is required to gain a thorough knowledge of all available tools, including training on Lexis, which facilitates legal research.

Form 3:2 *Continued*

POSITION DESCRIPTION *(Please Read Instructions on the Back)*			1. Agency Position No. 58483E
2. Reason for Submission: [X] Redescription [ ] Reestablishment Explanation *(Show any positions replaced)* GS-950-7 No. 58485E of 10/18/78	3. Service: [X] New [X] Dept'l [ ] Field [ ] Other	4. Employing Office Location: Washington, DC	5. Duty Station	6. CSC Certification No.
		7. Fair Labor Standards Act: [X] Exempt [ ] Nonexempt	8. Employment/Financial Stmt Required: [ ] Yes [ ] No	9. Subject to IA Action: [X] Yes [ ] No
		10. Position Status: [X] Competitive [ ] Excepted *(Specify)*	11. Position is: [ ] Suprvsry [ ] Managerial [ ] Neither	12. Sensitivity: [ ] Critical [ ] Noncritical [ ] Nonsensitive	13. Competitive Level Code
				14. Agency Use

15. Classified/Graded by	Official Title of Position	Pay Plan	Occupational Code	Grade	Initials	Date
a. Civil Service Commission						
b. Department, Agency, or Establishment						
c. Bureau	Paralegal Specialist	GS	950	9	JHH	
d. Field Office						
e. Recommended by Supervisor or Initiating Office						

16. Organizational Title of Position *(if different from official title)*: Paralegal Specialist

17. Name of Employee *(if vacancy, specify)*

18. Department, Agency, or Establishment: **Treasury Department**
 a. First Subdivision: **Internal Revenue Service**
 b. Second Subdivision: **Office of the Chief Counsel**
 c. Third Subdivision: **Office of the Deputy Chief Counsel (Gen.)**
 d. Fourth Subdivision: **General Legal Services Division**
 e. Fifth Subdivision: **Branch 1**

19. Employee Review — This is an accurate description of the major duties and responsibilities of my position.

Signature of Employee *(optional)*

20. Supervisory Certification. I certify that this is an accurate statement of the major duties and responsibilities of this position and its organizational relationships, and that the position is necessary to carry out Government functions for which I am responsible. This certification is made with the knowledge that this information is to be used for statutory purposes relating to appointment and payment of public funds, and that false or misleading statements may constitute violations of such statutes or their implementing regulations.

a. Typed Name and Title of Immediate Supervisor

b. Typed Name and Title of Higher-Level Supervisor or Manager *(optional)*

Signature s/   Date

Signature   Date

21. Classification/Job Grading Certification. I certify that this position has been classified/graded as required by Title 5, U.S. Code, in conformance with standards published by the Civil Service Commission or, if no published standards apply directly, consistently with the most applicable published standards.

22. Standards Used in Classifying/Grading Position

Typed Name and Title of Official Taking Action

Information for Employees. The standards, and information on their application, are available in the personnel office. The classification of the position may be reviewed and corrected by the agency or the Civil Service Commission. Information on classification/job grading appeals, and complaints on exemption from FLSA, is available from the personnel office or the Commission.

Signature s/   Date

23. Position Review	Initials	Date	Initials	Date	Initials	Date	Initials	Date	Initials	Date
a. Employee *(optional)*										
b. Supervisor										
c. Classifier										

24. Remarks

25. Description of Major Duties and Responsibilities *(see attached)*

Optional Form 8 (Revised 8/77)
U.S. Civil Service Commission, FPM Chap. 295

Form 3:2 *Continued*

PARALEGAL SPECIALIST — GS-950-9
Branch No. 1 — General Legal Services Division

I. Major Duties

The incumbent assists the Branch Chief and one or more attorneys in Branch No. 1 (Labor-Management Relations) of the General Legal Services Division by performing numerous tasks, as listed below:

A. Assisting the Branch Chief and/or attorneys by performing legal and other necessary research in cases relating to labor-management relations, unfair labor practices, disciplinary actions, adverse actions, and equal employment opportunity matters;

B. Preparing correspondence, affidavits, and memoranda relevant to quasi-judicial and civil litigation proceedings;

C. Aiding in the preparation of exhibits and pertinent administrative files;

D. Assisting in the interviewing of prospective witnesses before and during the administrative trial process;

E. Reviewing and analyzing arbitrators' decisions for determination of retention on the Panel of Arbitrators;

F. Monitoring the progress of assigned cases in the courts;

G. Maintaining a monthly report of changes in the litigation status of all Service EEO cases;

H. Writing a weekly internal newsletter reflecting all Regional and National Office administrative and judicial decisions involving unfair labor practices, disciplinary actions, adverse actions, and EEO matters;

I. Amending, revising, and rewriting notices, delegation orders, and GLS Division orders.

J. Monitoring Congressional Committee hearings in the House and Senate (CSRA) and providing progress reports;

K. Monitoring the progress of Congressional bills having far-reaching Service and Government-wide implications;

L. Searching Division files and records pursuant to requests made under the FOIA and Privacy Act; and

M. Performing other duties of a legal or quasi-legal nature, as assigned.

II. Knowledge Required by the Position

The technical skills and knowledge required to perform the duties and responsibilities of this position are:

A. Proficient knowledge and understanding of the organization and functions of the General Legal Services Division and the Regional GLS function;

B. Practical knowledge of certain laws, statutes, regulations, orders, notices, and other documents required to perform a diversity of duties in a very wide variety of GLS cases with emphasis on labor law and labor-management functions;

Form 3:2 *Continued*

    C. Proficient knowledge of basic principles, concepts, and methodology used in legal research;

    D. Ability to identify, evaluate, and extract pertinent information from a very wide variety of sources and documents;

    E. Ability to use mature judgment in analyzing complex issues and in determining alternate courses of action to obtain requisite information;

    F. Ability to communicate effectively, both orally and in writing.

III. Supervisory Controls

The incumbent is under the general supervision of the Branch Chief and/or attorney whom he/she is assisting, but is given wide latitude in performing assigned duties. The incumbent's research, legal analysis, prepared comments, and other work products are reviewed at the completion of an assignment by the Branch Chief or appropriate attorney for content, legal sufficiency, and compliance with office format.

II. Guidelines

The Paralegal Specialist (GS-9) in Branch No. 1 must be thoroughly familiar with the GLS Division's portion of the Chief Counsel's Directive System, the Department of Treasury's Directives, and the IRS' Manual system; laws, statutes, regulations, and court precedents that are applicable to specific cases or problems pending within the General Legal Services Division; changes brought about by enactment of the Civil Service Reform Act that have affected policies and procedures in the area of labor law; Treasury, IRS, and Chief Counsel policies and established office procedures; and specific instructions issued by supervisory personnel. In addition, the incumbent working in the area of labor law (Branch 1) must be thoroughly familiar with the provisions and application of the Federal Personnel Manual, and regulations and decisions of the Office of Personnel Management, Merit Systems Protection Board, Equal Employment Opportunity Commission, and Federal Labor Relations Authority. Although guidelines used are generally applicable, good judgment is required to interpret and apply them to specific cases and/or circumstances.

V. Complexity

The incumbent's work involves a combination of quasi-legal and legal tasks and is basically technical in nature. In addition, the duties require that the incumbent begins to exhibit an in-depth understanding of certain aspects of case procedures in the GLS Division particularly in the area of labor law. The incumbent must have the ability and technical knowledge to understand and participate in the procedural aspects of complex legal operations, as well as to make meaningful contributions of a technical nature to the professional work of the attorneys in the Division.

Form 3:2 *Continued*

VI. Scope and Effect

The Paralegal Specialist's primary responsibilities involve assisting the Branch Chief and other branch attorneys with a wide variety of tasks relating to the disposition of administrative and litigation cases in the area of labor law. The duties range from relatively complex tasks to providing complete segments of an attorney's final work product. The incumbent's assistance usually affects the accuracy of the attorney's work products and, at times, segments of the Branch's completed work product.

VII. Personal Contacts

On a day to day basis, the incumbent is required to deal effectively with staff of the branch and the GLS Division and on an "as need" basis with the Regional GLS field function and personnel of various IRS functions in order to obtain information, retrieve documents, prepare affidavits, and coordinate other necessary tasks. Depending upon the requirements of the cases, contact is made by phone or in person with personnel of the Office of Personnel Management, Merit Systems Protection Board, Equal Employment Opportunity Commission, Federal Labor Relations Authority, Congressional Committees and subcommittees, the courts, and other Government agencies.

VIII. Purpose of Contacts

Normally to give or receive facts and information which may range from those easily understood to those highly technical in nature.

IX. Physical Demands

No unusual physical requirements.

X. Work Environment

Work is performed in a normal office setting.

The Government Law Office — Forms

Form 3:2 *Continued*

POSITION DESCRIPTION *(Please Read Instructions on the Back)*	1. Agency Position No. **NY-801**

2. Reason for Submission	3. Service	4. Employing Office Location	5. Duty Station	6. CSC Certification No.
☐ Redescription ☒ New ☐ Reestablishment ☐ Other Explanation *(Show any positions replaced)*	☐ Dept'l ☒ Field	New York, N.Y.	New York	

7. Fair Labor Standards Act	8. Employment/Financial Stmt Required	9. Subject to IA Action
☒ Exempt ☐ Nonexempt	☐ Yes ☐ No	☒ Yes ☐ No

10. Position Status	11. Position is	12. Sensitivity	13. Competitive Level Code
☒ Competitive ☐ Excepted *(Specify)*	☐ Suprvsry ☐ Managerial ☒ Neither	☐ Critical ☐ Noncritical ☐ Nonsensitive	14. Agency Use

15. Classified/Graded by	Official Title of Position	Pay Plan	Occupational Code	Grade	Initials	Date
a. Civil Service Commission						
b. Department, Agency, or Establishment	Paralegal Specialist	GS	950	11		
c. Bureau						
d. Field Office						
e. Recommended by Supervisor or Initiating Office						

16. Organizational Title of Position *(if different from official title)*

17. Name of Employee *(if vacancy, specify)*

18. Department, Agency, or Establishment
Securities and Exchange Commission

a. First Subdivision
New York Regional Office

b. Second Subdivision
Office of Assoc. Regional Administrator (Reg)

c. Third Subdivision

d. Fourth Subdivision

e. Fifth Subdivision

19. Employee Review *This is an accurate description of the major duties and responsibilities of my position*

Signature of Employee *(optional)*

20. Supervisory Certification. *I certify that this is an accurate statement of the major duties and responsibilities of this position and its organizational relationships, and that the position is necessary to carry out Government functions for which I am responsible. This certification is made with the knowledge that this information is to be used for statutory purposes relating to appointment and payment of public funds, and that false or misleading statements may constitute violations of such statutes or their implementing regulations.*

a. Typed Name and Title of Immediate Supervisor

b. Typed Name and Title of Higher-Level Supervisor or Manager *(optional)*

Signature s/   Date

Signature s/   Date

21. Classification/Job Grading Certification. *I certify that this position has been classified/graded as required by Title 5, U.S. Code, in conformance with standards published by the Civil Service Commission or, if no published standards apply directly, consistently with the most applicable published standards.*

Typed Name and Title of Official Taking Action

22. Standards Used in Classifying/Grading Position

Signature s/   Date

Information for Employees. The standards, and information on their application, are available in the personnel office. The classification of the position may be reviewed and corrected by the agency or the Civil Service Commission. Information on classification/job grading appeals, and complaints on exemption from FLSA, is available from the personnel office or the Commission.

23. Position Review	Initials	Date	Initials	Date	Initials	Date	Initials	Date	Initials	Date
a. Employee *(optional)*										
b. Supervisor										
c. Classifier										

24. Remarks

25. Description of Major Duties and Responsibilities *(see attached)*

SEC-105   GPO : 1977 O - 241-530 (3051)   Optional Form 8 (Revised 8/77)
U.S. Civil Service Commission, FPM Chap 295

Form 3:2 *Continued*

Introduction

The primary purpose of this position is to provide paralegal, analytical and research assistance to the Associate Regional Administrator (Reg.) and his subordinate staff.

Duties

The incumbent independently performs any or all of the following duties:

1) Gathers facts and information for the use of attorneys engaged in the preparation of cases scheduled for administrative hearings, court proceedings, etc., or in connection with enforcement activities of the Commission.

2) Conducts searches in legal reference books for authorities and precedent cases on a specific point of law.

3) Performs preliminary research on interpretative questions or problems regarding the statutes administered by the Commission. On well defined issues or questions, incumbent drafts proposed reply or a legal memorandum if required. Some assignments will require a considerable degree of judgment in applying factual situations to legal principles and precedents which may not be exactly on point.

4) Digests or abstracts pertinent cases for use of attorneys engaged in the preparation of a brief, legal memorandum, decision or opinion, and otherwise performs other assignments in connection therewith.

5) Studies the records in non-complex cases and independently drafts memoranda on the law and facts thereof, as well as standard legal instruments such as notice of hearing, etc.

6) Assumes responsibility for the independent performance of such duties as research and analysis of new matters for possible enforcement action by conducting conferences with attorneys, company officials and interested persons; examines and analyzes material submitted in coordination with other local law enforcement agencies, prepares brief summary of relevant information of the investigation in order to justify recommendations and/or conclusions to the attorney.

7) Examines and analyzes Freedom of Information Act requests, coordinating them with the appropriate members of the staff of the regional office, and prepares responses.

8) Performs other assigned legal research or related duties.

Supervision and Guidance Received

Operates under the general supervision of the Associate Regional Administrator (Reg.) or the attorneys to whom assigned. Is apprised of any unusual circumstances surrounding the case or issue to which assigned, any background information

Form 3:2 *Continued*

which must be considered and any important policy considerations which will govern development of the case or issue. Works independently in investigating facts, defining legal and factual issues, drafting the necessary legal documents and developing conclusions and recommendations. Work is subject to review for soundness of approach, conclusion, application of legal principles and consistency with governing policies, procedures and regulations of the agency.

Guidelines include the securities laws and regulations, agency guidelines, legal dictionaries, encyclopedias, current looseleaf services, guides to legal periodicals and local court rules.

Qualifications Required.

Must be alert, resourceful and able to apply knowledge in the general field of law. Must be capable of understanding legal concepts under the statutes administered by the Commission and the rules and regulations promulgated thereunder. Familiarity with the activities of the Commission in a general way is required, especially with regard to legal phases of work.

Form 3:3 — Managing Litigation for the Federal Government.
Text — § 3.8.

Carol Essrick*

§ 3A3.1 Introduction. Litigation on behalf of the federal government often involves complexity of issues, responsibilities to both the public and private sectors, multi-level approval systems and above all size, both in staff and in volume of documents. All these factors make organization essential if litigation is to proceed in an orderly and timely fashion. Ability to meet deadlines must play a major role in shaping a workable system.

Although responsibility ultimately lies with the lawyer, actual control of many legal matters can be delegated to others. In addition, many lawyers handling government litigation report to other lawyers, administrative personnel and the agency's superior officers. Ultimate decision-making power may rest with commissioners who may or may not be lawyers.

The use of non-lawyers in conjunction with lawyers provides the most appropriate mix in terms of organization, time and money. One of the most effective systems is to use a team consisting of a lead trial lawyer, several junior lawyers, paralegals or legal assistants (on a two paralegals to one lawyer ratio), and legal technicians and secretaries.

Creating a workable system must involve people knowledgeable as to the substantive and procedural aspects of the litigation and adept in assigning people to the tasks required. The talent of selecting an individual with the right skill for the right job may in the long run make or break a system. A good system with the wrong personnel will create overlapping duties and lost time, while good personnel with strong skills may save a mediocre system by having abilities to compensate for design failure.

§ 3A3.2 The Team Approach to Litigation. A team approach allows for more consistency in the day-to-day administration of a case. Such an arrangement allows the senior lawyer to reassign personnel knowing that each individual is fully aware of what is happening to the case. By having a cohesive unit, each staff member can develop expertise in matters arising within his or her skills area. The following sections describe a model team system at each stage of litigation and the roles played by the various team members.

§ 3A3.3 Role of the Paralegal and Other Nonlawyer Support Personnel in Managing Litigation on Behalf of the United States Government.

§ 3A3.3.1 The Paralegal's Role. The paralegal is an integral part of the legal staff. Formal paralegal training or extensive legal work experience is essential to performance at higher levels of responsibility. Generally, the paralegal can perform any assignment delegated by a lawyer that does not require legal signature or direct client advice. The paralegal reports directly to the lawyer staff. As skills dictate, the paralegal may work independently and contribute a separate work product with only general guidelines and supervision from the legal staff.

---

* Law student, Golden Gate School of Law, San Francisco, California; formerly paralegal, Federal Trade Commission, Washington, D. C.

Form 3:3 *Continued*

§ 3A3.3.2 Duties Performed by the Paralegal. A paralegal can perform a variety of tasks in litigation. Duties to be performed by the paralegal should be decided after discussion among the senior lawyer, the junior lawyer supervising the final work product and the paralegal. Specific guidelines for preparing the work product may be helpful in directing the paralegal's efforts. During this initial meeting, the lawyers should brief the paralegal on the major issues that will govern the project's outcome.

With appropriate instructions, many tasks formerly performed by lawyers can be delegated to paralegals. Some such duties include, but are not limited to (1) reviewing and summarizing documents received in response to subpoena requests, (2) drafting specifications for subpoenas with further review by lawyers, (3) legal research on major issues in the case which may become incorporated in the trial brief, (4) interviewing witnesses and preparing interview reports, (5) preparing witness summaries of testimony and exhibit lists, and (6) preparing exhibits to be used by trial counsel. Other opportunities for paralegal assistance also exist. As a general rule, any task can be delegated to paralegals, providing their work is reviewed by the lawyers responsible for the case. Although more time may be spent initially in giving detailed explanations to a paralegal for work that would require less lawyer time, assigning the task to the paralegal will ultimately result in less time for both individuals in the long run.

§ 3A3.3.3 The Legal Technician's Role. The legal clerk or technician differs from the paralegal in terms of skills and responsibilities. Most of the technician's duties involve mechanical processing and compilation of the physical aspects of the case.

The technician's basic function is as a document custodian. Upon receipt of any documents, the legal technician should record their date of receipt, source and treatment by protective order. At this time, the clerk should assign a control number to the document. If the originals of the documents are to be used for other purposes, the clerk should establish a checkout system.

The legal technician should also prepare documents for introduction into evidence. A folder should be prepared for each individual exhibit, recording the document control number, the source and treatment of document. The technician and the paralegal together should also compile exhibit books for use at trial, a record book showing disposition of exhibits and witness folders if requested by trial counsel. The technician should also be responsible for the timely filing and processing of all pleadings in the case.

§ 3A3.3.4 The Legal Clerk's Role. While many of the legal clerk's responsibilities can be performed by a paralegal as well, separation of the two serves a distinct purpose. Often the paralegal will be involved in time-consuming substantive issue tasks, under extreme time constraints. Matters such as deadlines and coordination of document control are sometimes lost by those individuals having too much else to do. Having a person whose sole function is to handle the physical control of the documents and deadlines assures the timely handling of litigation responsibilities.

§ 3A3.4 Discovery. After staff discussion by the entire team, the junior lawyers and paralegals should develop guidelines for review of documents meeting

Form 3:3 *Continued*

discovery requests. Within general guidelines, erring on the side of inclusion, the bulk of review and document selection should be assigned to paralegals. Only major legal documents and sensitive documents under protective orders may require review by a lawyer.

At the end of selection process, the paralegals should prepare general discussions or written summaries of the records reviewed for use by lawyers. Such summaries enable the lawyers to assess compliance and significance of the data received through discovery without spending large amounts of time actually reading the documents. Paralegals may also tag documents according to what subpoena specification each document is responsive. At the end of discovery the documents should be sent to the team's document control clerk. The document control clerk in the federal government is called a legal technician. The role of this staff member differs from the paralegal both in the training and skills required. The legal technician may have no legal training. The technician's major tasks require maintaining technical accuracy as to the physical location of documents and the processing required as to each.

At the end of discovery the legal technician becomes custodian of the documents. Immediately upon receipt of documents, the clerk assigns each document a number. In addition, the clerk makes a notation either lightly in pencil on the back of the original or on a separate listing compiled for this purpose of the number, date of receipt, the source of the document and treatment as to protective order or confidentiality agreement.

Legal technicians should maintain custody of the documents at all times. If staff members are to use the originals, a checkout system controlled by the legal technician should be implemented. The legal clerk should also be responsible for preparing documents for admission into evidence. This may require reproduction of the documents. If any of the documents are illegible, the clerk should arrange to obtain better copies.

§ 3A3.5 Review of Documents in Preparation of Case-in-Chief. Most likely all staff members will become involved in this process. At early stages, review of large numbers of documents can be accomplished in several ways.

Document review and analysis can be assigned to paralegals under guidelines drawn up by the legal staff to aid in the selection process. One approach calls for paralegals to review large numbers of documents within a given area and then prepare written summaries analyzing their relevance to major issues in the case. Alternatively, paralegals may provide a brief summary according to key points for each document on a document summary sheet prepared by the paralegal and lawyer staff before review begins. If the staff has a good grasp of the subject matter and issues in the case at this time, it may be able to develop a coding system to speed the process. This is the suggested approach for a case involving 3,000 documents or more. Implementation of this system depends in part on the staff's ability to refine its thinking into major areas. Coding systems are most useful if designed for use in a computer system. Although computers have been used for retrieval of case law, their use during litigation has only recently begun.

Form 3:3 *Continued*

§ 3A3.6 Computers and Litigation. The major advantages of a computer over staff personnel are consistency and memory. While a staff member may leave for a better job, a computer program remains until destroyed. Similarly, a staff member cannot remember 3,000 documents in great detail. If programmed correctly, a computer can retrieve in seconds what would take a person days to find, even if a good indexing system has been established.

Although the decision to use computers in a case involving 1,000 documents may be debated, in cases involving 3,000 documents or more using the computer as a tool becomes a must. Designing a viable program should involve paralegals and lawyers in developing a workable code. A successful outcome is more likely if the systems analysts and programmers are government personnel. Even better would be use of team members if they possess computer background. Using computers results in both long-term and short-term productivity in litigation. Computers permit ready retrieval of documents in preparation for the case-in-chief and trial brief. In cases requiring post-trial findings, the computer also provides an invaluable tool in matching documents to evidence admitted.

§ 3A3.7 Preparation of the Trial Brief. Major writing of the brief, especially the legal analysis sections, should be done by the lawyer staff. Both paralegals and lawyers may perform the legal research required to support the legal analysis. Ideally, background legal research should be the paralegal's function. Final analysis and arguments should be left to the lawyer staff. Citechecking and Shepardizing should be performed by the legal technician, with close supervision from the paralegal. Citechecking for form should be performed jointly by the legal technician, paralegal and secretary. The same three staff members should also prepare an indexed table of authorities.

§ 3A3.8 Preparation of Exhibits. While the paralegal and lawyer staff are preparing the witness and exhibit list, the legal technician should prepare the documents for admission at trial. The legal technician prepares a folder for each document with the following notations: (1) exhibit number, (2) source, and (3) treatment, *e.g.*, under protective order, in camera treatment, confidentiality grant. The clerk should place the original and one copy within each folder — one to offer to the court, and one to offer to the other side or witness.

§ 3A3.9 Exhibit Books. The legal technician may also compile a series of looseleaf binder notebooks with copies of all the exhibits for use by the judge, respondents and trial counsel when the exhibits are prepared. Compilation in this manner facilitates introduction of documents with a minimum of paper shuffling.

§ 3A3.10 Witness Folders. The paralegal and legal technician should work together to compile materials relating to a witness's testimony. The paralegal should review all exhibits to be introduced by counsel, and compile lists of documents originated and received by the witness, as well as documents relating to incidents involving the witness. The paralegal should also gather and compile documents concerning interviews and notes relating to the witness. The lawyer staff may add documents to be introduced through the witness's testimony. The legal technician

Form 3:3 *Continued*

should be responsible for copying these documents and organizing the folders. After assembling, the lawyers should review all documents compiled for the witness in preparing questions for direct examination. Preparation of documents in this fashion should enable the lawyer better to prepare for or present each witness's testimony. In a particularly voluminous case such a compilation may not be feasible. A computer program including specific witness information could be the answer for cases having a large number of documents.

§ **3A3.11 Preparation of Trial Record.** The legal technician should prepare a trial record to record the disposition of all exhibits during trial.

§ **3A3.12 Preparation of Witness Testimony.** Lawyers should be responsible for drafting questions to be asked each witness on direct examination. Depending on the paralegal's knowledge, he or she may also prepare questions to be asked.

Form 3:4 — Guidelines for Retaining Paralegals.
Text — § 3.6.

Use and Misuse of Paralegals — or — How to Keep the Paralegal You Hired.

As with any employee, the attorney-manager will want to help the paralegal become an increasingly valuable employee.

1. Confront the problem of boredom head-on. Work with the paralegal to find a satisfactory solution.
2. Find out what legal training the paralegal has received and to the degree possible make the person feel that he or she is using it.
3. Provide or make available further education even if the job does not require it.
4. Develop areas for which the paralegal has responsibility.
5. Don't make the paralegal reliant solely on other attorneys for work load. Have regular suggestion-sessions to identify ongoing work projects for non-pressure periods.
6. If it fits the office and situation, encourage paralegals to behave as professionals. Do this in the same manner as one would encourage attorneys regarding attitude, hours, continuing education, etc.
7. Encourage the paralegal to think creatively about his or her job. Could he or she contribute something no one previously had time for, such as reading and reporting on trade publications?
8. Deal with the psychological needs of the paralegal as an employee.
    a. Allow the paralegal to operate as part of a team.
    b. Assign a supervisor-protector who has the authority to change bad working situations.
    c. Hold regular discussions with the paralegal regarding his or her perceived work needs. Unhappy people are not necessarily able to formulate, by themselves, reasons for their dissatisfaction.
9. Do not give in to the temptation to have paralegals do clerical work such as massive copying projects, cutting and pasting, or filing. Most paralegals have a professional attitude regarding their career and their role in an office, and take no more kindly to the idea of being a highly paid clerk than would an attorney. The goal is to have a paralegal for less than the price of an attorney, not for more than the price of a clerk.
10. Don't let the availability of paralegals become an excuse to avoid correcting office inefficiencies.

4

CREATING YOUR OWN LEGAL ASSISTANT POSITION

Karen J. Feyerherm*

§ 4.1 This Chapter's Scope. This chapter discusses several methods that can be used in obtaining employment and "creating" a position as a legal assistant. Although this chapter is written for and will be of interest primarily to aspiring assistants, it should also be beneficial to lawyers seeking to employ nonlawyer personnel for the first time. Unfortunately, many lawyers do not employ legal assistants, simply because they do not know how to work with them effectively. By hiring a person capable of creating his or her own position, a lawyer will be able to enjoy the benefits of an assistant without expending the time and money otherwise required in adding nonlawyer personnel.

§ 4.2 Before You Begin Your Search for Employment. You should not begin searching for a position until you have determined what type of work you would like to do as a legal assistant. Begin by talking to lawyers and assistants in diverse areas of practice. Inquire about the kinds of assignments you could expect to receive as an assistant in each of these areas. Also, learn to what extent past experience or formal training is required.

Many areas of the law require a great deal of specialization by the lawyer as well as the assistant. For example, probate, estate planning and taxation are highly specialized. You probably would not be able to perform effectively as an assistant in these areas without either formal training or past experience. There are, however, other areas, such as litigation, in which you may learn to perform competently with a general knowledge of the law, and a lot of determination and creativity.

If, after talking to people in the field, you decide you would like to pursue a career as a litigation assistant, you should be aware that most lawyers will not hire a legal assistant with no training or experience. It may be possible for you to acquire the necessary experience by working in a law office in another capacity. Many assistants have "trained" themselves by working first as secretaries or receptionists.

You may discover that the facet of law that interests you requires specialized education. In that case, you should consider attending classes at a community college. Most community colleges in larger metropolitan areas now offer courses in law specifically designed for legal assistants. Depending on your career goals, you may also want to consider formal training in an American Bar Association-approved legal assistant program. For a list of such programs see § 1.9.

---

*Student, University of Washington School of Law; former legal assistant. Copyright © 1980 by Karen J. Feyerherm.

§ 4.3 Where to Begin Your Search.
§ 4.3.1 Explore the Resources in Your Present Office.

§ 4.3.1.1 Promotion Possibilities. If you are working in a law office in another capacity and would like to become a legal assistant, you may want to consider the possibility of promotion within the office. If your office has a managing partner or an office manager, approach him or her and explain your proposal. If there is no designated office manager, as is often the case in an unstructured firm, go to the person most likely to be receptive to your plan. This may be the lawyer for whom you are presently working. Remember, though, that it may not be to the lawyer's immediate advantage to promote you and thereby lose an experienced secretary or receptionist. Be prepared for this response and be ready to explain that you would be willing to continue in your present capacity long enough to train another person to replace you. If you are satisfied with the office in which you are working and it agrees with your proposal, you have begun to create your position.

§ 4.3.1.2 Lawyers as Resources. You may not be able to convince the lawyers in your present office that they need a legal assistant or you may desire to work for a different office. If you have a good working relationship with the lawyers in your present office, they could still be an excellent resource in finding employment as an assistant. When you first approach them to inquire about "leads," assure them that you will not desert them without adequately training your replacement. In addition to asking for leads, you may want to ask one of the lawyers to prepare an introduction letter to be included with your resume. A letter of introduction from an employer — especially from a lawyer — will be given more weight than an application letter under your own name.

§ 4.3.2 Consult Reference Books.

§ 4.3.2.1 Law Firms. *Martindale-Hubbell* is a multi-volume reference listing names and addresses of lawyers and law firms in the United States, Canada, Puerto Rico and the Virgin Islands. Biographical sketches of the lawyers and brief descriptions of the firms are included, making this directory indispensable when searching for prospective employers as well as in preparing for interviews.

Local and state bar associations often publish membership directories. "Specialty" legal associations also publish directories of their members. For example, the Washington State Trial Lawyers Association has a membership directory of lawyers and legal assistants. Bar associations may also have lists of lawyers seeking legal assistants or resume files of individuals searching for such positions.

§ 4.3.2.2 Corporations. General business information can be obtained by consulting corporate reference books such as *Standard and Poor's* and *Moody's*. Additional sources of information available at most public libraries include *30,000 Leading Corporations* and *Contacts Influential*. The *Wall Street Journal* and *Business Week* provide more current and detailed information about the business ventures of major corporations. See C. Bruno, Paralegal's Litigation Handbook 477 (1980) (hereafter "Bruno").

§ 4.3.2.3 Government Agencies. Consult the annual *U. S. Government Handbook* or Bruno for extensive listings of executive departments, agencies and commissions with general counsel offices at the federal level.

Do not overlook the possibility of creating a position with the city attorney, the prosecutor or district attorney, the public defender or the solicitor at the local level. It may also be possible to create a position at the state level with the state attorney general, state legislators or state agencies. See Bruno at 447.

§ 4.3.4 Read the Local Newspapers. Don't neglect to use the local newspapers as a resource. Although law firms seldom advertise for legal assistants in the classified section, corporations occasionally list openings for assistants under "help wanted." Some metropolitan newspapers may also publish ads for employment agencies that specialize in legal employment. Be careful, though, if you are using an employment agency. It may require that you pay as much as 100% of your first month's salary in fees. Often the employer will pay these fees, but be sure you know the terms of any agreement *before* you sign on the dotted line.

A more creative way to use the newspapers as a resource is by reading the feature stories on local lawyers. Often a newspaper focuses on the lawyers in a feature story about a current trial. If you are looking for a job as a litigation assistant, call or write the lawyers who are featured concerning employment possibilities. If the lawyer has spent six months or more preparing for a trial that is now in progress, he or she may be willing to hire a legal assistant to help with the backlog of work piled up in the office. It may be advisable, however, to wait until the trial is concluded, since many lawyers do not wish to be disturbed while they are in trial.

§ 4.4 Arranging for the Interview. A resume accompanied by a letter of application is the standard approach used in arranging for interviews. Detailed descriptions of the contents of a resume and letter of application are beyond this chapter's scope. For samples, see Bruno at 458-76. This approach, however, may not necessarily be the best approach for your purposes. There is no one "right way" to make your initial contact with a prospective employer. You should at least consider some of the alternatives.

§ 4.4.1 Sending a Resume and Letter of Application. If you decide this approach best suits your needs, it is important that you conclude your letter by stating: "I will be telephoning you on (date) to arrange for a mutually convenient time for an interview." Otherwise, you will have to wait for the person to whom the letter was sent to take the initiative in arranging for an interview.

§ 4.4.2 Using the Telephone. Although there is some disagreement about the desirability of arranging for an interview by telephone (see Bruno), this method can be effective under certain circumstances. For instance, if you know of a specific opening, you may want to avoid the delay involved in sending a resume and application letter. By arranging for the interview over the phone and taking your resume with you to the interview instead, you may be able to get in ahead of the other applicants.

§ 4.4.3 Distributing Business Cards. Having business cards commercially printed for distribution to prospective employers is particularly important if you are seeking free-lance work as a legal assistant. Business cards may also be used effectively in a door-to-door search for permanent employment. Although "hitting the pavement" may not always be the ideal method of obtaining employment as a legal assistant, a professionally executed door-to-door job search may give you access to the maximum number of prospective employers and enable you to decide which office is best suited for you.

§ 4.5 Convincing the Lawyer of the Need for a Legal Assistant.

In order to convince the lawyer of the need for a legal assistant, you must be prepared to discuss the types of assignments you will be able to handle.

§ 4.5.1 Prepare a Portfolio.

The best way to demonstrate that you are capable of performing certain assignments is by taking a "portfolio" along with you to the interview. Include samples of interrogatories, settlement brochures, deposition summaries and other legal documents you have prepared.

If you have not drafted any legal documents, take a writing sample along, but do not select a scholarly dissertation. Choose something short and simple. Otherwise the lawyer may not take the time to read it, regardless of how fascinating you find the subject.

§ 4.5.2 Check Into Certification Procedures.

Before your initial interviews, check with the local bar association regarding any procedures for certification of legal assistants. Some local bar associations certify assistants who meet specified qualifications authorizing them to perform such tasks as presenting ex parte motions at the courthouse, checking out court files and using the courthouse library. Ordinarily these are privileges granted only to lawyers. The qualifications for certification will vary, but they usually require a college education or previous legal experience. The certification programs may also require the signature of a "sponsoring" lawyer as part of the application process.

Even though you may not be able to become certified before you find a position, you should explain the certification process if the lawyer with whom you are interviewing doesn't already know about it. Explain that you will apply for certification and that if you become certified you will be able to complete some of the time-consuming tasks now being performed by lawyers in the office.

§ 4.5.3 Make the "Unsuccessful" Interview Worthwhile.

If you are unable to convince a lawyer that he or she needs a legal assistant, don't consider the interview a waste of time. Instead, ask the lawyer for the names of others who might be interested in hiring an assistant. By doing this during each "unsuccessful" interview, you will add to your list of potential employers, and you won't run out of possibilities before you find your desired position.

§ 4.6 Creating the Position.

§ 4.6.1 Define Your Responsibilities.

Accept any reasonable assignment graciously during your first few weeks of employment. Remember, the lawyers are probably not quite sure what you are capable of doing, and it will take time for you to "prove yourself."

If you find that after two or three weeks you still are not getting the kind of assignments you desire, ask your supervising lawyer for additional tasks. Be assertive — but not aggressive — in requesting additional work. Most overworked lawyers will appreciate your willingness to accept more responsibility if you approach them with confident assertiveness.

If, on the other hand, you are asked to perform a task you have not done before, do not turn it down until you have determined that you would not be able to handle it. For example, if the attorney asks that you prepare a "request for production of documents" and you have never heard of one, do not assume immediately that you cannot draft one. Ask for the name of a file in the office that contains a similar document. Using this document as your guide, you shouldn't have much difficulty.

If you are unable to locate a certain type of document, refer to a set of form books for guidance. Check the office's library or the nearest law library for various commercial form books. These form books can be indispensable resources for the new assistant.

§ 4.6.2 Know Your Limits in Accepting Assignments. Once the lawyers in the firm discover the benefits of having a legal assistant in the office, you may find yourself swamped with assignments from every lawyer — all due on the same day. To prevent this from happening you will have to keep a detailed calendar of all assignments, estimating the length of time that it will take to finish each task and entering the projected completion date.

If a lawyer gives you an assignment and you are not certain that you will be able to finish it on time — say so. Do not wait until the day before it is due to explain why it will not be completed on time. If you explain your situation when it is assigned, the lawyer will be able to decide whether to give you the project with an extended deadline or handle it in some other way.

One solution to problems of juggling assignments may be to use a "broker." A broker is a lawyer or office manager who accepts assignments and divides them among the nonlawyer personnel. Some offices use this method for assigning research projects to legal interns. One advantage of having a broker is that it is often easier for him or her to explain to the lawyer that the desired deadline cannot be met. It may also serve as a convenient mechanism for ensuring that as many lawyers as possible will be able to use some of the assistant's time.

§ 4.7 Developing a System. In order to increase efficiency, it is essential that you eventually develop a system for handling your assignments. See, *e.g.*, R. Ramo, ed., How to Create-A-System for the Law Office (A.B.A. 1975), which includes guidelines for preparing routine documents in collections, divorces, incorporations, personal injury litigation, adoptions, probate and other areas.

§ 4.8 Conclusion. Creating a legal assistant position involves more than simply obtaining employment in a law office. By continually redefining your responsibilities and increasing your efficiency, you can achieve the satisfaction that distinguishes a career from a job.

5

INVESTIGATION AND FACT-GATHERING

Patricia S. Kottner[*]

§ 5.1 This Chapter's Scope. This chapter discusses the use of legal assistants in investigation and fact-gathering. It includes the assistant's role in interviewing clients and witnesses, and in obtaining source material. Although these tasks are often performed in conjunction with formal discovery, this chapter is limited to investigation and fact-gathering outside the discovery process. For discussion of the use of assistants in the discovery process see chapter 6. For illustrative purposes, the discussion and forms relate primarily to Arizona agencies. Independent inquiry should be made and corresponding forms developed for other states, including annotated checklists of procedures, fees required for obtaining information, and information required by the source.

This chapter does not discuss in detail the ethical considerations with respect to the use of legal assistants in investigation and fact-gathering. Nevertheless, lawyers should remember that the assistant, like the lawyer, is guided by the Code of Professional Responsibility. Those contacted by the assistant, whether agency personnel, witnesses or clients, should be made aware of the assistant's ethical limitations. For example, the fact that the assistant is not a lawyer should be disclosed. Lawyers should advise their clients that the legal assistant may not give legal advice or represent the client in an advocacy position.

§ 5.2 Establishing the Lawyer-Legal Assistant Roles. Investigation assignments given to legal assistants should first be thought through carefully by the assigning lawyer. A legal assistant well-trained in investigative procedures and armed with the knowledge of where and how to locate useful material and people is a valuable asset to the lawyer, the client and the firm. Guidelines should be established for the best division of responsibility between the lawyer and assistant so that both can use their time and talents most effectively. The working relationship should be based on a clear understanding of the assistant's role and function as an investigator/fact-finder. The lawyer should know in advance and advise the assistant concerning how the investigation's results are to be used. Assistants should know in advance whether the person being investigated is a client, a client's witness, an adversary witness or a potential party. Such advance knowledge is necessary to guide both the investigation and the reports prepared as the result.

§ 5.3 The Investigative Process: Initial Stages.

§ 5.3.1 Client Interview or Initial Conference with Lawyer. Since the client often provides the initial leads for an investigation, the legal assistant should, whenever practical, be present during the initial client interview with the

---

[*] Legal assistant, Lewis and Roca, Phoenix, Arizona.

lawyer. After the meeting with the client, the lawyer can have the legal assistant conduct additional fact-gathering. The type of case determines the precise information needed from the client. A client interview sheet illustrating the type of information frequently requested of a client is shown at Form 5:1. Each lawyer-assistant team can prepare variations of the client interview sheet to meet a wide variety of specific needs and problems. The assistant can then immediately begin to investigate to obtain any necessary information not directly supplied by the client.

§ 5.3.2 The Case's Background. The case's background should be outlined through an initial conference with the lawyer, a detailed memorandum directed to the assistant or both. If the assistant was not present during the meeting with the client, an assignment memorandum from the lawyer should provide the areas of concern that need to be investigated, together with enough background information to place the assignment in proper perspective. The lawyer and assistant should confer early in the investigation process so that the assistant clearly understands the purpose and scope of the case and what steps to follow in the investigation. Having been provided with the necessary background, the assistant should be encouraged and educated to handle any necessary investigative assignment as it develops.

§ 5.3.3 Objectives and Reporting. Conferences and memoranda between the lawyer and legal assistant are necessary to establish objectives and ensure that any required interim status reports are prepared during different stages of an investigation. In addition, such conferences allow additional ideas or suggestions to be considered fully. Any questions or concerns the assistant may have should be discussed with the lawyer at the earliest opportunity to avoid wasted time and effort.

The best method of conveying results of the investigation is through a memorandum to the lawyer. On more complex cases, interim reports should be prepared to keep the lawyer informed concerning how the investigation is proceeding. The lawyer and assistant will then be in a position to evaluate the strengths and weaknesses of the case at all stages.

§ 5.3.4 Checklists. The lawyer and legal assistant should develop and use checklists whenever appropriate to see what has been done and what needs to be done on a particular matter. For instance, a personal injury investigation checklist, Form 5:2, can be used at any stage of an investigation. Another example is the incorporation checklist, Form 5:3. The assistant should concentrate on obtaining certain items, such as the police report or incident report, as soon as possible. From such a report, the assistant can obtain other necessary data, including witness names and photographs. Checklists should be formulated for any general category of case on which the lawyer or legal assistant is working, as well as for specific assignments not fitting any particular pattern.

§ 5.3.5 File Organization. Prior to beginning the actual investigative work, the legal assistant should become familiar with and be responsible for organizing the file. For example, if the matter is a personal injury case, the assistant should see that the file contains the relevant filebacks, *e.g.*, police reports, photographs, investigative reports and witness statements. It is also helpful to use a file control sheet once a complaint has been filed, as shown on Form 5:4. Similar file control sheets can also be developed for other categories of law practice.

§ 5.4. Skip-Tracing: Location of Witnesses. Locating a potential witness often becomes essential. A legal assistant will often discover that a witness has recently moved from the address available from the file or other reports. By the time a lawyer becomes involved in a case, months or sometimes years may have elapsed from the date of the incidents at issue. Location of and communication with potential witnesses thus should be undertaken as soon as possible. A good sequence of steps to follow is outlined in the first five sources listed on the left on the investigative checklist or skip-trace worksheet, Form 5:5. This checklist suggests various sources that may be helpful in obtaining information about people, their whereabouts, and current business, social, legal and personal status.

§ 5.4.1 Telephone and Other Directories. The legal assistant can begin the search with the full or partial name (initials and last name) of the person to be found. The following sources should be checked initially: the local telephone directory, telephone directory assistance and the local city directory. The city directory generally is cross-referenced under name, last known address and phone number. It may also provide spouse's name, occupation (if available), and the names of neighbors, who may be helpful if an individual has moved.

§ 5.4.2 Post Office Check. Time naturally is a factor in determining what other steps to follow. If there is not an immediate hearing or trial date, a post office check can prove useful when the individual's last known address is available. This is most easily accomplished by submitting a form letter to the main United States post office covering the area concerned. In requesting a forwarding address, the individual's full name and last known address should be provided. A fee plus postage may be required. This information may be obtained more quickly by going in person to the post office branch serving the last known address of the individual the legal assistant is attempting to locate.

§ 5.4.3 Registrar of Voters. A registrar of voters check may also uncover valuable information. This generally can be accomplished over the telephone. As shown on Form 5:6, a voter registration affidavit, the residence address and mailing address, telephone number, occupation and physical description of the individual can be obtained. This agency, as well as others mentioned in this section, will provide certified copies.

§ 5.4.4 Motor Vehicle Department. Another source for obtaining the location of an individual is the state motor vehicle department. A motor vehicle department search can be performed either by mail or in person. There are two possible categories of searches:

1. A "T & R" (title and registration) search can be obtained by providing either name and address or license plate number. The address, spouse's name and vehicular information, including liens on vehicles, are shown. See Form 5:7, a copy of the Arizona T & R search report. The motor vehicle department is also a good source of information for an asset check.

2. An "MVR," or driver's license search, accompanied by a full name, last known address if available and date of birth, will provide the individual's most recent address, social security number and driving record. In addition, a copy of the individual's driver's license application can be purchased separately. This will show the person's occupation, if any, and physical description. There may be a fee for either a T & R or MVR, and an additional fee for certification.

§ 5.4.5 Credit Bureau. A local credit bureau can be a helpful source in locating an individual. Information can be obtained concerning all known credit, mortgage, lien and usually judgment data, as well as the spouse's identity. Such files can be reviewed at no cost. There is usually a charge to obtain copies of the file's documentation. The information required to review another's file is name, last known address, age and social security number. A legitimate professional purpose is also expected. This source is particularly helpful when performing an asset check on an individual.

§ 5.4.6 Other Investigative Sources. Another source for locating witnesses is the Social Security Administration, Bureau of Data Processing and Accounts, Baltimore, Maryland 21235. A letter directed to the witness can be put in an unsealed, unaddressed stamped envelope to the Social Security Administration, together with a $3.00 fee. The letter will then be forwarded by this agency to the witness's last known address.

The legal assistant must be resourceful and imaginative. For instance, if a witness is a registered nurse, the state registered nurses directory will have data concerning the witness's employment, and possibly a home address and telephone number. One source often leads to another. Perhaps the registered nurse is no longer working at the hospital or doctor's office given by the registry. However, in contacting the hospital or office the assistant might talk with someone acquainted with the witness who can provide a helpful lead. Other valuable sources are neighbors, relatives, former employers, friends and other witnesses.

§ 5.5 Agencies as Sources of Information.

§ 5.5.1 Court Property and Records. Court records for current or past lawsuits involving the client, other parties, witnesses or other interested persons should be examined. Generally the lawyer will discuss with the legal assistant whether a docket search would be necessary or helpful. The lawyer may ask the assistant to discover all property owned by an individual. The assistant can look at records in the local county assessor's office for the following: property ownership and location, legal description, full cash value and assessed value of the property, type of property, taxation and lien information. The assessor's records are normally indexed alphabetically by name. However, if one wants to determine property ownership the tax parcel number is necessary. Other agencies that can be helpful are title companies, the Bureau of Land Management (for federal land and mining claims) and the state land department (for information on state leases and water and mineral rights).

Title insurance or abstract companies usually can provide a legal description for any given tract address. The legal description is usually required to check on land. The Bureau of Land Management is presently in the process of computerizing its records. It will then have a master claim map for verifying claims with a legal description.

The county recorder's office will have records of the mortgages, deeds or liens concerning a piece of property. In Arizona, the county recorder also often has copies of the transactions entered into between parties including notes, loans, sales agreements and judgments. Since all indexes are by name only, it is helpful to know the names of the parties, and the date and type of transaction before making the search. The Arizona secretary of state's office provides Uniform Commercial Code filings pertaining to secured transactions, chattel mortgages and liens. Here, too, it is necessary to know the names of the parties. Trademarks and trade names, including assumed names ("aka"), can also be found at this office.

§ 5.5.2 General Sources. Numerous other sources can be helpful in investigating a person or business. These include the registrar of contractors, the corporation commission, the Better Business Bureau, consumer protection agencies, licensing and regulatory agencies, and law enforcement agencies. Newspaper articles, another valuable source, can be obtained either through the newspaper's own library or through public libraries, colleges or state archives. The information desk can help the assistant find the appropriate sources.

If a legal assistant needs to learn about a particular subject area, such as accident deaths in the United States, he or she can contact the public library's social science reference department. City, county, state and federal agencies also can provide information if the assistant knows the correct agency to contact. For example, if the lawyer needs to know the standing or status of a particular CPA, the assistant can call the state accountancy board. In each state numerous boards or commissions exist from which it is possible to obtain licensing information and other data on a given individual or firm. The state attorney general's office may also provide the assistant useful information in dealing with a case involving possible consumer or financial fraud.

The agencies to be contacted will depend on the legal area in which the assistant works. A probate assistant, for example, will be more likely to be in contact with insurance and real estate companies, the social security office, and funeral homes. A personal injury assistant, on the other hand, may more often contact law enforcement agencies, city or state highway departments, and hospital and medical facilities. An assistant asked to perform an asset check for a lawyer can consult a number of the agencies previously mentioned, including motor vehicle department, county assessor and recorder offices, credit bureaus, the appropriate UCC filing office, former and current employers, the corporation commission, Better Business Bureau and licensing departments.

The nature of the investigation necessarily will depend on the facts involved in a particular case. For example, if the lawyer or legal assistant suspects a person may have a monetary interest in a liquor store, the assistant can check with the city's privilege license department. This agency will tell the assistant whether the individual holds a liquor license, the precise location of the store and other pertinent data.

§ 5.6 Interviewing Witnesses.

§ 5.6.1 General Considerations. A frequent follow-up assignment to skip-tracing and background checks is interviewing witnesses. W. Statsky, Introduction to Paralegalism (West Publishing Co., 1974), contains two chapters on legal investigation and interviewing techniques. It also includes useful bibliographies on the arts of investigation and interviewing. Following these guidelines, the legal assistant can obtain much useful information. The most common procedure is then to report the details of the interview in memorandum form to the lawyer. If the lawyer anticipates in advance that the witness's testimony will be favorable, the assistant should be asked to prepare a statement for the witness to sign at the end of the interview. Alternatively, the lawyer may wait for the assistant's report before deciding whether to ask for a witness statement or affidavit. In either event, the lawyer should be specific as to how the statement will be used so that it will be prepared properly.

Once the potential witness is contacted, the assistant should state his or her identity and the purpose of the discussion. The witness should be assured that there is nothing improper in talking to either side or in giving statements. Most importantly, a professional and courteous approach should be employed. The assistant should always express appreciation for the witness's time. Any meeting should be scheduled at a place and time most convenient to the witness. Depending on the information desired, a telephone interview can be helpful in determining whether to meet with the person and to obtain a signed statement. The assistant frequently can learn in a telephone call the extent of a witness's knowledge about an occurrence and then report what has been learned to the lawyer. All details are important. Interviews should be conducted by the assistant with the attitude that he or she is looking for the truth. If damaging evidence is uncovered, it may save the lawyer and the client time and money in the long run. All such evidence should be reported to the lawyer as soon as possible.

§ 5.6.2 Taking a Written Statement. Prior to obtaining the statement, the legal assistant should discuss with the lawyer the facts to be obtained. The assistant then must use common sense in determining what should go into the statement. After developing the basic facts known by the witness, the assistant should prepare a statement for the witness to sign. When a witness is interviewed personally, the legal assistant should write down the information using the witness's words as much as possible. The notes become, in effect, the witness's statement. The final form, depending on the lawyer's instructions, will be the assistant's handwritten statement for the witness to sign, or a typewritten statement that can be mailed or hand delivered at a later time.

A legal assistant can conduct a telephone interview when a personal meeting is not feasible or convenient. The assistant can then read the contents of the drafted statement and make any necessary corrections in a follow-up call. The assistant should also review the final draft of the statement before mailing or delivering it. Important points to consider in taking witness statements are covered in R. Blanchard, Litigation and Trial Practice for the Legal Paraprofessional (West Publishing Co., Paralegal Series, 1976). Blanchard states that the information to be obtained should include the witness's identity, background, observations, contacts with the parties and any pertinent conclusions he may have. The assistant will also want to determine whether the witness has been interviewed by or given a statement to anyone else.

The statement should always begin with the witness's name, address, telephone number and age. If the witness is cooperative, his social security number should be included. Examples of the kinds of questions that might be asked of a witness to an automobile accident are shown on the witness questionnaire, Form 5:8. The questionnaire itself can be used. This is especially helpful when discussing an accident with a young child, an adolescent or an elderly individual, when a free-flowing statement can be difficult to obtain. A legal assistant may find that showing the witness the questionnaire makes it easier to recall certain events.

Blanchard also makes the following suggestions: it is helpful to inform the witness of facts or information already obtained since such a review might elicit the witness's cooperation or help the witness recall additional facts. A reluctant witness may be more cooperative if told that the case will not be tried for a year or more and that it would therefore be helpful to have a written statement to help him refresh his recollection at a later date. He can also be told that if he is unwilling to make an informal statement, the alternative would be a deposition, requiring him to respond to a subpoena and testify under oath. After the statement is written, the witness should be asked to read it to confirm that the information is correct and then sign it. In addition to the statement, the assistant should prepare a memorandum to the lawyer summarizing his or her impressions of the witness. The memorandum should include observations of the witness's appearance and credibility, as well as anything else the assistant believes might be important.

§ 5.6.3 Expert Witnesses. Depending on his or her experience, a legal assistant may be in a position to contact and interview expert witnesses. For example, an assistant who has been a registered nurse could contact and interview physicians or other health personnel in order to evaluate the witness's expertise and willingness to testify. In a contested automobile accident case, an accident reconstruction expert may be needed. In contacting the expert, the assistant should be aware of the following areas: determining speed from skidmarks, pedestrian speed, stopping distance, speed at impact, angle of impact, point of impact, condition of brakes, whether the tire exploded before or after impact, and negligent design of the auto or any specific parts. Some sources for expert witnesses are the classified ads in the back of *The American Bar Association Journal*, as well as other pertinent journals, periodicals and law reviews.

§ 5.7 Summary and Conclusion. This chapter demonstrates the numerous ways in which a lawyer can employ a legal assistant as a fact-finder and investigator. The assistant can be a valuable aid to the lawyer if properly oriented and educated in fact-gathering procedures. Checklists, a thorough approach and resourcefulness are essential tools. Close monitoring by the lawyer in the investigative process is necessary, particularly since the data obtained by the assistant may change, expand or limit the investigation's scope. Having an assistant interview and locate witnesses or source material can give the lawyer more time to meet other responsibilities.

Form 5:1 — Client Interview Sheet.
(Varies, depending on type of case.)
Text — § 5.3.1.

Interview Date _____
File No. _____
Case Name _____
Date of Accident _____

PLAINTIFF

1. Client _____
   (Spouse) (Parents) _____
   Address _____
   D/B _____
   Res. Phone _____
   Other Phone _____
   Social Security No. _____
   Driver License No. _____

   Nearest Relative _____
   Address & Phone _____
   School _____

   Statute of Limitations (calendar) _____

   Previous offer received _____
   Offer confirmed _____

DEFENDANT — (Specify whether individual, minor, agent, partnership, corp.)

1. Name _____
   Address _____

2. Name _____
   Address _____

3. Name _____
   Address _____

4. Name _____
   Address _____

AUTO AND NON-AUTO
OTHER FACTS AND WITNESSES

(Include all additional facts including witnesses — include post-occurrence)

_____
_____
_____
_____
_____

Form 5:1 *Continued*

NON-AUTO

General Facts _____

_____

_____

_____

_____

Time _____ Day of Week _____

People Present _____

Location _____

Specific Facts (including model numbers and other identifying facts, ownership, etc.)

_____

_____

_____

_____

_____

AUTOMOBILE

1. Scene (Including Directions) _____

_____

_____

2. Diagram:

3. Weather and Road Conditions _____
4. Time _____ Day of Week _____
5. General Facts of Occurrence _____

_____

_____

_____

_____

Form 5:1 *Continued*

Specific Facts

6. Police at Scene _____
   (State, County, City)

7. Arrests and Charges _____

8. Plaintiff Vehicle Type (Ownership) _____
   _____

   Photos _____

9. Defendant Vehicle Type (Ownership) _____
   _____

   Photos _____

PERSONAL INFORMATION — PLAINTIFF (one for each plaintiff)

1. Name _____ Age _____

2. Dependents:
   (Name)   (Address)   (D/B)   (Relationship)

   _____
   _____
   _____
   _____

3. Employment Information
   (a) Name _____
   (b) Address _____
   (c) Type of Work _____
   (d) Job Title _____
   (e) Foreman or Boss _____
   (f) Wage Rate _____

4. Time Lost From Work (dates; change in job) _____
   _____

5. Other Information: (significant previous illnesses, and doctors and hospitals last 15 years)

   _____
   _____
   _____
   _____
   _____

Form 5:1 *Continued*

MEDICAL INFORMATION
(one sheet for each plaintiff)

_____
(Name)

_____
(Address at time of hospitalization)

1. Plaintiff's Injuries
   (describe complaints)

   _____
   _____
   _____
   _____
   _____

2. Plaintiff's Doctors (indicate treating, company, consulting, etc.)
   (Name)   (Address)   (treating, consulting, etc.)

   _____
   _____
   _____
   _____

3. Hospitals (in-patient and out-patient)
   (Name)   (Address)   (Dates of Hospitalization)

   _____
   _____
   _____
   _____

4. Plaintiff's Insurance Coverage:
   (a) Plaintiff's Company (Adjuster)
       (Name)   (Address)   (Phone)

       _____
       _____

   (b) Type of insurance (liability, uninsured motorists, etc.)

   (c) Did plaintiff give statement, and if so, to whom and what type
       (Both companies)

   _____
   _____

Form 5:1 *Continued*

5. Defendant's Insurance Coverage:
    (a) Defendant's Company, Adjuster

        (Name)   (Address)   (Phone)

_____
_____

PRIOR INJURIES OR CLAIMS
(Include workmen's compensation — all types
including sporting, fall, childhood, etc.

1. (a) Type of injury _____
   (b) Where injured _____
   (c) Treated by _____
   (d) D/A _____
   (e) Claim or law suit described _____
   (f) Attorney who handled _____

   (Repeat if necessary)

Investigation and Fact-Gathering — Forms

Form 5:2 — Personal Injury Investigation Checklist.
Text — § 5.3.4.

(This checklist can be used several times during a case: at the initial interview, during the early stages of the investigation, while formulating interrogatories, before depositions and in preparing for trial.)

☐ Police Agency
   (a) Accident or incident report (diagrams) _____
   (b) Photographs _____
   (c) Parts of vehicles _____
   (d) Interview investigating officer (obtain officer's notes if available) _____

☐ Citation Disposition
   (a) Court date _____
   (b) Court reporter _____
   (c) Plea and fine entered _____

☐ Motor Vehicle Licensing Authority
   (a) Moving violation record _____
   (b) Ownership of vehicle _____

☐ Newspapers: (for photographs and witness information) _____

☐ State or Local Traffic Engineering Agency
   (a) Maps, including aerial maps _____
   (b) Photographs _____
   (c) Traffic control devices (time cycle), signs _____

☐ Prepare Client Diary (to check physical progress, medical visits, loss of time from work, etc.) _____

☐ Witnesses
   (a) Contact _____
   (b) Interview _____

☐ Photographs
   (a) Vehicles _____
   (b) Scene of accident _____
   (c) Injuries _____

☐ Autopsy, Coroner's Inquest Report _____

☐ Medical Bills, requested _____

☐ Property Damage Estimates and Bills (including receipts of payment) _____

☐ Statute of Limitations _____

☐ Investigation Agency Report _____

Form 5:2 *Continued*

☐ Police Records
  (a) Plaintiff _____
  (b) Defendant _____
  (c) Witnesses _____

☐ Insurance Company Statements (to health and accident carriers)
  (a) Plaintiff _____
  (b) Defendant _____

☐ Workmen's Compensation Records
  (a) Plaintiff _____
  (b) Defendant _____

☐ Hospital and Doctors' Records _____
_____

☐ Physician's Report _____

☐ Medical Authorizations Obtained _____

☐ Loss of Wages Letter _____

☐ Social Security Records _____

☐ Income Tax Records _____

☐ U.S. Weather Bureau (weather report) _____

☐ Interstate Commerce Commission _____

☐ Accident Reconstruction Expert _____

☐ Medical and Other Experts _____

☐ Bars, Restaurants or Taverns _____

☐ Accident Scene _____

☐ Weigh-In Station (trucks) _____

☐ Previous Owners of Vehicle _____

☐ Vehicle Maintenance, Repair Records _____

☐ Consumer Product Safety Commission _____

Form 5:3 — Incorporation Checklist.
Text — § 5.3.4.

A. ARTICLES OF INCORPORATION

1. **Corporate name (A.R.S. § 10-008):** _____
   a. Check for availability with Corporation Commission
      Yes _____ No _____
   b. Reserve proposed corporate name for 120 days ($10.00 fee) Yes ___ No ___

2. **Purpose**
   Should we use only the general purpose clause? Yes _____ No _____ If not, what specific purposes should be listed? (Any specific purpose suggested by the name of the corporation should be listed.)

3. Brief statement of the character of business which the corporation initially intends to conduct:

4. **Capitalization**
   a. Amount of authorized capital _____
   b. Number of shares authorized _____
      1) Par value per share: _____
      2) No par value: _____
   c. Class(es) of shares authorized:
      1) Common stock _____
         Pre-emptive rights: Yes _____ No _____
      2) Preferred stock Yes _____ No _____
         If yes, describe nature of proposed preferential rights with regard to:
         a. Voting:
         b. Dividends, cumulative or non-cumulative:
         c. Liquidation:
         d. Redemption:
         e. Conversion:
         f. Other:

5. **Statutory Agent**
   a. Use firm's statutory agent Yes _____ No _____
   b. Other:
      Name _____
      _____
      (Street Address)
      _____   _____
      (City)   (County)

Form 5:3 *Continued*

6. **Directors**
    a. Number of directors constituting initial board (one or more):

    b. Names and addresses (business or residential) of initial directors:

    c. Please specify terms if a staggered board of directors should be authorized (note: board must have nine or more members):
        1) Number of directors _____
        2) Length of terms _____
        3) Number to be elected each year _____

7. **Incorporators**
    a. Initial stockholders, not exceeding 10, must be incorporators to qualify for the exemption from registration of securities issued to incorporators, A.R.S. § 44-1844.10.
    b. At least two incorporators are required to form an Arizona non-professional business corporation.
    c. Names and addresses (business or residential) of incorporators:

8. Names, addresses (business or residential) and capacity of officers:

Investigation and Fact-Gathering — Forms

Form 5:4 — File Control Sheet.

Text — § 5.3.5.

Name: _____ Client No. _____
Attorney in Charge: _____ Cause No. _____
Attorney for Adverse: _____ Phone No. _____
Attorney for _____ : _____ Phone No. _____
Date of Loss: _____
Complaint Filed: _____ Answer Filed: _____
Offer of Judgment Filed _____ Amount: $ _____
Trial Date: _____ Jury? _____ Judge: _____
Client Notified: _____ Phone No.: _____ Company Notified: _____

Discovery Schedule

Interr. to Client Rec'd: _____ Ans. Due: _____ Ans. Filed: _____
Interr. to Adverse on: _____ Ans. Due: _____ Ans. Filed: _____
Trial Interr. to Adv. _____ Ans. Due: _____ Ans. Filed: _____

Depositions to be Taken   Date Taken   Summarized
  Adverse _____   _____   _____
  Client _____   _____   _____
  Witness _____   _____   _____
  Others _____   _____   _____

I.M.E.: _____ Doctor: _____ Date: _____

Adverse's Treating Doctors   Records Rec'd   Injuries Diagnosed
  1. _____   _____   _____
  2. _____   _____   _____
  3. _____   _____   _____

                                                        Records
Hospitals   Date   Req.   Rec'd
  1. _____   _____   _____ _____
  2. _____   _____   _____ _____

Documents to be Produced   Date Req.   Date Produced
  Adverse: _____   _____   _____
  Client: _____   _____   _____
  Others: _____   _____   _____

Reports or Things to be Produced Date Req.   Date Produced
  Adverse: _____   _____   _____
  Client: _____   _____   _____
  Others: _____   _____   _____

Witnesses' Name, Address & Phone Number   Statements Taken
  1. _____   _____
  2. _____   _____
  3. _____   _____
  4. _____   _____

Form 5:4 *Continued*

Exhibits   Location
    1. _____   _____
    2. _____   _____
    3. _____   _____

Trial Statement Due: _____ Prepared: _____
Preparation of Trial Book: _____
Special Legal Issues to be Briefed: _____

Reports to Company:
    Due _____ Sent _____
    Due _____ Sent _____
    Due _____ Sent _____
    Due _____ Sent _____

Investigation and Fact-Gathering — Forms

Form 5:5 — Investigative Checklist
  a.k.a. Skip Trace Worksheet,
  Asset Check, Background Check.
  Text — § 5.4.

Date Assigned Attorney's Initials Case Name

Name of Subject Last Employment or Other Identifying Date

Sources

- ☐ Telephone directory, directory assistance
- ☐ City directory check (Polk's, Cole's and others)
- ☐ Motor Vehicle Department
  1. T & R
  2. MVR (driver license service)
- ☐ Post Office Check U.S. Main Post Office (Last Known Address)
- ☐ Registrar of Voters
- ☐ County Assessor's Office
- ☐ County Recorder's Office
- ☐ Docket Search: Plaintiff and Defendant
  (a) Superior Court
  (b) U.S. District Court
  (c) Marriage License Dept.
  (d) Child Support Payment Division
  (e) Municipal and Justice Courts
- ☐ Credit Bureau, (*e.g.*, Credit Data of Arizona)
- ☐ Social Security Administration, Bureau of Data Processing and Accounts, Baltimore, Maryland, 21235

- ☐ Secretary of State, UCC
- ☐ Registrar of Contractors
- ☐ Corporation Commission
- ☐ Better Business Bureau
- ☐ Previous address visit, former neighbors, friends, relatives
- ☐ Previous employment check
- ☐ Newspaper articles
- ☐ Various licensing depts., Real Estate Dept., etc.
- ☐ Other sources unique to subject, *i.e.* police departments, licensing agencies, city, county and state offices
- ☐ Asset check

Working With Legal Assistants

Form 5:6 — Voter Registration Affidavit.
Text — § 5.4.3.

STATE OF ARIZONA
AFFIDAVIT OF REGISTRATION
MARICOPA COUNTY

SAMPLE

Registration Officer: TYPE or PRINT plainly with ink. LAST, FIRST and MIDDLE NAME must be shown in full using CAPITALS. Place all information within the space allowed.

Document Locator _____

Date of Registration _____ | Mo | Day | Year

(1) Full Name MR. MRS. MS. MISS. _____
Last Name | First | Middle | Jr/Sr/III

(2) Residence Address _____
House Number | Direction | Street Name | Type | Suff | Apt/Sp | Res. City | Zip Code

(3) Mailing Address If Different _____
House Number | Direction | Street Name or Rural Rt. or "P.O." | Type | Suff | Apt/Sp/Bx | Mail City | Zip Code
(Describe exact location of residence on diagram provided on reverse side.)

(4) PARTY PREFERENCE _____

(5) Telephone Number (Unless unlisted) _____

(6) Place of Birth _____ State _____ Country _____ Birth Date Mo | Day | Year

(7) Occupation _____ Indian Census Number (optional) _____

(8) Father's Name _____ Last | First | Middle

(9) Currently registered in _____ County | State | Prec.

(10) Precinct Name _____
(11) Office Code _____
(12) Prior Registration Information
Former Address _____
Former Party Preference _____
Former Name _____

State of Arizona }
County of Maricopa } ss

I, the undersigned registrant swear (or affirm) that I am a citizen of the United States, and a resident of the State of Arizona and the County of Maricopa; that before the next General Election, I will be eighteen years of age or more; that I have not been convicted of treason or a felony (or if so, my civil rights have been restored); and that all of the statements on both sides of this card are true to the best of my knowledge and belief.

Subscribed and Sworn To before me on this _____ day of _____, 19 _____.

_____ | _____ | _____
Signature of Registration Officer | Title | Signature of Registrant

NOTE: IF THE ADDRESS GIVEN ON THIS AFFIDAVIT IS ON A RURAL ROUTE OR POST OFFICE BOX NUMBER GIVE EXACT LOCATION OF THE RESIDENCE ON THE DIAGRAM AT LEFT. — INDICATE WITH AN "X".

NORTH

WEST ——————— EAST

SOUTH

NAME OF STREET RUNNING NORTH AND SOUTH

DISTANCE FROM RESIDENCE TO STREET RUNNING NORTH AND SOUTH

NAME OF STREET RUNNING EAST AND WEST

DISTANCE FROM RESIDENCE TO STREET RUNNING EAST AND WEST

NOTE: BE SURE TO INDICATE ANY LANDMARK ON DIAGRAM (CANALS, RIVERS, RAILROAD TRACKS, ETC.)

DISTANCE FROM RESIDENCE TO LANDMARK RUNNING NORTH AND SOUTH

DISTANCE FROM RESIDENCE TO LANDMARK RUNNING EAST AND W.

21-38 1/80

Investigation and Fact-Gathering — Forms

Form 5:7 — Arizona MVD Title Search Report.
Text — § 5.4.4.

```
                    MOTOR VEHICLE RECORD AS OF    08/18/80
LIC VTR266-73  TAB H26684  VIN TE51304528
VYR 78      VMA TOYOT   VST S   FUEL G  SC 26 47
CAT A       YFR 78      FLP  4708   GVW          EXP JUN-81      SEQ 3,128,745
                                                                 DCR 07/08/80 00
OWNER    VICTOR,J,KOTTNER           L/S    OR                    DPR 07/10/79 01
OWNER    PATRICIA,,KOTTNER          L/S                          B/D 07/07/80
M/ADDR   2007 N 38TH LN                                          BCH J534
S/ADDR
CITY     PHOENIX               ST AZ ZIP   85009  CO    07


26-VEH,OWN,REG RECORD       47-MVREN
```

Title No. **D338374** Date Issued **7-28-78**

Lienholder **Valley National Bank**

Address **P.O. Box 2947, Phoenix**

Amount $ **7556.16** Date **7-1-78** Kind **PMSA**

Arizona MVD, Title Records Section

Date **10-26-28** By **Dm**

Form 5:8 — Witness Questionnaire.

Text — § 5.6.2.

Your name has been given as a witness to the following described accident. It is only through the friendly cooperation of witnesses such as yourself that disinterested information can be obtained for the purpose of justly determining the rights of the parties involved. Therefore, it will be appreciated if you will answer each of the following questions and promptly return the completed statement in the enclosed envelope.

The accident referred to occurred on or about _____ at or near _____ between "A", which was a _____ owned by _____ and a _____ "B", owned by _____ . Hereafter the respective vehicles will be called A and B as indicated above.

Please state the following:

1. Your name _____
2. Your address _____
3. Your telephone number _____
4. Your occupation and employer _____
5. Location of accident _____
6. Date and time of accident _____
7. Did you see the accident occur? _____ . If not, how soon afterward did you arrive? _____
8. Where were you when you observed the accident or other events? _____
9. Where was A when you first saw it? _____

   Going what direction? _____
10. Where was B when you first saw it? _____

    Going what direction? _____
11. When you first saw the vehicles, what was the speed of A? _____ The speed of B? _____
12. When the collision occurred, what was the speed of A? _____ The speed of B? _____ .
13. Describe what you observed (use back of form if necessary). _____

Form 5:8 *Continued*

14. Was either vehicle on the wrong side of the road? _____
    If so, which one? _____ . How far? _____
15. If the accident occurred at an intersection, which vehicle entered the intersection first? _____
16. Did either vehicle fail to observe traffic or stop signs? _____
    If so, which one? _____
17. Describe any signals made by either driver. _____
    _____
18. What lights if any were burning on A? _____
    On B? _____
19. Was the view of either driver obstructed? _____
    If so, by what? _____
20. Had either driver been drinking intoxicating liquor? _____
    _____ . If so, which one? _____
21. Did either driver admit any blame for the accident? _____
    If so, which one and what was said? _____
    _____
22. Whom do you consider to blame for this accident, driver A or B? _____
    Why? _____
23. Are you acquainted with any of the parties involved? _____
    If so, with whom? _____
24. Do you have any other information you feel might be helpful? _____
    _____
    _____
    _____

_____
Name
_____
Date Signed

6

FACTUAL RESEARCH, ANALYSIS, DISCOVERY AND DOCUMENT CONTROL

Evelyn E. Rasmussen*

§ 6.1 This Chapter's Scope. This chapter considers the legal assistant's role in performing factual research and analysis, and in organizing and coordinating documents and discovery in complex cases. It discusses the use of assistants to research, organize and analyze documents and information obtained through informal investigation or formal discovery, and to implement systems for management of complex litigation. It does not include investigative procedures. These are discussed in chapter 5. Sources of information are described in relation to the assistant's roles as researcher and analyzer, rather than as investigator. The use of legal assistants in trial practice is discussed in chapter 7.

§ 6.2 Research and Analysis Based on Informal Investigation.

§ 6.2.1 Publicity Research and Analysis. Litigation involving well-known figures, public agencies and major corporations often results in extensive publicity. In a large law firm, a member of the support staff might be assigned to clip news articles and editorials from newspapers and magazines concerning the litigation or the parties. In a small law firm, such a task might be assigned to the legal assistant. In either case, the legal assistant can then be asked to review the articles to determine whether publicity adverse to the client is sufficient to justify a motion for change of venue, whether public or corporate hearings or meetings have been held on the subject of the litigation, whether there have been changes in policy or procedure as a result of such hearings, and to obtain leads for further investigation based on the research already performed by investigative reporters.

The purpose of the investigation and the nature of the desired work product should be clearly defined. Since publicity research is open-ended, the lawyer might ask the legal assistant to prepare a preliminary summary in memorandum form. The summary could include a proposed work assignment checklist suggesting possibilities for the form of the final work product or possibilities for further investigation. For example, if a motion for change of venue seems appropriate, the assistant might be asked to prepare a chart or pretrial book illustrating adverse publicity. If further investigation is necessary, the assistant can be asked to obtain and summarize transcripts or minutes of hearings, or to obtain transcripts and videotapes of radio and television broadcasts. The assistant can then review and edit the materials, deleting the extraneous and irrelevant information and summarizing the important points of the hearings or broadcasts.

§ 6.2.2 Historical Research and Analysis. Frequently major litigation requires extensive historical research. Legal assistants can greatly aid the lawyer in

---

* Legal assistant, Lewis and Roca, Phoenix, Arizona. Copyright © 1980 by Evelyn E. Rasmussen. All rights reserved.

such research, performing most, if not all, of the background work. The examples listed below are merely illustrative of the many types of research tasks the lawyer might assign.

§ 6.2.2.1 Research of Territorial, Water and Mineral Rights. Litigation involving territorial, water and mineral rights often requires historical research to establish chains of title or rights. The legal assistant should be asked to prepare a checklist of sources for such historical information. He or she can then perform the research, reporting as necessary to the lawyer if obstacles are encountered and for further guidance. Early historical and legal records were often poorly recorded and maintained, particularly in rural areas. The assistant may thus need to compile an oral history based on interviews with the area's older residents. The lawyer will need to guide the assistant carefully in the preparation of the oral history, taking into account its potential use.

The results of the assistant's research of historical title or rights may be presented as a preliminary memorandum to the lawyer; as a draft of a statement of the case to be used in conjunction with a pretrial or trial memorandum; as a chart, graph, overlay map or other visual portrayal of the historical developments; or any combination of these. The format should be governed by the substance of the case and the lawyer's purposes. However, the general approach to a narrative report based on historical sources should include footnote and bibliographical references, and exhibits, appendices and charts or diagrams in support of the findings.

§ 6.2.2.2 Research of Governmental Agency Jurisdiction. Often in the early stages of a case or even prior to its commencement, it may be necessary to establish which governmental agency or agencies had jurisdiction or control over a matter at any particular time. Examples are jurisdiction over Indian tribes and reservations, civil rights, atomic power and work safety. This type of research also usually involves defining the extent of the agency's regulatory and enforcement powers. A legal assistant without formal training in legal research can perform the initial background work. At all stages, however, the lawyer should carefully guide the research, since it usually involves subjects unfamiliar to the average person.

If the research involves seeking information pursuant to the Freedom of Information Act, 5 U.S.C. § 552, a simple but useful tool is C. Marwick, ed., Litigation Under the Amended Federal Freedom of Information Act (Center for National Security Studies, 4th ed. 1978). Both the lawyer and the legal assistant should be familiar with the statute's provisions and limitations, particularly the obstacles imposed by the Privacy Act of 1974, 5 U.S.C. § 552A. After carefully determining the required information and obstacles, the assistant can prepare a request under the Freedom of Information Act.

A useful procedure for the legal assistant to follow in seeking information from government agencies is to make direct personal contact with the person in charge of handling such requests. The assistant will invariably find that it helps to make a "friend" at the agency prior to actually sending the formal request. That person can assist the legal assistant in properly phrasing the request and in narrowing or broadening its scope. In addition, that person can explain the agency's legal or other limitations, *e.g.*, lack of computer or indexing capabilities, manpower or information. Although government agencies normally treat requests for information on a first-come, first-served basis, personal contacts with agency officers often result in more rapid and efficient processing of requests.

§ 6.2.2.3 Historical Research of Business Entities and Enterprises.

Cases involving land and securities fraud typically involve transfers between multiple corporations or partnerships. As described in Chapter 5 on investigation, much information often can be obtained from agencies such as the corporation commission, real estate department, county recorder or county assessor. The lawyer may ask the legal assistant to compile that information in chart or summary form. That preliminary investigation may reveal possible dilution of real estate and personal property assets through corporate or partnership transfers and mergers. The assistant should be able to recognize evidence of such transactions in searching titles and reviewing legal descriptions. Although a litigation assistant may not usually become involved in real estate transactions, it may be necessary to become familiar with the documents recorded in a real estate transaction. From the investigation, the assistant can prepare flow charts or diagrams showing transfers of real and personal property. Dilution of real estate assets or other transactions can be demonstrated by preparing transparent overlays or sequential colored maps.

§ 6.2.3 Statistical Research and Analysis.

A properly guided legal assistant can readily handle the investigation and analysis required to prepare a statistical summary. The fact-gathering process may involve the review of business or public records. If it is likely that a statistical analysis will be required in the future, the assistant should prepare a checklist of sources of information. The checklist would include national, state, local and other agencies having statistical information on such facts as employment of minorities, new housing starts and sales, cattle water consumption or annual rainfall. The checklist should be annotated with respect to the procedures and information applicable to a given agency. For example, claims filed at the Arizona registrar of contractors' office are generally indexed by the name of the contractor, the year and the number of the regulation allegedly violated. It is thus possible to review the index for rule violations to determine the number and disposition of all cases involving the violation of the particular rule.

If a contractor client appears to have received an unusually harsh penalty for violation of a particular rule, the lawyer may wish to move for a new hearing and for reduction of the penalty. To establish statistical support for the motion, the lawyer may ask the legal assistant to review the claims index. The assistant's initial summary should be stated in the form of a memorandum or chart setting forth the procedure followed and the statistical findings. If the findings are favorable to the client, the lawyer may then have the assistant prepare an affidavit, a chart or both supporting the motion. The assistant should also obtain copies of any agency indices; any findings of fact, conclusions of law and orders of the hearing officer; and any other source documents used to prepare the summary affidavit or chart.

Whenever the legal assistant is asked to prepare a statistical summary or analysis, he or she should also be asked to prepare an annotated checklist of the sources of information and the procedures to be followed in obtaining that information. C. Bruno, Paralegal's Litigation Handbook, 101-13 (Institute for Business Planning, Inc., 1980), contains samples of such an annotated checklist. In addition to the information provided by an agency, the legal assistant should include in the checklist the specific procedure to be followed in acquiring that information.

§ 6.2.4 Research in Other Substantive Law Areas.

Assignments and procedures usually performed by real estate, probate and corporate legal assistants are not included in this volume. However, litigation assistants should be at least generally familiar with the substantive law and procedures in those areas. As discussed at § 6.2.2.3, the litigation assistant should be aware of the basic procedures followed in real estate transactions. On occasion, probate cases result in litigation. For example, litigation might reveal a fraudulent or a faulty transfer of assets through a will. In such instances, the litigation assistant may be required to review a probate file. The assigning lawyers should ascertain and if necessary supplement the assistant's knowledge of probate law and procedures. Litigation assistants must also be familiar with basic substantive law concerning the formation and operation of corporations, partnerships and sole proprietorships. Business litigation of all types often involves determining whether a corporation has been properly incorporated, whether the required annual reports have been filed, and whether minutes and notices of meetings have been prepared and distributed. The lawyer should confirm the assistant's understanding of such matters to direct any such assignments properly.

§ 6.3 Research and Analysis Based on Formal Discovery. The legal assistant's participation in the discovery phase of smaller cases and subsequent assistance in the trial stage is described in detail in chapter 7. This section concerns the legal assistant's role in more complex litigation involving multiple parties and witnesses, and large numbers of documents.

§ 6.3.1 Systems for Coordinating Discovery. Without a carefully considered approach, discovery in a complex case can result in a morass of useless information and an endless flow of paper. Many states have adopted uniform interrogatories for routine matters such as personal injury and domestic relations cases. Other states have placed limitations on the number of interrogatories or sets of interrogatories that may be served. With or without these limitations, a coordinated use of the various discovery methods can be highly efficient and effective. The legal assistant can be valuable to the lawyer at both the drafting and summarizing stages after answers and documents have been received and depositions taken.

Statutory or rule limitations, the nature of the case itself and the lawyer's preference may all dictate whether interrogatories, requests for admissions and requests for production should be combined in one, two or three separate documents. It is generally easier to keep track of responses to discovery by serving three separate documents and requesting three separate responses. A second reason for keeping the documents separate is that rules relating to failure to answer or respond are usually distinct as to each form. Nevertheless, by following simple principles, the three forms of discovery can be coordinated by the legal assistant to provide the desired information. Following receipt of the requested information, the assistant can summarize the answers and make suggestions for further discovery, including the taking of depositions. The examples described below are for illustrative purposes only. Any applicable federal, state and local court rules for format and content should be strictly followed. In addition, individual firms and lawyers may have their own preferences as to format and language techniques. The assigning lawyer should make certain that the assistant is aware of all such rules and preferences.

§ 6.3.1.1 Drafting Interrogatories. Written interrogatories are generally regarded as the least expensive method for identifying relevant documents, establishing dates and facts, and identifying persons who have knowledge of the facts. Interrogatories may also be used to inquire concerning a party's legal contentions and the allegations in the pleadings. Interrogatories are most useful when one has particular questions that may require research, gathering background information, or lengthy and complex answers. Properly phrased interrogatories may also be used to require the opposing party to compile data not previously assembled. The lawyer should see that the legal assistant follows a specific procedure rather than randomly approaching the task of drafting interrogatories. Suggested steps are as follows:

1. The assistant should first learn the legal issues of a case in order to inquire concerning the facts on which those issues are based. The assistant should read the pleadings carefully. The lawyer should then verify that the assistant has a clear understanding of the issues.

2. The assistant should next correlate the issues of the case with the known or established facts, both from the client's point of view and from information based on previous investigation or discovery. The lawyer should verify that the assistant understands the facts and how they relate to the issues.

3. Having applied the known facts to the issue, the assistant, guided by the lawyer, should determine areas about which more information is needed. A checklist of areas of inquiry might include such items as parties and witnesses, places and things, relief sought or damages, and possible defenses.

Interrogatories inquiring about the bases for allegations should be phrased to coincide with the wording used in the pleadings of the opposing party. For example, an interrogatory inquiring about an allegation of misrepresentation might read:

> Interrogatory No. 1. With respect to the allegation in paragraph IV of the Complaint that the defendant's agent represented that said insurance would be at a good price, state specifically and with particularity:
>
> . . . .

Form sub-interrogatories may be designed to elicit the facts underlining the allegation. See Form 6:1 for sample form sub-interrogatories.

The legal assistant should work from the pleadings themselves and from the checklist of areas of inquiry to prepare interrogatories in draft form. They should then be presented to the lawyer for review and editing prior to preparation of their final draft. If the lawyer has worked on cases of a similar nature, the assistant should be provided with samples of interrogatories reflecting individual preferences in format and style. Form files of interrogatories should also be prepared relating to specific subject areas and individual lawyers' preferences. See Form 6:2.

§ 6.3.1.2 Drafting Requests for Admissions. A simple rule of thumb for drafting discovery documents is that interrogatories are based on the opposing party's pleadings, while requests for admissions are based on one's own pleadings. This rule is best illustrated by pointing out the different purposes of the two types of discovery. Interrogatories are designed to enable one to learn as much as possible about the facts on which the opposing party's allegations are based. Requests for admissions are designed to establish as binding the facts set forth in one's own pleadings. The legal assistant should be asked to prepare a checklist or chart of all allegations, admissions, denials and affirmative defenses in all pleadings, including counterclaims and cross-claims. The request for admissions can then readily be drafted by the assistant. For example, the plaintiff may have alleged misrepresentation as to the terms of an insurance contract on personal property. The defendant's request for admissions might be drafted as follows:

> 1. On or about September 17, 1979, Fred Smith as insurance agent for Black Insurance Company issued an insurance policy on the subject property to the plaintiff.

2. A true and correct copy of the insurance policy is attached to the Complaint.
3. The insurance policy provides in pertinent part that . . . .
4. As of the date that plaintiff received the insurance policy plaintiff knew or had notice that the policy did not include coverage against theft of the subject property.

Service of the request for admissions with interrogatories and requests for production requesting the facts and evidence upon which the allegations are based can be an effective means of forcing early dismissal or settlement of a case that has little or no merit.

§ 6.3.1.3 Drafting Requests for Production of Documents or Things. The purpose of a request for production of documents is to require the opposing party to provide documented evidence in support of the allegations in the pleadings. Various approaches in drafting are possible:

1. Having required an identification of the documents in previously served interrogatories, the lawyer can ask the legal assistant to draft a subsequent request for production, using the opposing party's own description of the documents. This procedure is more useful when it is not known whether particular documents even exist, or if so, in what form. For example, an interrogatory might ask:

Interrogatory No. 1. Do you have in your custody or control or are you aware of the location of any maintenance records on the airplane? (Sub-interrogatories should require the name, description and location of the documents, and the name of the person who has custody or control of them.)

When affirmative answers are received, the legal assistant can easily draft a request for production, specifying the documents described in the answers.

2. If the existence and description of a particular document or documents is known, the request can be combined with the interrogatories in the same or separate documents. Thus, interrogatories directed toward allegations of breach of contract might be accompanied by a request for copies of all correspondence between the parties prior to execution of the contract.

3. An effective alternative is to serve with the interrogatories a request for documents which, like the interrogatories, is also based on the allegations in the opposing party's pleadings. Such a request might be phrased as follows:

Request No. 1: Please produce all contracts, agreements, records, correspondence, memoranda or other communications between the parties which refer to, denote or reflect:
   A. The basis upon which you allege the defendant misrepresented the terms of the contract.
   B. The basis upon which you allege that the defendant is an expert in the real estate business.

Coordinated discovery requires the opposing party to assemble documents and other evidence based on the legal issues raised in his or her own pleadings. One advantage is that the lawyers on both sides can readily evaluate the merits of the case and the strength of the evidence, which may lead to early settlement or dismissal. A potential disadvantage is that it may also inspire the opposing party to prepare the case more carefully than he or she might have otherwise. Such preparation may lead the opposition to discover facets of the case not previously considered. The lawyer should carefully review the documents drafted by the assistant to determine whether there are suggestions of defenses or causes of action not already raised by the opposing party.

§ 6.3.1.4 Summarizing Answers to Interrogatories and Requests for Admissions. Although many state and local court rules require that interrogatories and requests for admissions be retyped or otherwise stated in the answers, some recalcitrant or unknowing lawyers simply set forth the answers. A second problem arises when the same answer applies to two or more interrogatories, and opposing counsel simply refers to a previous answer, *e.g.*, "See answer to interrogatory no. 5(b)." It becomes very time-consuming for the interrogating lawyer to have to refer to many interrogatories or sets of interrogatories to find the answer. The legal assistant can be asked to summarize the responses to show the content of the question along with the response. Such a summary might read as follows:

> Interrogatory No. 1. We asked the defendant to state the facts upon which he bases his allegation of contributory negligence. He has responded that the plaintiff left the motor running while connecting the starter cables.

The summary should also reflect inconsistencies in responses:

> Request No. 1. The defendant admits he is president of Black Company [in his answer to Interrogatory No. 4 he denies knowing the officers of Black Company].

§ 6.3.2 Digesting Depositions. V. Watenmaker and S. Faber, Fundamentals of Civil Procedure (Charing Cross Publishing Co., Inc., 1976), discuss important points to consider in digesting depositions (see chapter on discovery procedures). A deposition digest with page and subject references can be a valuable aid to lawyers in preparing for subsequent depositions and for trial. Because there is so much extraneous material in a deposition, a digest can save time in locating a deponent's specific testimony on the important facts and issues of the case. In large cases involving many witnesses and many events, topical and chronological digests can also be prepared.

§ 6.3.2.1 Preliminary Considerations. In assigning the legal assistant to digest a deposition, the lawyers should first consider: how and by whom will the digest be used; how many digests must be prepared, and whether they must be cross-indexed; and how much time the assistant will require to complete the assignment. If the digests will be used only by those in the firm who are very familiar with the facts and issues of the case, an index listing topics of testimony and page numbers may be sufficient. In this case, the digest would serve simply as a guide or index to the testimony. If the digest will be shared with clients, co-counsel or others working outside the firm, a more detailed narrative digest may be needed. This situation arises most often in complex cases with many depositions in which the digest may aid lawyers unfamiliar with all the facts of the case to prepare for subsequent depositions. In such cases, it may be necessary to have the assistant digest everything said by the witness, eliminating only extraneous and transitional comments. This type of digest is time-consuming and expensive to prepare, but can save the lawyer and the client much time and expense over the course of a major lawsuit. The client also can prepare for his or her own deposition by reading the digests of the testimony of other witnesses.

A full narrative digest, with complete sentences, can generally be prepared by an assistant at the rate of 100 to 200 pages of testimony per day, depending on the subject's complexity. The result should be approximately one page of digest for every six to ten pages of testimony. A detailed narrative digest should impart the flavor of the testimony in addition to the facts. If rearranged into a chronological digest or with extraneous material deleted, it has a continuity that the deposition itself may lack. The lawyer can easily refresh his or her memory by reviewing a digest without rereading the deposition many times. However, the digest should not be used by the lawyer as a complete replacement for reading the deposition itself. The digest should be used as a research aid and a fact organizer.

§ 6.3.2.2 Language Techniques. The lawyer should caution the assistant to follow closely the language used by the deponent. Words such as "think," "recall," "remember," "know," "believe" and "assume" should be carefully used. If the witness has used them in his testimony, then the assistant should use them in the digest. If the deponent answers "yes" or "no" to the lawyer's question, the assistant should repeat the lawyer's words in the digest, *e.g.*, "Mr. Smith, did you see the light turn green? A: No." should be translated in the digest to "Mr. Smith did not see the light turn green," or "Mr. Smith confirmed that he did not see the light turn green." If the response is "I believe so," the digest should read "Mr. Smith believed he saw the light turn green."

The legal assistant should not ordinarily use quotations in digesting the testimony unless the witness makes a very significant admission, or unless his statement is oddly phrased or otherwise incomprehensible. If the deponent is an adverse witness, the lawyer may ask leading questions, *e.g.*, "Q: Mr. Smith, is it not true that you saw the light turn green?" In order to preserve the testimony's true flavor, the digest should phrase a straight "yes" or "no" answer to such a question as an admission or a denial, *e.g.*, "Mr. Smith denied that he saw the light turn green." Sometimes an answer is not directly responsive or is absolutely evasive, *e.g.*, "A: Well, I'm pretty sure I saw it turn green"; or "A: Well, I can't really be sure because I was hung over at the time." Depending on the total context and atmosphere, the digest might read "Mr. Smith was 'pretty sure' he saw the light turn green," or "Mr. Smith couldn't really be sure he saw the light turn green because he was hung over at the time."

Mistakes in transcribing testimony often occur. If the reporter has not correctly heard a contraction, the difference between "did" and "didn't" can seriously affect the meaning of the testimony. If it seems possible that there is an error in the transcript, the assistant should make a note to that effect in the digest. Such notes should be put in brackets so that it is clear to the lawyer that it is not part of the testimony. The assistant should be cautioned that the same type of error can occur in one's own dictation. The assistant should therefore proofread the digest carefully against the original deposition to make sure that the transcriber did not mishear a word or phrase.

The use of abbreviations, except the commonly recognized ones, should be kept to a minimum. Abbreviations tend to stop the flow and continuity of the digest, and the lawyer's concentration. Page references, especially in a detailed narrative style digest, are important. Since a deposition page may contain only 28 or 30 lines, it should not generally be necessary to make line references. The assistant should be advised to keep sentences concise and paragraphs short. The paragraphs should be limited to one topic only. While this may result in some one- or two-sentence paragraphs, it allows the lawyer to scan a page more easily. In addition, if it is later necessary to separate all testimony on specific topics, material in short paragraphs is easier to locate.

§ 6.3.2.3 Format. Even well-organized lawyers seldom follow a straight-line chronological order in taking a deposition. Nevertheless, the assistant should be instructed to digest the deposition sequentially (in the order in which it appears) rather than editing it to put the testimony in chronological or topical order. This procedure should be followed even if the deponent or the examining lawyer jumps from one topic to another. It is extremely difficult to skip around in the deposition itself and too easy to overlook something.

If necessary, a copy of the digest can be cut up and arranged to place the testimony in chronological or topical order. For those having access to more sophisticated word processing or computer equipment, the traditional "cut and paste" procedure can be done by a machine. See Forms 6:3 and 6:4 for sample sequential and subject matter digests. In the alternative, by using brackets, the assistant can refer back to previous discussions on the same topics. The lawyer and the assistant should determine early in the case whether the digest will be reorganized under subject or issue categories. If so, every paragraph of every digest should have the deponent's name, the volume number if there is more than one (or the dates if separate volumes of a deponent's deposition are not assigned volume numbers) and the page references.

§ 6.3.2.4 Information in the Digest. The lawyer should decide what information to include in addition to the testimony of the witness. Some lawyers prefer to have virtually all of the information that is contained within the deposition, including the names of those present, exhibits, objections and colloquy between counsel. Other lawyers prefer not to have extraneous material included. The lawyer should decide and then advise the assistant whether to include all exhibits, a description of them and any comments the deponent makes about them. The deponent's background may or may not be significant. If he is an expert witness, his education and experience would be considered significant. It might be necessary to have the assistant describe those in detail, along with any awards or special recognition he has received. The education and experience of lay witnesses may or may not be significant, depending on whether they are eye witnesses to an accident or officers and directors of a party corporation.

Colloquy between counsel may be summarized as follows: "Colloquy between counsel re continuation of deposition." It is rarely necessary to summarize discussions between lawyers, unless they make major stipulations, objections or decisions. Simply noting an objection, without going through all of the grounds, is generally sufficient. However, the assistant should be advised to note in brackets any refusal by a witness to answer a question, or an instruction by his lawyer not to answer, *e.g.*, "Smith instructed not to answer because of attorney-client privilege."

Usually the lawyer will assign a legal assistant permanently to a large case involving many depositions. Extensive knowledge of the facts and issues becomes as important to the assistant as to the lawyer. The assistant can note testimony that conflicts with previous testimony or with the evidence revealed in documents produced in the case. Similarly, he or she can note important admissions by adverse parties or witnesses. The assistant should be instructed to note such testimony in brackets, along with references to the conflicting testimony or evidence, *e.g.*, "Mr. Smith denied that he saw the light turn green. [Conflict: Mr. Green stated at page 10 of his deposition that Mr. Smith admitted to him that he saw the light turn green.]"; or "[conflict: In his signed statement to the investigating officer, Mr. Smith said he saw the light turn green.]"; or "[conflict: This is the first time in three rounds of depositions that Mr. Smith has denied he saw the light turn green.]."

§ 6.3.3 Summarizing a Deposition.

A summary of a deposition contains no page references. It may or may not include subject or topic references. The purpose of the summary is to keep clients, co-counsel, corporate counsel or other interested persons informed as to what a particular party or witness has said in his deposition. A second purpose is for the lawyer to determine rapidly what subjects have already been covered in previous depositions of the same deponent, so he can avoid asking the same questions again. This is particularly important in cases involving continuing depositions or depositions of many people on the same subject. The summary is usually prepared after the digest is prepared. It is a brief (two to five page) narrative account, using full sentences, of the substance of the deponent's testimony.

The lawyer may find it helpful to have the assistant attend the deposition and take notes of the deponent's testimony. Following the deposition, and before the transcript of the deposition is prepared, the assistant can prepare a summary from the notes for the same purpose. For various reasons, transcripts of depositions may not be prepared. In such cases, the notes and summary of the deposition made by the legal assistant become even more important. The assistant should be instructed to summarize the notes carefully, since they may well be the only record the firm may have of what a deponent said on a particular subject. Such a summary should be as detailed as the notes, and far more detailed than a summary might otherwise be.

§ 6.3.4 Digesting the Trial Transcript or Trial Notes.

The rules outlined previously for digesting a deposition also apply to digesting a trial transcript. However, the legal assistant should be instructed to give careful attention to objections and rulings made during the course of the trial. See §7.9 *et seq.* for a discussion of taking trial notes. All other rules for format and style outlined above should be followed for a trial transcript. Digests of trial transcripts are not often prepared. The exception is for the very long trial resulting in many volumes of transcripts.

If the assistant is with the lawyer at trial, it is useful to have a daily summary of the testimony prepared from the assistant's notes. That summary can then be used later to aid in the examination of witnesses and presentation of evidence. Following a trial, there may be insufficient time for the court reporter to prepare the transcript before a motion for new trial or other post-trial motions must be filed. The assistant's summary of the trial notes, or the notes themselves, can be an invaluable aid to the lawyer in citing testimony and exhibits. If the verdict or judgment is appealed, the assistant's digest of the trial notes or transcript will assist the lawyers in preparing the briefs. When an appeal is restricted to a single issue, the assistant's digest of notes can be used to order only the portions of the transcript related to that issue.

§ 6.4 Document Management in Complex Cases: Discovery.

Major litigation increases the problems of management, control and retrieval of great numbers of documents. Many law firms have turned to the use of in-house computers or commercial litigation support services to manage the documents in such cases. The use of computer-oriented litigation support systems is outside the scope of this discussion. For a good reference, see Use of Computers in Litigation (A.B.A. 1979).

Nevertheless, many of the principles used in computer-supported litigation may be employed in manual indexing and control systems. Under the lawyer's guidance, the legal assistant may have a significant role in the design and implementation of such systems. The systems described in the following sections are for illustrative purposes only. Each case presents its own special problems requiring analysis by its litigation team.

§ 6.4.1 System for Depositions and Exhibits to Depositions.

§ 6.4.1.1 The Court Reporter. Whenever possible, counsel should stipulate to the use of the same court reporter throughout all discovery proceedings in a major case. Knowledge of what has previously transpired greatly improves the reporter's service and efficiency. In addition, such an arrangement enables the lawyers and legal assistants to design uniform and efficient systems for the marking and indexing of exhibits. Implementation of the system can then be delegated to the assistant and the reporter.

§ 6.4.1.2 Marking and Indexing Exhibits to Depositions. When a case requires multiple parties and witnesses to review or discuss the same document or documents, duplication of documents results in awkward cross-indexing and retrieval. One solution is to assign each separate deponent a sequential number in the same order that the depositions are taken. The number is retained throughout the discovery process. Each exhibit is then marked with the number of the deponent, followed by its own sequential number, *e.g.*, 1-1, 1-2, 1-3, etc. If an entire file, book, or series of documents is marked as one exhibit, it can be numbered as 1-1.1, 1-1.2, 1-1.3, etc. Counsel may stipulate as to whether they desire individual pages to be marked immediately or later. Duplication is avoided because each separate, unique document, once it has been marked, retains its identification number throughout the litigation rather than being renumbered. The document can be referred to subsequently by that number, *e.g.*, "Mr. Smith, I show you what has been marked as exhibit 2-3" or "Mr. Smith, I show you what has been marked as exhibit 2-3 to Mr. Jones' deposition."

Arrangements can be made with the court reporter to have the exhibits copied onto 8½" by 11" paper and prepunched with an index using the master numbering system. In the alternative, the legal assistant can prepare the index, preferably annotated.

A similar system involves simply numbering exhibits sequentially throughout the litigation and avoiding marking any unique document more than once. For example, the exhibits to Mr. Smith's deposition might be numbered 1 through 6, the exhibits to Mr. Jones' deposition 7-10, etc.

Both these systems require that the legal assistant and the court reporter have current lists or indexes of the deponents and the exhibit numbers. They should also have copies of the exhibit indexes in order to avoid having identical documents marked more than once. See Form 6:5 for a sample master index of depositions.

A second advantage to these systems is at the pretrial and trial stages. If the legal assistant keeps an index of both depositions and exhibits, the pretrial statement or memorandum can easily be prepared. The assistant has a ready list of the witnesses the lawyers want to call and of the exhibits they want to use with each. The deposition exhibit numbers can be used, avoiding the confusion of having separate numbers for depositions, pretrial statements and trial.

§ 6.4.2 Systems for Handling Productions of Documents.

§ 6.4.2.1 The Court Reporter. The court reporter's role at a production of documents in a major case is similar to his or her role in marking exhibits to depositions. The reporter makes a record of the documents produced and then marks them with an identifying number. If the documents are produced at a deposition, they can be marked using the system described above. If they are produced in response to a specific request for production, they may be marked using a simple variation on that system. If cost or other considerations do not permit the use of a court reporter at a separate production of documents or if the documents are simply delivered to the lawyer's office, the legal assistant may be asked to take responsibility for marking and indexing the documents.

§ 6.4.2.2 Marking and Indexing Documents Produced. The initial marking and indexing of documents produced by either party is simply for the purpose of making a record of what has been produced. The system probably will not have any relation to what is ultimately done with the documents, some of which will become exhibits to depositions and at trial. A simple way to handle the initial production is to use a variation of the system for marking the exhibits to depositions. For example, documents produced in response to the first request for production can be identified as 0-1, 0-2, 0-3, etc. If there are subsequent productions, the documents can be identified as 00-1, 000-1, etc. In the alternative, one can use letters of the alphabet to denote documents produced, *e.g.*, A-1, A-2; B-1, B-2, etc. If multiple parties are producing documents, their initials can be used to identify them as the source. Thus, documents produced by Fred Smith at a first production can be identified as FS 0-1, FS 0-2; or FS A-1, FS A-2. See Forms 6:6 and 6:7 for sample sequential and chronological indexes.

The lawyer should determine the system preferred early in the case. Some lawyers prefer to use a paginator and simply maintain a record of where they left off at the previous production. If the source of the documents but not the order or form in which the documents are produced is significant, it may be sufficient merely to place the party's initials on them, without sequential numbers. The documents can later be arranged in chronological order according to the source. The lawyer should consult with the legal assistant at each stage to make certain that the principles for identification are understood by all those working on the case.

§ 6.5. Manual Systems for Control and Retrieval in Complex Cases: The Legal Assistant's Role Throughout the Case.

§ 6.5.1 The Role of the Legal Assistant in Relation to Other Support Personnel. Traditionally, lawyers have assigned large cases to one or more legal assistants, who immediately or eventually work full-time on that case alone. Careful evaluation of the case and of the individual assistant will dictate whether such an assignment is the most efficient or effective use of the assistant's time. Early in the assistant's career, it is generally desirable to assign him or her to one case. The potential for boredom is outweighed by the value of learning how all phases of investigation, research and discovery fit together. In addition, if the assistant is directly involved in investigation, research and the discovery process throughout the litigation, he or she will become an invaluable resource person, with the ability to assemble all facts and evidence relating to any legal issue.

One disadvantage of this procedure is that requiring the assistant to work on one case at a time for extended periods can result in boredom and "burn-out." An intelligent, well-educated and well-trained legal assistant can become little more than a file clerk, responsible only for locating a given document. An experienced assistant also usually has a higher standard hourly billing rate, thus increasing the cost to the client of having the assistant manage the entire control and retrieval system.

An effective means of avoiding the problem of boredom for a legal assistant experienced in complex litigation is to employ the assistance of other support personnel. Law firms handling major cases generally have a separate records department. An efficient system is to assign at least one person in that department to the assistant working on large cases. By using a simple routing and numerical filing system, the tremendous flow of on-going correspondence and documents can be handled by the records department. A routing slip with the names of the lawyers and the assistant working on the case can be attached to each document. The assistant in charge of control and retrieval should be the last person to receive the document. The assistant or the assistant's secretary should then mark a code number on the document, identifying it as general correspondence, legal research or the like, and send it on for filing in chronological order. The person assigned in the records department need not know anything about the case or the document. A second advantage to the routing system is that all members of the litigation team can be continually aware of the course of the litigation. If any of the members do not need to read the document, their names can be crossed off or they can simply pass it on without reading it.

A second person assigned to the legal assistant may be one who specializes in indexing and tabbing or marking of documents. Although this role is generally assigned to the assistant early in his or her career, it may become prohibitively costly at higher billing rates. The assistant, with the help of temporary or full-time support personnel, can maintain control over the documents in several major cases at once. In a smaller firm, the two roles described may be filled by one person or by the assistant's secretary. The advantage to using support personnel for indexing and tabbing is that it frees the assistant to perform the research and analysis tasks described previously.

§ 6.5.2 Considerations and Guidelines for Control and Retrieval Systems. Traditional record-keeping systems involving filebacks for legal documents, correspondence and work papers are insufficient to meet the demands of a complex case. Lawyers have attempted unsuccessfully to deal with the mass of documents by simply creating new filebacks with new titles, without careful consideration of the unique issues and facts of the case, its potential for growth or how they will find a given document three years hence. Rarely are documents produced in a form usable at trial or even at depositions. Once a record has been made of what has been produced, the problem arises of how to arrange the documents to facilitate control, retrieval and their ultimate use at the trial stage. The members of the litigation team, whether one lawyer and one legal assistant or many, should carefully evaluate the legal issues and facts of the case to determine what documents are important and how they should be evaluated and organized. Certain guidelines should always be considered, as outlined in the following sections.

§ 6.5.2.1 The System Should Be Simple. An overly complicated filing system invites needless duplication and frustration in trying to learn the system. A master index should be maintained by the legal assistant and any other support personnel which shows the location of categories of documents. Sub-indexes can list the documents in a particular category. The sub-indexes should be kept with the master index in a book, as well as with the documents themselves. Code numbers or letters can be assigned to categories of documents, parties, witnesses, legal issues or subject matter. The lawyer should determine early in the case the likelihood of requiring documents in any given category so that the indexing system may be designed accordingly.

§ 6.5.2.2 Legal Documents. A single fileback of pleadings, motions and discovery documents is rarely sufficient for a major case. Consideration should be given to separating discovery requests and responses from substantive pleadings and motions. In a case involving many separate legal issues, consideration might also be given to separating substantive pleadings and motions from each other according to legal issues.

§ 6.5.2.3 Legal Research and Investigation. The same guidelines for filing and indexing legal documents apply to the system for handling legal research and investigation. The lawyers should consider whether they want research separated by legal issues, internal memoranda, cases or subject matter. If the issues are few, it may be sufficient simply to create a file labeled "Legal Research." However, it is often more efficient to separate research and investigation into legal issues or subject matter areas.

§ 6.5.2.4 Documents Produced. As described at § 6.4.2.2, a permanent index should be made of documents produced by any party to an action. Similarly, a permanent index should be prepared of documents obtained from outside sources such as witnesses, and government and private agencies. Other considerations will dictate whether the documents should be duplicated and arranged in some other fashion:

1. Is the chronology of events significant to the legal issues of the case? If so, a chronological index of documents should be prepared showing the location of the documents. If advisable, the documents might themselves be duplicated and rearranged in chronological order.

2. Is it preferable to organize the documents by legal issue or subject matter? If so, issue or subject matter indices should be prepared. These can be combined with chronological indexes by simply listing documents chronologically under a given issue or subject.

3. Is it important to know what information is available from a particular party or witness or what was said about a person at a given point in time? If so, an index and witness book or file should be prepared of documents that a particular person wrote or received or that contain references to that person.

Sample master indices for major cases are shown at Forms 6:8 and 6:9. The issues and facts of any given case should be carefully reviewed to determine both the content and form of the files and indexes.

The principles for preparation of documents to be offered in evidence at the trial stage are described in chapter 7. Such presentation can greatly be facilitated by designing a control and retrieval system at the pretrial stage which focuses on triable issues. If guidelines have been carefully drawn and followed by the litigation team, the pretrial statement or memorandum can be drafted based on the system itself. At all stages, the legal assistant should be kept apprised of the course of the litigation and the strategies for further proceedings. Although the assistant can be responsible for implementing the system, the lawyers on the litigation team should be directly involved in its design.

§ 6.6 Summary and Conclusion. The legal assistant can and should perform a great variety of tasks in every stage of litigation. In performing factual research and analysis, coordinating the various discovery processes and implementing systems for the management of major cases, the assistant will enable the lawyer to devote his or her time to the purely legal aspects of the case. As the legal assistant acquires experience and expertise, and as checklists and forms are developed, less direct supervision from the lawyers will be required, resulting in greater time and cost savings to the client and to the firm, and more efficient delivery of legal services.

Working With Legal Assistants

Form 6:1 — Form Sub-Interrogatories. Interrogatories Based on Allegations.

Text — § 6.3.1.1.

Mr. Smith's Form

a) Each and every fact upon which you base the allegation;

b) Each and every document upon which you base the allegation and in this regard, please state with particularity sufficient to support a request for production of documents:

   (i) The name or title of the documents;

   (ii) The name, business address and business telephone number of the sender or preparer of the documents;

   (iii) The name, business address and business telephone number of the addressee or receiver of the documents;

   (iv) The name, business address and business telephone number of all persons possessing or in control of the original or a copy of the documents.

Mr. Jones' Form

a) Each fact known or believed by you to exist which may support your allegation;

b) The name and street address of each person known or believed by you to have information which may support your allegation;

c) The identity, location and custodian of each document, item or thing which contains, or which you believe contains information that may support or tend to negate your allegation and whether, with respect to each such document, item or thing, you will attach a copy thereof to your answers to these interrogatories without the necessity of a separate request for production;

d) The name and street address of each person you may call as an expert witness at trial in support of your allegation and, with respect to each such person, state specifically and with particularity:

   (i) The subject matter on which the expert is expected to testify;

   (ii) The substance of the facts and each opinion to which the expert is expected to testify;

   (iii) A summary of the grounds for each opinion of such expert.

Form 6:2 — Checklist and Form Interrogatories.
Text — § 6.3.1.1.

Checklist and forms for interrogatories based on allegations of breach of contract or other written agreement.

A. Meetings (telephone conversations) between the parties.

   1. State whether there were any meetings (telephone conversations) between the plaintiff and the defendant involving negotiation of the terms of the lease.

   2. If your answer to interrogatory no. 1 is in the affirmative, state specifically and with particularity:

      (a) The date and location of all the meetings (telephone conversations);

      (b) The substance of all the meetings (telephone conversations), including oral agreements; and

      (c) The names, business addresses and telephone numbers of all persons attending the meetings (involved in each telephone conversation).

B. Whether the substance of the meetings (telephone conversations) was committed to writing.

   3. State whether the substance of the meetings (telephone conversations) described in interrogatory no. 1 was committed to a written document or documents.

   4. If your answer to interrogatory no. 3 is in the affirmative, state with particularity sufficient to support a request for production of documents:

      (a) The name, title or nature of the document;

      (b) The name, business address and business telephone number of the sender or preparer of the document;

      (c) The name, business address and business telephone number of the addressee or receiver of the document; and

      (d) The name, business address and business telephone number of all persons possessing the original or a copy of the document.

C. Written communications between the parties.

   5. State whether there was any correspondence, memoranda or other written communications between the parties involving negotiation of the terms of the lease not previously described in your answer to interrogatory no. 3.

   6. If your answer to interrogatory no. 5 is in the affirmative, state with particularity sufficient to support a request for production of documents: . . .

D. Facts upon which allegations or defenses in the pleadings are based (each allegation should be separately set forth).

E. Specific terms of the contract or agreement reflecting allegations in the pleading.

Form 6:2 *Continued*

    7. With respect to your allegation in paragraph II of the complaint that the defendant "realized" that it was in the best interest of all parties that the alleged ownership be insured, state specifically and with particularity:

       (a) Each and every fact upon which you base the allegation;

       (b) The specific wording in the lease which reflects the allegation that the defendant wished to protect the ownership interest of the plaintiff;

       (c) Each and every document which reflects the defendant's wish to protect the plaintiff's ownership interest in the equipment, and in this regard, please state with particularity sufficient to support a request for production of documents: . . .

F. Existence of previous contracts or agreements of a similar nature.

    8. State whether, prior to the lease of the equipment, you had ever leased any other personal property in this or any other jurisdiction.

    9. If your answer to interrogatory no. 8 is in the affirmaive, state specifically and with particularity:

       (a) The jurisdiction in which the property was leased;

       (b) whether any of such leases required insurance coverage on the leased property;

       (c) List by date and nature of property each such lease;

       (d) State the name, business address and business telephone number of all persons possessing the original or a copy of each such lease.

Form 6:3 — Deposition Digest: Sequential.

Text — § 6.3.2.

Smith, II 66-68 Loss of Business	Smith claims loss of business in Kalamazoo to Black Company. In 1976-77, production with Brown Company increased substantially. Life insurance premiums increased from $150,000 to $250,000. Smith attributes this to his many agents in Kalamazoo having brought business other than just group insurance. The other types of insurance were an ancillary business. When group business dropped off, so did the other types.
Smith, II 68-70 Loss of Goodwill	Smith believes there was a stigma attached to his contract being terminated. He stated he does not mean to imply that Brown Company maligned or said anything slanderous about him. But the insurance profession is tightly knit and people surmise things if a contract is cancelled, resulting in a loss of goodwill.
Smith, II 70-71 Business Disruption	Smith sold out in Kalamazoo because he couldn't afford to build the business back up. The group insurance aspect of Brown Company was profitable to Black Company in 1977 and 1978. Then Brown Company's business dropped off and they weren't anxious to get any more business. They increased the premiums to a point where it was impossible to write any business because they were so much higher than the competition.

Form 6:4 — Deposition Digest: Subject Matter.
Text — § 6.3.2.

Dr. Green's opinion of Dr. Brown's surgery.

Red, I
43-45
Dr. Green
Evaluation

Red stated that she was told by Dr. Green that the previous surgery had been "botched so badly" that the kidney had grown and attached itself to the adjacent organ. Dr. Green also told her that he didn't think the first surgery was necessary.

Red, II
58-59
Dr. Green
Opinion

Red stated that following his surgery, Dr. Green told her he found "the biggest mess he had ever seen in his years of operation." He told her the earlier surgery should not have been done because even if there is a blockage in the tube it is possible to correct without that kind of major surgery.

Dr. Green
27-28
Opinion of
Surgery

Dr. Green stated that the X-rays taken prior to Dr. Brown's surgery showed minimal obstruction. Dr. Green probably would not have performed that surgery, but confirmed that it was a "judgment call." He does not ascribe the scar tissue he found to any error or fault on the part of Dr. Brown.

Form 6:5 — Master Index of Depositions.
Text — § 6.4.1.2.

Smith v. Jones
File 12345-001
C 54321

Deponent	Date Taken	Exhibits	File Location
1. Smith	11/27/78	1-1 through 1-18	600
2. Jones	12/06/78	2-1 through 2-6	700
3. Brown	2/02/79	3-1 through 3-9	600
4. Black	3/06/79	4-1 through 4-44	600
5. Green	4/01/79	5-1 through 5-3	700
6. Red	6/07/79	6-1 through 6-7	700

NOTE: Information in the index can be expanded to include categories such as: Noticed By, Case, Comment (whether exhibits are complete, on file, etc.), and Digest (whether digest has been prepared).

Form 6:6 — Index of Documents Produced: Sequential.

Text — § 6.4.2.2.

Sequential Index of Documents Produced
By Plaintiff - Request No. 1

Smith v. Jones
File 12345-001
C 54321

Number	Date	Author	Addressee	Description	Location
0-1	3/11/76	Smith	Black	Letter re opening escrow	630
0-2	4/15/76	Black	Brown	Memo re election of officers	630
0-3	9/15/75	Brown		Articles of Incorporation	630

Form 6:7 — Index of Documents Produced: Chronological.

Text — § 6.4.2.2.

Chronological Index of Documents
Produced by Plaintiff

Smith v. Jones
File 12345-001
C 54321

Date	Author	Addressee	Description	Number	Location
4/12/76	Black	Brown	Letter re Purple Property	CB 000-21	632
4/13/76	Smith	Black	Memo re Board Meeting	BB 0-27	630
5/12/76	Black	Smith	Memo re purchase agreement	FS 00-2	631

NOTE: A chronological index might include documents produced by several parties. The categories should be expanded accordingly to include the source or initials of the party may be used, as above.

Working With Legal Assistants

Form 6:8 — Master File Index.
Text — § 6.5.2.

Smith v. Jones
File 12345-001
C 54321

Code No.	File Name
00-99	Correspondence and Costs
FBs 00-09	General Correspondence
FBs 10-19	Intraoffice Memos
FBs 20-29	Costs
100-199	Legal Research
FBs 100-109	Cases
FBs 110-119	Research Memos (may be separated by legal issue)
200-299	Legal Proceedings
FBs 200-209	Legal Proceedings Except Discovery (may be separated by legal issue)
FBs 210-219	Discovery Legals (may be separated by type of discovery and by sets)
FBs 220-229	Minute Entries
FBs 230-299	(may be used for related cases)
300-399	Workpapers
FBs 300-309	Brown Workpapers
FBs 310-319	Black Workpapers
FBs 320-329	White Workpapers
400-499	Clients' Documents
FBs 400-409	Clients' Documents — General (may be separated by issue or subject matter)
FBs 410-419	Clients' Photographs
FBs 420-499	(May be used for multiple clients, or types or subject matter of documents.)
500-599	Discovery Against Plaintiff
FBs 500-509	Depositions of Plaintiff's Witnesses
FBs 510-519	Exhibits to Depositions, Plaintiff's Witnesses
FBs 520-529	Deposition Digests, Plaintiff's Witnesses

Form 6:8 *Continued*

FBs 530-539	Documents Produced by Plaintiff
600-699	Discovery Against Defendant
FBs 600-609	Depositions of Defendant's Witnesses
FBs 610-619	Exhibits to Depositions, Defendant's Witnesses
FBs 620-629	Deposition Digests, Defendant's Witnesses
FBs 630-639	Documents Produced by Defendant
FBs 700-799	Documents from Other Sources

et seq.

(Numbers may refer to folders, filebacks or both.)

Form 6:9 — Master File Index.

§ 6.5.2.

Text —

Red v. Green
67890-001
C 09876

A. Correspondence
   1. Fileback #1, 2/22/79 — 6/29/79
   2. Fileback #2, 7/6/79 — 12/12/79
   3. Fileback #3, 12/13/79 — 7/7/80

B. Intraoffice Memos
   1. Fileback #1, 2/22/79 — 1/5/80
   2. Fileback #2, 1/13/80 — 6/27/80

C. Legal Proceedings Except Discovery
   1. Fileback #1, 2/15/79 — 7/28/79
   2. Fileback #2, 8/1/79 — 12/9/79
   3. Fileback #3, 1/6/80 — 6/30/80

D. Research Cases
   1. Fileback #1
   2. Fileback #2

E. Research Memos

F. Workpapers
   1. Fileback #1
   2. Fileback #2

G. Discovery
   1. Fileback #1 — Defendant's Answers to Plaintiff's Interrogatories, First Set
   2. Fileback #2 — Plaintiff's Answers to Defendant's Interrogatories, First Set
   3. Fileback #3 — Plaintiff's Response to Defendant's Request for Production, First Set

H. Clients' Documents
   1. Folder #1 — Documents re Lease Agreement
   2. Folder #2 — Documents re Insurance Coverage
   3. Folder #3 — Documents re Liens

I. Documents Produced by Opposing Party
   1. Folder #1 — Documents re Lease Agreement
   2. Folder #2 — Documents re Damages
   3. Folder #3 — Documents re Personal Property

7

TRIAL PRACTICE

Thomas H. Watkins*
and Cathy Logue**

§ 7.1 This Chapter's Scope. This chapter concerns the use of legal assistants in the courtroom. It discusses the mechanics of using assistants in the litigation process, particularly in the trial itself and in the management of litigation files. The chapter will also describe the assistant's relationships with the various court personnel and lawyers, which enable the assistant to be effective in processing litigation files. Its purpose is to provide both a general approach and some specific suggestions concerning the various roles an assistant can play in litigation.

§ 7.2 The Trial Book. The fundamental aid for trying lawsuits is the trial book, the basic form of which is shown in Forms 7:1, 7:2, 7:3, and 7:4. For further information on the trial book and its use see H. Feder, *How to Get a Case Ready for Trial*, in Manual for Managing the Law Office ¶ 7075 (Prentice-Hall, Inc., 1970).

There are many different methods for organizing a trial book, but each method should include several essential elements. The first is a loose-leaf binder which contains all the information pertinent to the trial and is readily available for use. This means, for example, having a separate section in the book for the jury list, a section for outlines of opening and closing arguments, a section for current pleadings, and a section for deposition, witness and exhibit indexes. The legal assistant needs to design the trial book's organization in a fashion that is comfortable for both the lawyer and the assistant. Either of the unit divisions shown in the forms following this chapter is effective, depending on the lawyer's and assistant's preference. The divisions of the trial book will vary at times with the type of case.

The lawyer and the legal assistant should be flexible in designing the trial book. The theory, however, is that adequate preparation for trial is ensured if each section in the trial book is completed prior to trial. The assistant should be responsible for preparing and supervising each section of the trial book. The trial book thus functions as the principal checklist to ensure that the case is ready for trial. See the master trial checklist, Form 7:5.

§ 7.3 Jury and Argument. One section of the trial book should be devoted to information concerning the jury. If jury information sheets or other types of jury information are available, these should be placed in the trial book. The legal assistant should participate fully in each jury trial, including selection of the jury. It is essential that the assistant pay specific attention to all information obtained during voir dire, recording that information accurately for each juror. This allows the lawyer to concentrate fully on each juror while obtaining necessary information. The assistant should also observe the reactions of the panel while the lawyer is questioning indi-

---

* Shareholder, Hilgers, Watkins & Kazen, Austin, Texas.
** Legal assistant, Hilgers, Watkins & Kazen, Austin, Texas.

vidual panel members. The assistant may well notice either positive or negative attitudes which might otherwise escape the lawyer. The assistant also should express specific opinions about particular jurors; the lawyer thus can measure his or her own opinions by another person's reactions. This accomplishes the same result obtained when two lawyers try a lawsuit, but reduces the cost to the client.

Another advantage of the legal assistant's participation during trial is post-trial communication with jurors. Trial participation will have created sufficient identification and rapport to allow the assistant to investigate any jury misconduct effectively. The assistant can often obtain affidavits from jurors more easily than can lawyers involved in the trial.

If a wide voir dire examination is permitted, an outline of the specific questions to be asked of the panel should be placed in the trial book under the section labeled "Argument." This allows the lawyer to conduct an examination of the jury panel, to review whatever jury information has been given and to ask specific questions from the outline in an orderly fashion. The lawyer should not try to take notes concerning prospective jurors' responses. Doing so interrupts the examination's flow and diminishes the lawyer's ability to communicate and persuade. The assistant's function is to record and evaluate this information accurately.

In addition to preparing the voir dire examination outline, the lawyer and assistant should complete the trial book's opening and closing argument sections. This forces the lawyer to think through the entire case, trying to make the voir dire examination as close to opening argument as permissible under the local rules.

§ 7.4 Exhibit System.

§ 7.4.1 Requirements. In whatever manner exhibits are organized, the system has to accomplish several things:

§ 7.4.1.1 Index. The system must have an index which enables the lawyer or assistant to find the exhibit by a narrative description.

§ 7.4.1.2 Cross Reference. The system must provide a cross reference between the index number assigned and the exhibit numbers assigned by the court reporters during the course of a trial.

§ 7.4.1.3 Reconstructable. The system must be "reconstructable," meaning that during the trial, after the system has been taken apart by the introduction of various exhibits, it can be put back together at the close of testimony each day in a functional manner.

Except for complex cases involving numerous exhibits, it is not necessary to index exhibits by any method other than a narrative description and a number. An example of an exhibit list is shown at Form 7:6. Attempts to accomplish more by the index seem futile. An attempt to list exhibits chronologically will result in finding later exhibits which will not fit the chronology. An attempt to group exhibits around particular witnesses or evidence will severely limit the ability to find an exhibit which suddenly becomes material to a point not anticipated. In a case having fewer than 50 exhibits, a random listing of exhibits with a good narrative and simply using the next number available allows expansion of the exhibit list without having to redo the list as new exhibits are added.

§ 7.4.2 Preparation of Exhibits. The legal assistant should place every exhibit in a separate file folder and make at least two copies of each. If the evidentiary impact of an exhibit is not worth the cost of two copies and a file folder, it is not worth introducing. One copy of the exhibit should be bradded into the file folder; the label on the file folder should contain the same narrative and number as listed on the exhibit list. The original and the other copy should be placed loosely in the file folder, the copy to be handed to opposing counsel and the original to be marked as an exhibit. As the exhibit list enlarges, the file folders are kept in permanent expandable folders, the number of which is determined by the number of exhibits required to try the case. As each exhibit is added to the exhibit list, the number and narrative are added to the master exhibit list in the trial book and to at least one other copy of the exhibit list kept with the exhibits.

§ 7.4.3 **Number of Exhibits.** Ideally, discovery should have produced every document to be introduced by any party to the lawsuit. See the trial manual discovery section, Form 7:9. If a document is likely to be introduced by another party, it should be recorded as an exhibit so that it can be identified and labeled as a court exhibit. Theoretically, by the time the exhibit list has been completed in preparation for trial, it will include all the documentary exhibits to be offered. However, there are always a few surprises. The exhibit list should have sufficient space or additional pages to permit the legal assistant to list those exhibits offered by other parties during trial which have not been previously incorporated in the exhibit list.

§ 7.4.4 **Use of Exhibits During Trial.** At the time of trial, the more carefully the exhibit list is used, the better the lawsuit will be controlled. Offering any exhibit should have a very mechanical pattern. The more habit involved in offering an exhibit, the less likely a mistake will be made and the more likely the judge is to admit it in evidence. The process for offering an exhibit is as follows:

1. Remove the exhibit from its file folder.
2. Hand a copy of the proposed exhibit to opposing counsel and a copy to the court reporter for marking, stating something such as, "I ask you to mark this as Plaintiff's Exhibit 4 for purposes of identification."
3. Hand the file folder to the legal assistant, who will place the court's number on both the master exhibit and the file folder.
4. Then hand the marked exhibit to the witness with a statement such as, "Can you identify Plaintiff's Exhibit No. 4, please?"
5. Proceed with sufficient questioning of the witness to establish the exhibit's admissibility (subject matter not covered by this chapter).
6. Offer the exhibit with a statement such as, "I offer Plaintiff's Exhibit No. 4."
7. If the exhibit is received into evidence, the legal assistant marks on the master exhibit list and the file folder that it has been admitted. As the lawyer returns to the table, the assistant hands the file folder to the lawyer. Now the lawyer, the witness and opposing counsel each have copies of the same exhibit for the questions which relate to that exhibit.
8. If this procedure is used with each exhibit, the lawyer will appear more competent and there will be far better control over every exhibit.

§ 7.4.5 **Maintaining the Exhibit System During Trial.** At the end of each day's testimony, all the exhibit folders should be regrouped by index number. The information contained on the legal assistant's master exhibit list as to the court number and the admission of the exhibit should be checked against each file folder and the exhibit list in the trial book. The assistant should then review with the court reporter the original exhibits introduced during the day to confirm each exhibit's number assigned by the court and whether the exhibit has been admitted.

Each trial lawyer will have to alter whatever exhibit system is used to fit particular style, habits and tendencies. The above system is simply a suggested one with the recommendation that *a* system be developed and that the system be used in every case.

§ 7.5 Depositions. Many trial lawyers believe that most lawsuits are won or lost at the deposition stage. Even if that were 100% true, many lawsuits are lost because a lawyer cannot transfer a victory at the deposition stage into a victory in the courtroom. Just as with exhibits, effective use of depositions in the courtroom depends a great deal upon a system which is used consistently and effectively. Searching for that wonderful quote while trying to filibuster a witness is a miserable way to try a lawsuit. The ability to find the appropriate sections of a deposition quickly and accurately is the key to an effective deposition system. Whenever a deposition is taken, a standard procedure should be followed as to the use of the deposition from that point forward.

§ 7.5.1 Indexing the Deposition. A legal assistant should index the deposition prior to the time the lawyer reads it. This requires the lawyer to familiarize the assistant with the critical facts in that particular deposition prior to its indexing. The assistant should then read and underline a copy of the deposition while creating an index for the deposition, using a deposition analysis form such as that shown at Form 7:7.

§ 7.5.2 The Lawyer's Use of Depositions. Prior to trial, the lawyer should carefully read the depositions, noticing what has been underlined and comparing it to the entries on the deposition analysis. The lawyer should then correct, change, add to or delete from the analysis those portions which are individually useful in preparation for trial. This system will enable a competent trial lawyer to have "learned" the deposition thoroughly in only one reading by using the deposition analysis. Most other techniques require at least two and sometimes three readings of the deposition for the lawyer to become comfortable and familiar with it.

§ 7.5.3 Witness's Use of Depositions. Once the deposition analysis is completed, the deposition and the analysis should be provided the witness to be read just prior to trial. Reviewing those portions of his testimony underlined in the deposition analysis increases the witness's understanding of how the case is viewed by others. Such a review will also reduce the time required to prepare the witness for trial.

§ 7.5.4 Use of Depositions in Trial. There are three different purposes for the use of depositions in trial. The most prevalent is the effective cross-examination of adverse witnesses. The second is to prevent effective cross-examination of a friendly witness. The third is to present testimony from an unavailable witness. The final deposition analysis must be prepared so as to be effective for all three purposes. Significant portions must be underlined accurately and neatly. The page and line number should be accurately placed on the deposition analysis. The lawyer must learn to read from the deposition while keeping an eye on the analysis so the correct line and page numbers may be given when necessary.

§ 7.5.4.1 For Cross-Examination. When presenting cross-examination material, the proper predicate for impeachment must be established. When the lawyer is preparing to read from the deposition, he or she can use the deposition analysis to provide the line and page number, saying, "I am going to read from page 25, line 6 through page 28, line 7." This enables opposing counsel to determine where in the deposition the material will be read and enables the court reporter to determine what is going to be in the record.

§ 7.5.4.2 In Cross-Examination of Own Witness. When opposing counsel is cross-examining a witness, the only way to combat impeachment effectively is to be aware by a quick review of the deposition where the witness has explained away the seeming contradiction. This testimony can then be presented to the jury to indicate where this contradiction was eliminated. Often, this explanation may be pages away from the seeming contradiction. Only with an effective analysis can it be found in time to help the situation.

§ 7.5.4.3 To Present Testimony. When preparing a deposition for direct testimony, the assistant should see that two copies of the material to be read are made and processed as an exhibit. These copies must be identically underlined. The most effective presentation is to have the assistant or another lawyer take the stand. The lawyer then reads the question and the person in the witness stand reads the answers. This is effective only with two very carefully prepared copies of the deposition analysis. The use of depositions at trial using the system described in this section will increase those victories obtained in the deposition stage.

§ 7.6 Witness List. A witness list should be prepared by the assistant for each trial with name, address and telephone number (both work and home) for each witness on the witness list. This enables the lawyer or assistant to reschedule witnesses effectively at the last minute by having all the available information on one list. The witness list is also helpful in preparing last-minute subpoenas.

§ 7.6.1 Individual Witness Statements. For each witness who is to testify, whether friendly or not, a witness statement should be prepared. The witness statement should include a list of those topics or questions that are to be covered during direct or cross-examination. This witness statement should be kept in the trial book along with a deposition analysis and any other signed or sworn statement from the witness which might be used during the examination. If there are a number of exhibits to be introduced through a particular witness, the witness statement should include information concerning the exhibits to be introduced through that witness. If there is an adverse witness and impeachment testimony is available, the witness statement should include a list of the topical matter and segments of that deposition analysis where that material is contained. This provides a ready cross-index between documentary evidence, deposition and live witness testimony.

Just prior to trial, the witness should be taken through the exhibit system, particularly familiarizing him with the exhibits he is to identify. Sometimes reproduced copies of exhibits do not look like originals. Without proper preparation, the witness may become confused when asked to identify them on the stand.

§ 7.7 Legal Authorities and Case Decisions.

§ 7.7.1 Use of a Trial Brief. A trial brief should be prepared for controlling legal issues. If one is necessary, it should be mailed to the court and opposing counsel at least one week prior to the trial. If a trial brief is presented at the time of trial, it usually results in a delay in ruling. Either the court may delay its decision to review the trial brief or opposing counsel may request a delay in order to respond to the brief. Consequently, a trial brief should be prepared and submitted in advance on those legal issues which have been obvious in the case since its inception.

§ **7.7.2 Use of Major Cases.** For most legal issues, a trial brief is not advisable and is sometimes not possible. In most situations, there are two or three cases to be brought to the court's attention in order to obtain a ruling, either on the admissibility of evidence or in attempting to determine certain special legal issues. Sometimes the number of such issues requires a management system for case authorities similar to the system for exhibits. The simplest method is for the assistant to build a legal index similar to the exhibit index. Legal issues in narrative form should be outlined with the case citations relating to each issue listed in the index by folder number. Three copies of each case should be reproduced, underlined identically and placed in the file folder. At the time the legal issue arises, copies of the case may be handed both to opposing counsel and to the court. The argument can be conducted by directing everyone's attention to the underlined portions of the case. This accomplishes three things:

1. It gives the court a great deal of confidence that the case is being quoted correctly and that nothing is being omitted, even though the court is not obliged to read the whole case at that time;

2. It creates the maximum opportunity for the court to rule at that moment; and

3. It reduces the opportunity for opposing counsel to ask for additional time to respond to the legal theory since the court will usually ask for a response to that case at that moment.

§ **7.7.3 Use of Other Authorities.** The system just described can be used for those major cases which are controlling on a particular point. Other case citations may be listed on the legal index to be read to the court and opposing counsel. If quotations from other cases are particularly significant, reproduced copies of particular pages may be handled in the same fashion. Selected portions of three or four cases on the same point may be placed in one folder and indexed together into the master legal authorities index. Using the legal authorities index in the trial book permits access to the names of major case citations and all other citations. It also provides a means of locating the copies of those cases which relate to the point at issue. If legal authorities are handled in this manner, the court should be given copies of all relevant authorities with a minimum amount of search time.

§ **7.8 Instructions.**

§ **7.8.1 Preparation of Instructions.** A special section in the trial book is designed for proposed instructions or special issues as governed by local rules. See Form 7:8. A copy of all proposed special issues or instructions should be placed permanently in that section. Additionally, the assistant should place three copies of each requested instruction in a file folder marked "Instructions" and kept with the folders in the exhibit system. At the time the trial book is being assembled in preparation for trial, instructions can be prepared quickly as they occur to the lawyer during trial.

§ **7.8.2 Instructions and Other Sections of Trial Book.** The folder containing the instructions should be the first item created by the lawyer and assistant in preparing for trial. By reviewing the proposed instructions, the lawyer can prepare for trial an outline of voir dire examination, opening statement and closing argument. A good test of trial skill is how accurately the lawyer anticipates the instructions during his voir dire examination of the jury.

§ 7.8.3 Presentation of Instructions. When the court is ready to settle the jury instructions, the lawyer should request his proposed instructions by delivering complete sets to opposing counsel and to the court, working from the set permanently placed in the trial book. After the instructions have been completed, a copy should be placed in the instruction section of the trial book, along with any notes made so that necessary formal objections can be read into the record. This reduces the amount of time required to respond to the court's request for objections.

§ 7.9 Trial Notes. As described at § 6.4.3, summaries of the legal assistant's trial notes or the notes themselves may be used in a variety of ways, including the examination of witnesses and the preparation of post-trial motions. Although there is no set format for the taking of trial notes, the following elements should be included:

§ 7.9.1 The Date and Hour. It is important for the assistant to note the date of each day's notes, the time of day for each new witness, and each recess for lunch or in-chambers discussions. This enables the lawyer or assistant to aid the court reporter in locating rapidly any portions of testimony that must be transcribed.

§ 7.9.2 The Witness and Examining Lawyer. The assistant's notes should reflect the name of the witness in a prominent location on the page, the name of the lawyer conducting the examination, and whether it is direct or cross-examination. A simple procedure is to put the lawyer's name and type of examination in the right-hand margin.

§ 7.9.3 Exhibits. Whenever a witness is questioned about a specific exhibit, the assistant should note the exhibit's number and a brief description. Testimony about any given exhibit can be readily located by using the left-hand margin for exhibit references.

§ 7.9.4 Objections and Rulings. It is essential that the assistant note all objections to the admission of exhibits or testimony, and the rulings on those objections. These should also be highlighted, either by location on the page, underlining, or the use of a different-colored pen. Much time can be saved when the assistant can rapidly locate a ruling. Furthermore, the lawyer's credibility is enhanced by his or her ability to cite to a specific day, hour, witness or exhibit when repeating an objection and ruling previously made.

§ 7.9.5 Stylistic Considerations. The general language techniques described at § 6.3.2.2 for digesting depositions should be followed in taking notes of trial testimony. The difference is that in trial, the assistant is under much greater time constraints. These require the use of formula initials and abbreviations for frequently used names and words (assuming the assistant does not know shorthand or speedwriting). When taking notes of direct examination, it is usually easier to note the witness's answer, since the question is generally implied in the answer, *e.g.*, "After the light turned green, went through intersection." The same principle applies to short leading questions on cross-examination, *e.g.*, "Denied saw light turn green" implies the leading question, "Isn't it true that you saw the light turn green?" However, complex leading questions, lengthy hypothetical questions or series of leading questions followed by one-word admissions or denials can usually best be noted by simply writing the questions and answers themselves as nearly verbatim as possible. For example, the assistant might write:

"Assuming the following:
1. That Smith saw the light turn green,

2. That Smith entered the intersection one second after he saw the light turn green and

3. That the light turned red before he left the intersection,

Brown believes the yellow light time too short by two or three seconds."

§ 7.10 Relationships With Court Personnel. Developing proper relationships with court personnel is essential if the case is to proceed efficiently. Consequently, the legal assistant should ensure, where appropriate, that a first-name basis relationship exists with as many court personnel as possible.

§ 7.10.1 Clerks. The legal assistant needs to learn which of the assistant district or county clerks are responsible for setting cases for trial; which are responsible for issuing subpoenas and writs of garnishment, attachment and execution; and which are responsible for the district or county clerk offices' accounting functions. The assistant should know for whom to ask when calling the clerk's office concerning any such matters. The caliber of service received from any office at the courthouse increases immeasurably if a cordial relationship is established prior to the time the service is requested. If court personnel deal with the assistant on an anonymous basis, they simply will not provide the same quality of service.

When contacting a clerk's office the assistant should understand the nature of the request and what is actually involved within the clerk's office to respond to the request. For example, if a call is made to determine whether answers to interrogatories have been filed, it is helpful to know whether some particular person handles the docket sheets containing that information without having to remove the court's file. On the other hand, if the assistant must know whether a particular exhibit is contained in the file, it is helpful to know who can review the file and answer the question. If the assistant is aware prior to the time the request is made what work it will require, better cooperation from the clerk's office will result. Conveying to court personnel knowledge and appreciation of what their job is and how much work is involved in a particular request, and framing the request in a way that minimizes their burden, is the essential element for maintaining good relationships.

§ 7.10.2 Court Reporters. The official court reporter will soon come to rely on a well-prepared legal assistant for accurate information regarding each exhibit's court number and admissibility. In appealing a case, the proper relationship between the assistant and the court reporter is essential in obtaining accurate and candid information concerning the timely filing of any statement of facts and the possible need for obtaining an extension of any of the appellate deadlines. The assistant's role in this situation is not to threaten or cajole the court reporter, but to help communicate a sense of cooperation that the lawyer and the reporter are attempting jointly to prepare the statement of facts timely.

§ 7.10.3 Bailiffs. Involving a legal assistant with the bailiff in the coordination and management of witnesses who are yet to be called is an effective way to reduce the number of items a lawyer has to keep in mind while attempting to try a case. If the assistant keeps the bailiff informed as to how many witnesses are expected, their names and when they are likely to arrive, the bailiff can do his job more efficiently without additional demand on the lawyer's time.

§ 7.10.4 Constables, Sheriffs and Other Process Servers. Proper cooperation between the clerk's office and the constable's office or other process servers is essential to issue subpoenas effectively during trial. This cooperation does not happen accidentally. The legal assistant should have a good working relationship with both offices so that, on an emergency basis, the transfer of writs or subpoenas between the two offices occurs efficiently. Service of papers by constables, deputy sheriffs or other process servers will not occur as efficiently as the case demands unless the legal assistant develops a good working relationship with them.

§ 7.11 Relationships with Lawyers.

Litigation lawyers are often egotistical prima donnas. Although some can deal with other professionals without having to prove their talent, others cannot. Some are willing to deal personally with employees of opposing counsel to get the job done; others are willing to do so only after their status has been established. The legal assistant is forced by these tendencies to vary the method and approach required to deal with different lawyers according to the manner exhibited by the particular lawyer. The assistant will quickly be able to determine whether or not the lawyer is trying to establish a status prior to seriously discussing the subject at hand. Some lawyers are quite comfortable in dealing with legal assistants and have no particular reservations about setting depositions or discussing trial dates with non-lawyer personnel. Ironically, some of these same lawyers become difficult to work with when they think they are dealing with an assistant, simply because the idea is new or unusual to them. There are still other lawyers who will not deal with anyone other than another lawyer. If so, the assistant needs to learn this as quickly as possible. However, the longer an assistant participates in litigation, the more credibility and rapport is developed with a number of different lawyers. The assistant thus increasingly can perform many functions that do not require lawyer-to-lawyer communication.

The legal assistant should differentiate between those lawyers with whom this relationship is possible and those with whom it is not. If the assistant is careful to identify the proper status when asked, concentrates on communication which involves the administration of a lawsuit rather than its contested issues or settlement, and is flexible enough to respond in the most productive manner to opposing counsel, then major difficulties should be avoided. The distinction between what is administrative and what is substantive in the handling of a lawsuit requires the most careful ethical consideration by the assistant. Eventually, however, the assistant should become an effective communication center for a number of trial lawyers in coordinating their schedules, obtaining discovery and managing their litigation files, significantly reducing the number of lawyer hours necessary for these tasks.

§ 7.12 Summary and Conclusion.

The groups to whom a legal assistant must relate all have specific characteristics requiring thought as to how best to maintain good relationships. The lawyer's ability to concentrate on the lawsuit's essential elements is sharpened if the assistant can relate to the judge, a constable, a real estate appraiser or a court reporter on an efficient and professional basis.

The habitual organization of a trial book is the key to effective preparation for trial. The legal assistant who develops this organization and ensures its completion prior to trial will increase the lawyer's control and understanding of all facets of the trial. An experienced litigation legal assistant is the most valuable resource an active, competent trial lawyer can employ in providing the best possible quality of legal services at a lower cost to his or her clients.

Form 7:1 — Trial Book Outline.
> Text — § 7.2.

I. **JURY**
   A. VOIR DIRE EXAMINATION
   B. ARGUMENT
   C. OPENING ARGUMENT
   D. CLOSING ARGUMENT

II. **TESTIMONY**
   A. WITNESS LIST
   B. CLIENT'S STATEMENT
   C. WITNESSES' STATEMENTS

III. **EVIDENCE**
   A. DEFENDANT'S DEPOSITION
   B. PLAINTIFF'S DEPOSITION
   C. EXHIBIT LIST
   D. INSTRUCTIONS
   E. LEGAL AUTHORITIES AND CASE DECISIONS

IV. **PLEADINGS**
   A. PLAINTIFF'S ORIGINAL PETITION OR COMPLAINT
   B. DEFENDANT'S ANSWER
   C. LAST-MINUTE PLEADINGS (MOTION IN LIMINE)

Form 7:2 — Docket Control Entries.

Text — § 7.2.

I. RESPONSE TO PLEADINGS

A. Plaintiff's original petition or any citations received (answer date noted).

B. Answer date for request for admissions.

C. Answer date for interrogatories.

D. Objections to interrogatories (filing deadline).

E. Plea of privilege (filing controverting affidavit).

F. Motion for summary judgment
   1. Time in which to file response (7 days prior to hearing).
   2. Hearing not to be set prior to 21 days after motion filed.

G. Notice for deposition — time and date.
   1. Note duces tecum requirements.
   2. Note time in which to file motion for protective order if necessary.

II. SETTINGS

A. Trial date.
   1. Note last day to amend (7 days prior to trial).
   2. Note docket call information Thursday before trial.
   3. Note last day to file interrogatories prior to trial.
   4. Note last day to schedule depositions prior to trial.
   5. Note last day for request for admissions.
   6. Note last day for filing motion for summary judgment.

B. Depositions.
   1. Note reminder for confirmation of court reporter.
   2. Note reminder for compliance w/duces tecum.
   3. Note reminder for attendance at deposition by client/witness/attorneys involved.

C. Motion for summary judgment hearing.
   1. Deadline for filing affidavits.

D. Post-judgment discovery settings.
   1. Motions to compel.
   2. Motions for attachment.
   3. Motion to produce.
   4. Applications for writ of garnishment.

III. DEADLINES

A. Statute of limitations.

Form 7:2 *Continued*

      B. Appellate deadlines.
          1. Appellant's and appellee's briefs.
          2. Filing of transcript and statement of facts.
          3. Oral argument.
          4. Bond deadlines.
          5. Motion for rehearing deadline (CCA).
          6. Application for writ of error deadline.
          7. Motion for rehearing deadline (Supreme Court).
      C. Tax deadlines.

IV. **FILE REVIEW**
      A. Wills.
      B. Judgment renewals (10-year).
      C. Corporate review.

V. **FIRM COMMITMENTS**
      A. Professional commitments per lawyer (bar associations, civic responsibilities, meetings, etc.)
      B. Various civic commitments per lawyer.
      C. Office and staff meetings.

Form 7:3 — The Trial Book.
Text — § 7.2.

1. **VOIR DIRE**
   1.1 Type of juror wanted
   1.2 Particularly applicable voir dire questions

2. **ARGUMENT**
   2.1 Opening argument
   2.2 Closing argument
   2.3 Argument on motions

3. **TESTIMONY**
   3.1 Witness list
   3.2 Client's statement
   3.3 Witnesses' statements
   3.4 Defendant's deposition
   3.5 Expert witness reports

4. **EVIDENCE**
   4.1 Exhibit list
   4.2 Damage evidence
   4.3 Photographs
   4.4 Official documents
   4.5 Legal authorities
   4.6 Case decisions
   4.7 Instructions

5. **PLEADINGS**
   5.1 Complaint
   5.2 Answer
   5.3 Pre-trial order
   5.4 Damages

Form 7:4 — Procedures for Preparing the Trial Book.
Text — § 7.2.

INTERROGATORIES
Paste each question on blank sheet followed by the answer.
Cut and punch and put into book.

DEPOSITIONS
Prepare deposition analysis and put into book under "Testimony."

WITNESS LIST
Set up the columns as follows: **Name, Address and Telephone Number, Topic, and Time/Date for Testimony.**
Prepare witness list before pre-trial conference.
Take one copy of witness list with you to trial — leave one copy with your assistant/secretary.
Assistant/secretary will locate and schedule all witnesses.
Fill in the list as each witness is scheduled.

EXPERT WITNESS CONFERENCE
Organize the experts' testimony so that they buttress each other, cover gaps and eliminate inconsistencies.
Conference will be set by the secretary, she should attend and take notes.
The position of each expert should be summarized.
Background data on each expert must be itemized.
A memo of the expert witness conference should be circulated among all of the experts.
Place conference memo in Testimony Section.

PREPARING AND SERVING SUBPOENAS
Secretary should prepare subpoenas.
Use a standard form.
Send to process server.

EXHIBITS LIST
Set up the columns as follows: **Exhibit Number, Description, In/Out.**
Name of case and our file number should appear at the top.
Prepare before pre-trial conference.
Use In/Out for admission or rejection.
Use exhibit numbers the same throughout pre-trial and court for cross-referencing.

COLOR CODING
Red:	Our client's testimony outline, deposition analysis, interrogatories.
Yellow:	Adverse party's deposition analysis, statements and interrogatories.
Green:	General trial matters such as outline of the case, voir dire opening argument.
Blue:	Legal authorities relevant on evidentiary and substantial law points.
Purple:	Procedural portions.

Form 7:5 — Master Trial Checklist.
Text — § 7.2.

Date	Event
Six weeks prior to trial.	1. Confirm availability of witnesses for trial. 2. Determination and acquisition of all necessary evidence and documents. 3. Complete the taking of all oral depositions.
One month before trial.	1. Review pleadings for any possible amendments. 2. Make decision in regard to additional pre-trial discovery. 3. Review any depositions.
Three weeks before trial.	1. Complete all deposition analyses. 2. Arrange for the appearances of witnesses, including making any hotel reservations needed.
Two weeks prior to trial.	1. Complete the research of any legal questions (read carefully all pleadings to determine the legal questions involved in the lawsuit.) 2. Conduct pre-trial client conference, or complete the arrangements for pre-trial client conferences.

One week prior to trial.	1. Complete preparation for direct and cross-examination of witnesses, including expert witnesses, if any.
	2. Docket call.
	3. Organize trial exhibits.
	4. Organize evidence in regard to attorney's fees.
	5. For jury trial:
	   a. Prepare motion in limine.
	   b. Complete voir dire outline.
	   c. Complete preparation of special issues.
	   d. Prepare written stipulations.

Day before trial.	1. Meet with client in preparation for testimony at trial.

Form 7:6 — Exhibit List.

Text — § 7.4.1.3.

PLAINTIFF INSURANCE COMPANY	X	IN THE 201ST DISTRICT
VS.	X	COURT OF
DAN DEFENDANT	X	TRAVIS COUNTY, TEXAS

EXHIBIT LIST

NO.	DESCRIPTION	COURT NO.	IN/OUT
1.	State Board of Insurance — certified copy (License Status)	D#3	In
2.	State Board of Insurance — cert. copy (Form 100A- "Application of Incorporated Local Recording Agency for License 8-1-72)		
3.	State Board of Insurance — cert. copy (Letters from Time Ins. & State Board Inc. re directors)	D#1	In
4.	Client's list of accounts still in force from original list		
5.	Client's list of "items paid but no commission received"		
6.	Contract of Sale (9-1-76)	P#1	In
7.	List of companies att'd to contract (plus census figures)		
8.	Certified Copy from Comptroller re 1976 through 1979 franchise tax reports	D#2	In
9.	Tax Return (corporate) — 1979		
10.	Telephone Bills		
11.	Financial Statement (corporate) 1976		
12.	Telephone message (re Rand-Houston)		
13.	Note of expired binder (4-6-79)		
14.	Note re surplus market — 3-27		
15.	Installment payment notice (4-14-79)		
16.	Message re _____ call (4-3)		
17.	_____ memo to _____ re expired binder (3-30-79)		

Trial Practice — Forms

Form 7:7 — Deposition Analysis.

Text — § 7.5.1.

PLAINTIFF BUILDING CO.	X	IN THE DISTRICT COURT
VS.	X	201ST JUDICIAL DISTRICT
DEFENDANT RESORT, INC.	X	TRAVIS COUNTY, TEXAS

DEPOSITION ANALYSIS — PAUL PLAINTIFF

Page	Line	Description
11	6-15	In regard to the _____ agreement proportion and interest was 50%.
11	21-23	_____ interest in the _____ agreement was 50%
14	5-8	Relieved that there would be no other contracts that were not included in the two former contracts.
16	6-12	_____ responsibility under the agreements.
16 17	17-25 1-9	_____ responsibility for cost overruns.
17	10-18	The duties of the other partners: interim financing and sales.
17 18	19-25 1-14	It was understood who had responsibility for sales even though it was not mentioned in the contracts.
20	15-23	He usually was contacted about sales decisions after the fact. No actual discussion of plans for proposed sales. (Prior to entry, assuming _____ was not agent.)
21	6-7	Satisfaction with the approach and sales results.
24	5-10	Estimate of _____ proportion of profit if homes had sold the instant completed.
28	2-9	First felt the deal was going sour after visit with Mr. _____, a representative of _____
28	16-24	Meeting was in Houston in January of 1974.
29	4-11	His concern was caused by a feeling of conflict between Mr. _____ and Mr. _____, and the fact that sales had stopped.
29 30	22-25 1	Mr. _____ advised him they were going to run the project as they saw fit.
30	7-14	This statement was not in the form of "You back out," but rather gave a feeling that they weren't that concerned about the project at that time.

Form 7:7 *Continued*

31	17-24	On the basis of information available to there have only been three sales from March of '74 until January of '76.
31 32	25 1-13	Neither _____ nor _____ have received any money of distribution. There have been distributions that have gone into the joint venture account.
34 35	22-25 1-9	Assuming DX-3 to be true, any money received from the Title Company is a result of the closing that has been deposited in the joint venture account in the City National Bank.
35 36	15-25 1-3	$143,000 put back in and used as the interim on finishing out the townhouses.
36	9-14	At the closing after interest and principal were paid on the interim loan, _____ received whatever balance was left in the ____ account.
36 37	21-25 1-8	$143,000 used for construction cost rather than making draw on the interim loan.
37	13-21	Manner in which draws were made.
37 38	22-25 1-10	A substantial portion of the two million interim financing and the additional $143,000 was used to pay interest on the land.
38 39	22-25 1-5	Money not taken directly out of the $143,000 to make payments on the land. Joint venture account used to pay various costs, and no draws make on this unless joint venture was depleted.
39	15-22	Description of original purchase of the land.
39 40	23-25 1-15	Description of how interest on land was handled as an accounting debit from the partners.
40	16-23	No carry overs from previous developments concerning the cost of land.
41	1-15	Description of how interest payments were made.
41 42	24-24 1-6	Money for cost of land drawn out in first draw by the partners.
42 43	22-25 1-8	Amounts drawn out for the land on _____ and _____
44	5-13	Cost of construction at _____ cost did not involve anything dealing with merchandising, marketing or interest.

Trial Practice — Forms

Form 7:8 — Requested Special Issue.

Text — § 7.8.1.

PAUL PLAINTIFF	X	IN THE 167TH DISTRICT
VS.	X	COURT OF
DAN DEFENDANT	X	TRAVIS COUNTY, TEXAS

REQUESTED SPECIAL ISSUE NO. _____

ACCEPTED _____

REFUSED _____

_____
JUDGE PRESIDING

Form 7:9 — Trial Manual Discovery Section.

Text — § 7.4.3.

MEMORANDUM

TO: Office Manager

FROM: Cathy Logue

SUBJECT: Discovery Section of Trial Manual

The following is an outline checklist of the steps to be taken in the various forms of pre-trial discovery, including requests for admissions, interrogatories and depositions, both oral and on written questions. This section can best be described as that section which deals with the question of trying to obtain, in a form that is admissible, all information you want to get into evidence which will not come from a live witness. This is the process in which we determine what facts can be proven and in what form we are going to prove them.

I. INTERROGATORIES

A. Purpose — The specific purpose of interrogatories can best be summed up in a term known as "wheelbarrowing," in effect, loading up with all kinds of evidence. This is the method by which you find out as early in the case as possible what the disputed facts are.

B. When We Prepare Interrogatories.

1. Review allegations and defenses pled so far by both sides.

2. Gather documents to be proven up (such as contracts, memoranda, any supporting documentation).

3. Determine the facts to be obtained, keeping in mind the future witnesses to be deposed and special issues to be submitted.

4. Consult Bender's Forms of Discovery or other discovery aids and check under several categories for sample interrogatories.

C. Mechanics of Outgoing Interrogatories.

1. Determine to whom the interrogatories are to be directed (counsel for defendant or plaintiff or witness).

2. Prepare interrogatories beginning with opening paragraph including necessary instructions and dictate the individual interrogatories. After this has been completed, review the interrogatories with attorney involved before mailing.

3. After interrogatories have been approved, prepare for mailing. Send original to the clerk of the designated court, and copies to adverse attorney and all other parties involved in the lawsuit.

The certificate of service needs to indicate all parties receiving copies of the interrogatories, and the certified mail receipt must be filled out with the correct mailing information for each party receiving the interrogatories.

Form 7:9 *Continued*

    4. Calculate the time allowed for filing answers and mark on calendar.

    5. If request for extension of time is filed or an informal request for extension of time is made, be sure to mark new answer date on the calendar and request that a letter be written confirming extension by the other side.

    6. If answers are not filed by the due date, prepare a motion to compel answers and place on attorney's desk for approval and instructions.

    7. When answers are received, review to determine whether there are any exhibits to be requested or any answers improperly submitted. It is also a good idea at this time to determine whether or not answers have been directed to all parties involved.

    D. **When We Receive Interrogatories.**

    1. Immediately determine due date.

    2. Notify client for an appointment to go over interrogatories and set as soon as possible. At this time, inform him that he will be receiving a copy of the interrogatories to review prior to the interview.

    3. Determine immediately upon receipt if extension is necessary. If the client is out of town and it appears that there will be a timing problem, check with attorney for extension instructions.

    4. If client is out of town and appointment is not practical to go over the interrogatories:

        (a) Immediately forward copy of interrogatories to client, plus any material (contracts, memos, letters, etc.) he will need to prepare answers.

        (b) If time does not allow, request client to phone answers so formal answers can be prepared and mailed to him for signing before a notary public; otherwise, have client send his answers to you.

    5. Immediately upon receipt, in addition to mailing copy of interrogatories to client, review contents of our file, and when receiving answers from client, collate our answers with file information and prepare draft for approval. This is an appropriate time to watch for any discrepancies in the file and in the answers submitted by the client, and if any are noted, this should be brought to the immediate attention of the attorney involved.

    6. After the answers have been approved and prepared in final form, have the client come into the office to sign the answers to interrogatories before a notary public before filing.

    7. The original is filed with the clerk and copies of the answers are mailed to all parties involved, along with copy of cover letter addressed to clerk accompanying answers. Again, be sure to keep accurate certified mail receipts and attach receipts to file copies.

II. REQUEST FOR ADMISSIONS

    A. **Purpose** — This discovery tool is a device used to prove up those things

Form 7:9 *Continued*

which are not contested but which are essential to the case. The request for admissions acts as a tool to gather these facts into an admissible form before you get to the courthouse. Requests for admissions in most cases should be prepared immediately upon receipt of the answer. The main function of the request for admissions is to force the other side to tell you what they are going to fight about.

B. **When We Prepare Request for Admissions.**

1. We need to review the pleadings and the allegations and defenses which have been pled so far.

2. Determine the basic facts to be obtained.

3. Prepare each request to be answered in the affirmative, and be sure that there is not more than one fact to be admitted or denied in each request.

4. Gather documents to be proven up by requests.

5. Consult Bender's Forms of Discovery sample request for admissions or other discovery aids under several categories for guidelines and omissions.

6. Think. Be sure to include every fact that would be favorable to your case in the instance where a set of requests are deemed admitted for failure to answer.

C. **Mechanics for Outgoing Requests for Admissions.**

1. Determine to whom the requests are to be directed (counsel for the defendant).

2. Calculate the time allowed for filing answers to requests. At this time mark on the calendar the due date for the answers to the requests.

3. Be sure to fill out the certificate of service, including copies sent to all parties involved in litigation.

4. Fill out the certified mail receipt and attach to file copy of request for admissions.

5. If an extension of time is filed, or an informal extension is requested, be sure to note the new answer date on your calendar.

6. If the answers are not filed by the due date, the requests may be deemed admitted.

7. Upon receipt of answers to request for admissions, immediately cut and paste the requests and the answers so that the attorney can have the facts to work with in preparing for trial.

D. **When We Receive Incoming Request for Admissions.**

1. Immediately determine the due date for the request.

2. Notify client for appointment to go over request for admissions, if necessary, and set appointment as soon as possible.

3. Determine if extension of time is necessary.

4. If client is out of town and needs to review the requests before submitting answers:

Form 7:9 *Continued*

    (a) Immediately forward copy of request for admissions, plus supporting documents, to client and advise him that he needs to prepare answers as soon as possible.

    (b) Have client either phone his answers to requests as soon as possible so that formal answers can be prepared, or have him mail his answers to the office.

  5. When client's answers are received, collate these answers with the file material to determine any discrepancies in admitted or denied facts.

  6. Prepare formal answers for review by attorney and client and have signed before a notary public.

  7. After answers have been signed, send original answers to the court with copies to all parties. Again, keep accurate certified mail receipts and attach to file copies.

IMPORTANT THINGS TO KNOW ABOUT REQUESTS FOR ADMISSIONS

  1. A refusal to admit a fact is permissible when the inquiry involved solely an issue of law but refusal to respond to an inquiry of fact may cause the fact to be admitted.

  2. Refusal to admit a fact is not permissible in the event that the information necessary to respond is available.

  3. Admissions of fact are not binding on other defendants and not admissible in other proceedings.

  4. After a fact is admitted, the admitting party may not introduce controverting evidence.

  5. **Failure to answer or deny specifically a requested fact inquiry may result in the fact being deemed admitted.**

III. ORAL DEPOSITIONS

  A. **Purpose** — The purpose of an oral deposition is for the lawyer to obtain in written form the other side's version of the disputed facts and to force testimony of the adverse party and his witnesses before the trial about those facts. It can more accurately be said that one of the purposes of a deposition is to freeze the lawsuit. In other words, once testimony is in deposition form, it cannot easily be changed to something other than what is contained in the deposition. The following are general facts to know about depositions.

  1. A deposition is to be taken in the county of the witness's residence or where he is employed "or at such other convenient place as may be directed by the court." A non-resident or transient person may be required to attend in the county where he is served with a subpoena, or within 100 miles from the place of service (according to local rules).

  2. Written cross-questions may be directed to the witness who is to give an oral deposition.

Form 7:9 *Continued*

3. Where a deposition has been on file for at least one day, no objection to form or to the manner of taking can be heard unless objections are in writing.

4. Either party may use the deposition at trial.

5. Depositions in another suit which has been dismissed or involves the same subject matter and the same parties may be used in later actions. Out-of-town witnesses to be deposed are to be paid mileage and per diem expenses.

B. **When We Set Depositions.**

1. Contact adverse party for a mutually convenient time for deposition (optional).

2. Determine if notice for oral deposition to be filed with the court is necessary.

   (a) If subpoena duces tecum is required

   (b) Not by agreement

   (c) Deposition of a witness

3. Contact the court reporter to arrange for taking of deposition, and advise of forthcoming subpoena duces tecum if applicable.

4. Prepare the notice for oral deposition (if necessary) as per notice attached.

   (a) The original goes to the court

   (b) Copies to all parties

   (c) Copy to client

   (d) Copy to court reporter along with letter confirming taking of the deposition and requesting subpoena duces tecum if necessary.

5. If no notice is necessary, prepare letter to adverse attorney agreeing to deposition by agreement, including details of deposition, court reporter arrangements, and send copies to client, court reporter and all parties involved.

6. In our situation, we use a specific court reporting firm who takes care of having the subpoena duces tecum issued. We simply advise them in our notice for oral deposition and in the letter confirming the deposition arrangements and request that a subpoena duces tecum be issued.

7. Mark the deposition date on the schedule.

8. When scheduling an out-of-town deposition, determine if there are any other depositions in any other lawsuits which could be taken enroute to the deposition location or in the same town.

9. Notify the client of the deposition and advise him we will be in touch after taking deposition.

C. **When We Receive Adverse Deposition Notice.**

1. Immediately check calendar for conflict.

2. Notify client of deposition setting and arrange for an appointment to discuss deposition procedure and facts to be disclosed prior to deposition date.

Form 7:9 *Continued*

    3. If subpoena duces tecum is involved, advise client of material to be produced.

    4. Determine if deposition date would be a convenient time for us to take the deposition of the adverse party.

    5. If client is coming from out of town, discuss travel arrangements with him.

    6. Be sure to note the deposition requirements (100-mile radius rule) for any problems concerning depositions.

IV. DEPOSITION ON WRITTEN INTERROGATORIES

    A. **Purpose** — The purpose of a deposition on written interrogatories is to obtain testimony from any third party who might be a witness where that person's testimony is not controversial, where he can prove up written documents, or he is out of town and you know he will not be available at the time of trial. This is an expensive and time-consuming procedure, but is not as expensive as an oral deposition. The following are facts concerning depositions on written interrogatories:

    1. Party proposing to take the deposition upon written questions is required to give ten days' notice.

    2. Notice should state name and residence of witness, or place where he is to be found, suit description, name and address of officer before whom deposition is to be taken, and designation of documents to be produced under subpoena duces tecum.

    3. A set of interrogatories to be asked should be prepared.

    4. If public or private corporation is named, the matters to be inquired into must be described with reasonable particularity, in which event the corporation must designate one or more officers, directors or managing agents to testify and answer interrogatories.

    5. Where designation is made, the person so designated must testify as to matters known or reasonably available to that organization or corporation.

    6. Cross-questions must be filed within ten days of the filing of the written interrogatories.

    7. Re-direct questions may be filed within five days of cross-questions.

    8. Re-cross may be filed within three days of re-direct.

    9. A letter should be prepared to the reporter taking the deposition. Enclose a copy of the interrogatories and a copy of the notice and envelope prepared with style of suit and other information as per Texas Rules of Civil Procedure 196 and 198.

    10. A cover letter should be prepared to the clerk enclosing the notice to take written deposition with interrogatories attached.

Certified mail receipts should be used in forwarding all correspondence and filing with the clerk and attached to the office file copies.

V. DEPOSITION ANALYSIS

    A. As soon as a deposition is received in the office, the trial assistant should prepare a deposition analysis after instructions from the attorney.

Form 7:9 *Continued*

    B. In analyzing the deposition, you need to understand the basis of the lawsuit — which facts are relevant to the suit.

    C. Before analyzing the deposition, read with particularity the most recent pleadings filed by both sides. It might be a good idea at this point to check with the attorney for the specific testimony elicited in deposition.

    D. Use the deposition analysis form and dictate each individual entry.

    E. Pay particular attention to discrepancies in testimony and facts pled by pleadings filed to date.

    F. Analyze the deposition as soon as it comes into the office. This is particularly important in reducing the amount of time that the attorney has to spend in determining the strengths and weaknesses of the lawsuit.

                                                                          CATHY LOGUE

8

INSURANCE DEFENSE LITIGATION

Larry L. Gollaher*

§ 8.1 This Chapter's Scope. This chapter concerns working with legal assistants in the more routine "bread and butter" insurance defense case. It does not discuss their employment in complex litigation requiring a team of lawyers and assistants. The type of case discussed in this chapter is one that can be prepared and tried by a single experienced lawyer assisted effectively by a single assistant. However, a second lawyer occasionally may be necessary to take depositions or handle motions and other preliminary court matters. Such an insurance case may involve either the defense of an insured under a liability policy or the defense of the insurer in an action brought by the insured or other policy beneficiary. The defense of a self-insured party may also be within this chapter's scope.

§ 8.2 Introduction. The use of legal assistants in insurance defense litigation is an idea whose time has come. Most insurers supply a high volume of cases and prefer the lowest possible charge for legal services. A properly educated assistant can perform a variety of routine tasks at a lower billing rate than a lawyer would require. Since there is generally a great variety of cases, the assistant should not become bored or "burned out." Instead, an assistant can be employed in increasingly complex tasks as he or she becomes more experienced and proficient.

§ 8.3 The Legal Assistant File. The litigation assistant should be responsible to and work under the supervision of the lawyer handling the particular case. The assistant may also aid other lawyers who assist with the file from time to time. The assistant may work only for one defense lawyer or may work on defense files for more than one lawyer. He or she also may have duties other than as a defense litigation assistant. Some insurance defense cases may not require use of an assistant. A file referred to an assistant will be referred to as a "legal assistant file" to distinguish it from other files. Given this framework, the following pages summarize the litigation assistant's performance of the tasks customarily involved in a routine insurance defense case.

§ 8.4 The Litigation Assistant's Checklist. The foundation for a litigation assistant program is a system of checklists which summarize the usual order of a routine case in litigation. Such checklists may be in outline form or state in step-by-step order the tasks to be performed by the lawyer or the assistant. These tasks logically divide a case into three stages. A separate checklist should be prepared for each. Examples of such checklists, "The Initial Defense Checklist," "The Discovery Checklist," and "The Trial Checklist," are shown at Forms 8:1, 8:2 and 8:3, respectively. Separate checklists may be designed for appeals and for closing a file after a settlement has been negotiated. For appeals, see generally § 13.4.3.

---

*Shareholder, Larry L. Gollaher, P.C., Dallas, Texas.

The discovery and trial checklists can also be used in other types of cases, either for the plaintiff or defendant. As each step is completed by the litigation assistant or the lawyer, the date of completion is entered on the checklist. Each checklist should fit on a single sheet of paper so that it can be placed in each legal assistant case file.

Under the lawyer's guidance, the assistant should prepare a comprehensive instruction manual, keyed to each checklist. The manual should explain in detail what is required of the litigation assistant to accomplish each step on the checklists. The assistant should refer to the manual frequently until he or she is fully familiar with it. The assistant should also become responsible for revising the manual should any changes be made in either the checklists or the firm's procedures in such cases.

§ 8.5 The Legal Assistant Reference Directions. In most offices, not all files are assigned to legal assistants. Specific defense cases should be referred to the assistant by a written memorandum. See Form 8:4, "Legal Assistant Reference Directions." Form 8:4 is designed to be used in other litigation files as well as in routine defense files. Its purpose is to define clearly the tasks assigned to the assistant. The assigning lawyer can delete any steps on the checklists not required in any particular case. The litigation assistant thus knows precisely what tasks on the various checklists are his or her responsibility. Form 8:4 can also be used to identify any anticipated special problems and to convey other special instructions to the assistant.

§ 8.6 The Litigation Assistant's Responsibilities. The litigation assistant is a valuable addition to the insurance defense legal team. Experience demonstrates that a fully trained and experienced assistant can perform many insurance defense tasks. An assistant may not give legal advice to clients and may not appear in court or at other formal legal proceedings, such as deposition sessions, on behalf of clients. The only other restrictions imposed on the assistant by professional ethics considerations are that he or she may not finally evaluate the worth of a case for the client or attempt to negotiate settlements with the claimant's representative without express authority from a lawyer to do so.

The legal assistant should record and meet all applicable deadlines on every file for which he or she is responsible. Each specific deadline must be entered on the firm's master calendar, on the individual lawyer's diary and on the assistant's own calendar or docket system. One such system requires the assistant to maintain a 3" x 5" suspense card on each file. These suspense cards are used not only to record all procedural deadlines by date but also to schedule and organize the assistant's own work schedule, including periodic status reports to clients.

§ 8.7 The File Summary Memorandum. One of the first steps to be accomplished by the assistant after a file is referred is to prepare a comprehensive memorandum both summarizing the material contained in the insurance company's claim file and listing any obviously missing items or additional investigation required. The assistant should read the plaintiff's complaint, calendar the return or answer date required by the summons or citation and study the insurer's claim file. Next, the case should be summarized as it existed when received by the firm. The respective insurance coverages should be stated, the facts of the claim summarized and the damages (particularly any medical special damages and lost wages) set forth. Any apparent disability, the history of any and all settlement demands from the claimant and offers by the insurer, probable defenses and a list of needed items should all be described.

Some insurance companies may send poor quality photocopies of documents or photocopies of photographs, fail to enclose original signed witness statements or neglect to state the specific coverages provided by their policy. The assistant should check for such missing items and note them on the summary memorandum. The assistant often may also make definitive investigative recommendations, such as contacting particular witnesses to obtain statements. The entire file should be submitted to the lawyer for review when the memorandum has been completed.

The file summary memorandum can serve many purposes during the defense file's existence. Initially, it records basic information about the case and permits the lawyer to determine whether the assistant understands the nature of the lawsuit and its potential problems. The assistant's list of needed items and investigative recommendations should be helpful to the lawyer in developing the file at this initial stage. Later, the memorandum may be reviewed to refresh one's memory about the case. Should the file be assigned to another lawyer to present or resist a motion in court, the summary will quickly provide the necessary factual background to handle the matter with a minimum of review time required.

§ 8.8 Preparing Pleadings. Drafting both initial responsive pleadings and later amended answers where required should be well within the capability of the experienced assistant and a time saver to the busy lawyer. A looseleaf form book should contain, on separate pages, suitable sample form paragraphs to be included in the defendant's answer or motion to dismiss. After consulting with the lawyer, the assistant can then prepare a proposed pleading on the basis of this form book and his or her own experience. The lawyer should review the rough draft of the pleading along with the file and then check, edit and supplement it as required before it is prepared in final form. The lawyer thus maintains primary responsibility for the pleading's content. After the pleading has been prepared in final form, the assistant should have it filed and served as required by the applicable court rules.

§ 8.9 Preparing Correspondence. A correspondence form book similar to the pleading form book, with samples of letters for every aspect of the defense file, should also be maintained. These letters can range from rather simple acknowledgement letters to the insurance company to more detailed transmittal letters to the clerk of the court, and finally to complex correspondence such as reservation of rights letters or excess notice letters to the insured. These, as well as routine letters to opposing counsel, can all be prepared by the litigation assistant using a well-written form book. Many lawyers once were reluctant to allow such letters to be sent out over an assistant's signature. Now that assistants have been accepted as an integral part of the legal service system, letters are often signed by the assistant when appropriate. In all instances the assistant must be clearly identified as such and not as a lawyer. An assistant having any question regarding the propriety of sending any such correspondence should check with the lawyer before signing the letter. Complex correspondence clearly affecting legal rights or giving legal advice should always be reviewed and signed by the lawyer.

§ 8.10 Interrogatories. Discovery should be a primary task for the litigation assistant. Unlike the complex or major litigation file where the assistant may be more of a librarian or coordinator than a participant in discovery, on the routine insurance defense file, a major part of the assistant's time may be spent in preparing discovery questions or responses. See generally the discussion of discovery in chapters 6 and 7 and Form 7:9.

When interrogatories or similar instruments are received, the assistant should immediately calendar the answer date and then forward them to the client for response. The assistant may prepare proposed answers to the interrogatories based solely upon the lawyer's file. It is best for the assistant to confer with the client in person to obtain the information necessary to prepare a draft of the response. If a personal interview is not practical, a telephone interview or written responses supplied by the client should enable the assistant to prepare the response for the lawyer's review and approval. The lawyer then has the opportunity to compare the proposed final answers with the client's answers and the tentative answers prepared from the file, make any needed changes and then forward them, if necessary, to the appropriate person for signature under oath.

The litigation assistant should also aid in preparing interrogatories to other parties involved in the litigation. See the discussion at § 6.3.1.1. After the lawyer reviews and approves them, the assistant should have them served and filed if filing is required. The assistant should also calendar the due date for the answers to the interrogatories. If answers are not timely filed, the assistant should notify opposing counsel that they are late and should be completed promptly. In the event that the answers are excessively delayed, the assistant should prepare a motion to compel answers or for appropriate sanctions for the lawyer's review. After the motion is approved, the assistant should see that it is filed, served, set by the court for hearing and that notice of the hearing is given to all other parties.

When answers are received, the assistant should review them, note any new and useful information received and report to the insurer. Unresponsive and omitted answers should be called to the lawyer's attention. If appropriate, the assistant should draft a suitable motion to compel. The assistant similarly may also be responsible for preparing or responding to requests for admissions and for production of documents. See the discussions at §§ 6.3.1.2 and 6.3.1.3.

§ 8.11 Depositions. Depositions may be scheduled by the assistant by coordinating the lawyer's schedule with the opposing lawyer and the witnesses. After a date has been set, the assistant or secretary should arrange for a court reporter or make certain that the other side is doing so, attend to any necessary travel arrangements, and then confirm all agreements and arrangements by letter. Where the depositions must be taken upon formal notice, the assistant should prepare and arrange for service of the notice and any required subpoenas. When the firm's client is to be deposed by opposing counsel, the assistant should remind the client of the appointment, provide a preliminary explanation of deposition procedures and schedule an appointment for a pre-deposition conference with the lawyer representing him at the deposition. By this time, the assistant should have a good understanding of what should be developed from the plaintiff's deposition. The assistant should prepare a list of specific areas or questions for the lawyer's use as a reminder during the plaintiff's examination.

After the transcribed depositions are received, the assistant should be responsible for the mechanics of obtaining the witness's signature, filing the deposition or returning it to the the court reporter for filing if required, paying the court reporter's invoice and taxing any appropriate court costs with the court clerk. If the deposition transcript shows that the witness was to fill in blanks left in the deposition or supply requested materials, the assistant should either attend to those details or, if they are the adversary's responsibility, remind opposing counsel's office of them until they are fulfilled. The assistant should also prepare a digest or summary of each deposition received. See §§ 6.3.2 and 6.3.3; Forms 6:3 and 6:4. A copy of that digest may be forwarded to the insurance company when the deposition report is made by the lawyer or assistant. A copy also should be kept inside the deposition for later use by counsel taking additional depositions, during final trial preparation and at trial.

§ **8.12 Investigation.** The litigation assistant also may be employed to a varying extent for investigation or legal research in a routine defense case. Some insurers are able to do any outside investigation requested by counsel through its own staff, an independent adjuster or a private investigator. Others make a limited investigation before sending the file to the lawyer. In such instances, the legal assistant should conduct any additional investigation required. Most insurers will agree that this be done, since an experienced assistant can structure an interview to develop the information most helpful in defending the case. The assistant's hourly billing rate also compares favorably with that of an independent adjuster and duplication of effort is avoided.

Since many insurance defense lawyers are in court or at depositions much of the time, some believe the litigation assistant should remain in the office as much as possible to coordinate responsibilities among counsel, witnesses and clients. They believe outside investigation can be counterproductive if the assistant is required to be away from the office for any length of time and that the assistant should direct any outside investigation from the office in the lawyer's absence. Others, however, believe that the lawyer's secretary should be fully capable of handling the coordination responsibility and that the assistant is better employed in interviewing witnesses, locating and preparing experts, and handling other more responsible tasks. Those lawyers who assign their assistants increased responsibilities as they become more experienced find that the assistants are more pleased with their work and that they perform better than those limited to more repetitive, boring tasks.

§ **8.13 Final Trial Coordination.** Assistance given to busy defense counsel in last-minute trial coordination can be most valuable. The assistant or secretary should check the docket position of each case on the lawyer's weekly trial calendar to determine which are likely to go to trial and which require an actual appearance by the lawyer. The assistant should remain in contact with the client and all witnesses until the case is reached for trial or is passed. When subpoenas are required, the assistant should be responsible for having them issued and served. When a case is actually in trial, the assistant or secretary should coordinate the various witnesses' appearances by advising them when they are actually to be in court. The assistant may also aid by meeting with witnesses to reassure them and to prepare them for trial. The assistant should also be responsible for thanking witnesses for their cooperation.

§ **8.14 Settlements and Satisfaction of Judgments.** After a case has been tried and judgment entered, or after a settlement has been reached, the assistant should instruct the insurer as to whom the settlement draft should be payable. The assistant should then prepare a draft of a suitable release and judgment for the lawyer's approval. When the entire settlement package has been completed, the assistant should forward it to claimant's counsel and thereafter follow through to see that the release is executed, that the judgment has been filed and the case properly closed, that court costs are taxed or paid, and that the firm's client is appropriately billed for all services and expenses. If the insured is not already aware of the settlement, the assistant should notify the insured and any witnesses that have been alerted that the case has been concluded. If expert witnesses have spent time on the file for which they have not been paid, the assistant should ask that they forward their bills promptly so the file can be closed.

§ 8.15 Monthly Report by Legal Assistant. A monthly or other periodic report by the litigation assistant is useful as both a management tool and to keep the lawyer informed of the status of every file for which the assistant is responsible. A sample of such a report is shown at Form 8:5. For example, on the first day of each month, a list of active cases being worked on by each legal assistant for a particular lawyer should be prepared. Each case should be listed on this report by its file name. A very brief current status report of that file should then be given. The assistant should list any current work in process, the date of any pending trial setting, any outstanding settlement negotiations and the date on which the next discovery step, if any, is to be completed, for example: "Our interrogatory answers due on 11/20." After referring to this written report, the lawyer should discuss each case on the list with the assistant. During this conference, any action required on each file should be discussed and assigned to the appropriate person. All cases referred to a litigation assistant should thus remain current and be pursued actively towards final disposition.

§ 8.16 Summary and Conclusion. The use of legal assistants in defense litigation is rewarding to both the assistant and the lawyer. Such use permits the lawyer to manage a greater volume of work than he or she could perform alone and allows the client to be billed at a rate often more commensurate with the work actually being done. Of utmost importance, the lawyer is better able to meet deadlines and other obligations occurring in a busy defense practice. By having the assistant report to clients periodically, the lawyer also meets the responsibility to keep clients informed as to the progress of their legal business. As a result, the lawyer is much better able to concentrate upon those areas truly requiring legal experience and expertise.

If a file is not referred to an assistant shortly after it is sent to the firm, the question arises as to when to begin using a legal assistant for discovery and discovery analysis. Some lawyers tend to wait until they know the case is going to trial before having an assistant become involved in the matter. The better use of the assistant, however, is from the beginning and throughout the course of the defense file from the time it is first received in the lawyer's office. By this means the assistant can aid not only in cases that are in fact tried, but also with gathering and analyzing the facts necessary for advantageous settlements and in keeping the client informed of the case's progress from its inception. The latter task is most important to the client but often neglected by a busy lawyer.

If a firm employs a sufficient number of assistants, it may assign the day-to-day responsibility for all defense files to them. Doing so, however, requires a well-trained and well-managed team. The system discussed in this chapter will work for insurance lawyers regardless of the number of persons involved or whether the day-to-day file responsibility rests with the lawyer or the assistant.

Form 8:1 — Initial Defense Checklist.

Text — § 8.4.

RE: _____

_____

Date Done:

_____ 1. Check citation or summons for answer date and insert that date in the following space: _____ Suspense file for three work days prior to answer date. Read entire file. (If answer due immediately do step 2, proceed to step 5 forthwith and then return to steps 3 & 4.)

_____ 2. Send simple acknowledgment letter to client unless answer will be filed and first six steps will be completed within 3 days of receipt of file, in which case acknowledgment is deferred until step 7.

_____ 3. Prepare file summary memo.

_____ 4. Present file summary memo to counsel and confer with him on the entire file.

_____ 5. Prepare defendant's answer; when signed by counsel, go to step 6.

_____ 6. Transmit answer to court and opposing counsel.

_____ 7. Send deferred acknowledgment letter to client if not yet acknowledged. Include therein, or send separate letter if file already acknowledged, request for any needed information, investigation or originals. If liability defense, send or request client to send excess letter or send standard cooperation letter to insured.

_____ 8. Initiate any required inside investigation. Send standard letter notice to expert witnesses, independent adjuster or important witnesses revealed by file.

_____ 9. Make jury demand.

_____ 10. Amend original answer, if needed, as shown by investigation, such as adding plea in abatement, or asserting counterclaim or crossclaim. Assert third party action where appropriate.

_____ 11. Preliminary evaluation to client with respect to future course of action. Current pleadings if not previously sent to be enclosed. Request client to furnish any needed information, investigation or originals not previously obtained.

Working With Legal Assistants

Form 8:2 — Discovery Checklist.

Text — § 8.4.

RE: _____

Date: _____

_____ 1. Request setting on merits if we represent plaintiff in district or county court of Dallas County. Request pre-trial if defendant and exceptions filed.

_____ 2. Note trial setting _____.

_____ 3. Special exceptions setting _____.

_____ 4. Preliminary interrogatories to opposing parties prepared.
_____   a. Date served _____ .
_____   b. Date due _____ .
_____   c. Reminder letter to opposing counsel if not timely answered.
_____   d. Motion for sanctions if no result from reminder letter.
_____   e. Interrogatory answers received, evaluated and sent to client.
_____   f. Motion to compel answers to specific interrogatories or motion for production prepared.

_____ 5. Consider amending pleadings to join additional defendants (including third party), to plead cross or counterclaims, or plead in abatement.

_____ 6. Set any pending dilatory pleas or preliminary motions down for hearing.
_____   a. Date hearing set _____

_____ 7. Order entered on dilatory pleas and/or motions.

_____ 8. Appointment for opponent's deposition by agreement or notice.
_____   a. Court reporter secured or opposing side will secure.
_____   b. Date of depositions and place _____ .
_____   c. If deposition of our party-witness requested at same time — our witness notified of deposition date.
_____   d. Conference with our party-witness held.
_____   e. Particular areas to be covered on deposition prepared.
_____   f. Depositions taken.

_____ 9. Depositions received, checked and invoice forwarded to client.
_____   a. Arrangements made for our witnesses to sign depositions.
_____   b. Our witnesses' depositions signed and returned and changes noted; file with court.
_____   c. Written digest of depositions prepared.
_____   d. Reminder letter to opposing counsel about information to be furnished.

_____ 10. Report to client on content of depos. and discovery, bill any expenses; request client to authorize any needed investigation and/or experts.

Form 8:2 *Continued*

Date:

_____ 11. Consider motions for production, inspection, and med. exam.
_____ 12. Consider written depos. to pick up records from non-parties.
_____ 13. Consider further depos., *e.g.*, non-party witnesses.
_____   a. Appointment made, notice and subpoena served.
_____   b. Arrangements for court reporter made.
_____   c. Depos. received, checked and invoice sent to client.
_____   d. Written digest of depositions prepared.
_____ 14. Requests for admissions or stipulations of fact.

Form 8:3 — Trial Checklist.

        Text — § 8.3.

                              RE: _____

Date: _____

_____ 1. Consider requesting trial or pre-trial settings;

_____ 2a. Date of pre-trial setting _____.

                b. If assigned to new lawyer, state name _____.

_____ 3. Consider performing step 14 now, particularly as a needed predicate for or to resist motion for summary judgment, or to comply with pre-trial order establishing early date for pleading amendments, in which case put our pleading deadline here _____.

_____ 4. Consider moving for summary judgment.

_____ 5. Prepare working draft of trial memorandum.

_____ 6. Trial setting received. Case set for trial _____.

_____ 7. Notify or remind our witnesses, client and party of specific date, and confirm party and all witnesses' availability by phone.

TWO WEEKS BEFORE TRIAL:

_____ 8. Serve trial interrogatories and if warranted motions or requests for production and admissions re formal facts.

_____ 9a. Date that interrogatories due or motion set _____.

_____   b. Reminder letter sent to opposing counsel.

_____   c. Motion to compel or to dismiss filed.

_____ 10. If necessary, follow-up on any trial discovery sent adversary.

_____ 11. Prepare final trial pleading where amendment is necessary.

_____ 12. File final trial pleading with the court.

_____ 13. Finalize trial memorandum.

_____ 14. Consider supplementing our interrogatory answers.

ONE WEEK BEFORE TRIAL:

_____ 15. Check on all subpoenas for proper service.

_____ 16. By telephone, remind all friendly witnesses of trial.

_____ 17. Docket call _____ Number on docket as of_____.

_____ 18. Advise witnesses of docket position by telephone and keep them current until trial completed.

Form 8:4 — Legal Assistant Reference Directions.

Text — § 8.5.

To: _____
Legal Assistant

Date: _____
Re: _____

The captioned matter is referred to you as directed below:

1. ☐ You are to assist specially
   - ☐ on this file normally following the format of the checklists noted.
   - ☐ as hereafter directed.
2. ☐ You are to serve as coordinator of this major litigation file.
3. ☐ This file is generally referred to you for complete development in accordance with the checklists noted.
4. ☐ _____

CHECKLISTS:

☐ Initial _____
☐ Discovery _____
☐ Trial _____
☐ _____
☐ _____

Start at first step on first list checked unless later beginning # follows here: _____

Delete #'s: _____

Additional directions _____

_____, 19____   _____
                                                Counsel

Form 8:5 — Active Case Status List.

Text — § 8.15.

To: LLG
From: LS

ACTIVE CASE STATUS LIST FOR MONTH (Prepared 4/2/80)

COMMERCIAL UNION/Bobby Wood	Case passed but not reset; settlement negotiations in progress; diaried 4/7/80 status check.
EMPLOYERS MUT/Swann	Interrogatories served 11/22/79; no answers rec'd to date; reminder letter written; diaried 5/1/80 status check per instructions.
FARMERS/Bell v. Bolding	Diaried per instructions for 6/6/80; citation not served on Beal to date.
FARMERS/Weckwerth	Awaiting instructions from client re appeal; notice of appeal deadline 4/14/80.
FIRST OF GA/Hinton	Closed on my list.
INTERSTATE/Todd	Judgment & release amended to reflect all parties and correct opposing counsel; awaiting receipt of remaining 2 drafts before sending judg. & release; USF&G draft for $4,000 rec'd.
KEMPER/Allen v. Jeff	Depositions set for 4/18/80; Def. notified & to be here at 1:00 p.m. that date; areas to be covered at Pl's deposition will be prepared.
RELIANCE/Ford vs.	Case set for trial 6/5/80; Mr. Stone assigned to try case; all witnesses notified of trial.
TRINITY/Coker v. Chisum	Set for trial 4/28/80; all W's except Mr. Brown notified; subpoena for Brown in process. Pl. has not answered interrogatories re expert W's. Do you want motion to compel?

Assistant's cases:
 Total cases for you: 8
 Total cases for firm: 54

9

MEDICAL-LEGAL PRACTICE

Carol J. Morris*

§ 9.1 This Chapter's Scope. This chapter concerns the selection, training and use of legal assistants in law offices where medical knowledge is important, such as in personal injury or worker's compensation practice. The assistant in this field specializes in medical fact-gathering, analysis, interviewing, interpretation, record-keeping and reporting of medical data. As in other categories of practice, the assistant works within the limits of assigned authority and under a lawyer's supervision. A suggested job description is shown at Form 9:1.

§ 9.2 Selection of Employees. Choosing a potential legal assistant with past medical experience or education will reduce the time required for on-the-job orientation. Previous experience brings familiarity with medical vocabulary, the functioning of a health care facility and the problems of professional ethics. For other discussions concerning selection of assistants see §§ 1.3 and 2.5.2.

§ 9.2.1 Education Requirements. The legal assistant will require orientation both to the legal aspects of the position and to the firm's specific requirements. The following suggestions include general, medical and legal knowledge considered necessary for an assistant to function effectively in the medical-legal field. A plan is also offered for the lawyer to supervise education by the firm in both medical and legal areas.

§ 9.2.2 Special Medical Knowledge Necessary. (1) Medical terminology and abbreviations; (2) medical and surgical procedures and facilities; (3) anatomy and physiology; (4) health insurance; (5) medicolegal limitations and requirements; (6) pharmaceutical and therapeutic terminology; (7) medical research tools; (8) trial aids; and (9) public health agencies, medical welfare benefits, eligibility and application procedures.

A beginning assistant might have only a portion of these skills and learn the others while performing simpler tasks. He or she would then advance to more complex duties when the necessary education had been completed.

§ 9.2.3 Education by the Firm. If the firm undertakes an education program, the subjects and texts shown at Form 9:2 are recommended as minimal education. Materials selected should meet four criteria:

(1) They should be of a nature to be largely self-taught (individualized instruction methodology), with audiovisual aids whenever possible;

(2) They should be usable as reference tools for future legal assistant research tasks;

(3) They should be up-to-date and practical in scope; and

(4) They should be interesting.

---

*Medical and legal secretary instructor, Missoula Vocational Technical Center, Missoula, Montana.

§ 9.2.4 Continuing Education Programs.
The firm should conduct continuing education programs using the suggested materials to supplement whatever formal education, legal and medical continuing education is otherwise available. For other discussions of the importance of continuing education programs see §§ 1.6 and 2.5.3.

§ 9.3 Analyzing the Need for Legal Assistants.
Based on daily time records, a time use and task analysis study can be made to determine the extent to which medical knowledge is required within the firm. An accurate tally should be attempted for at least sixty days and the results evaluated. Lawyers and assistants should mark their time sheets with the letter "M" each time a duty requires medical knowledge. Copies of all papers requiring medical knowledge should be collected from the firm's work product. This should permit the firm to determine the extent to which medical knowledge is required by the firm's lawyers and assistants.

§ 9.4 General Suggestions.
Whatever the scope of the legal assistant's tasks, some general suggestions and precautions may help prevent problems. The lawyer must establish clear boundaries within which the assistant is to function and supervise and discuss both progress and problems regularly. The assistant should take care not to give medical advice, or to suggest medications or treatment. For more extended general discussions of the importance of lawyer supervision see §§ 1.4.1 and 2.3.1.

§ 9.4.1 Obtaining Authorization Forms.
The legal assistant must obtain a signed patient release form for every item of information sought from a physician, hospital or other facility, including requests for itemized bills.

§ 9.4.2 Ownership of Medical Records; Subpoenas.
The legal assistant should appreciate that although the contents of patient records technically belong to the patient, it is important to develop and maintain good relationships with medical records personnel. A subpoena to obtain such records should be used only when the information contained in the records cannot be obtained by other means.

§ 9.4.3 Obtaining Hospital Information.
The medical records department is the heart of the hospital information system. Its medical records administrator (supervisor) is accustomed to receiving written requests and subpoenas to release records. A subpoena duces tecum is often required in order to have records copied at a bonded copying service or to obtain the records themselves for court use. The assistant should not question anyone outside the medical records department concerning a particular patient's case or medical condition unless the lawyer has expressly authorized doing so. The assistant should not violate hospital rules regarding the patient's right to privacy. Unless the privilege of confidentiality has been waived, it is unethical for hospital employees to discuss a patient's condition outside the medical relationship.

§ 9.4.4 Obtaining Information from Physicians.
When the legal assistant appreciates the ethical and legal limitations placed on disclosures by medical facility staff members, there is an improved likelihood of establishing a successful relationship. The assistant should display tact, good rapport, dignity and discretion in order to maintain good working relationships with members of the medical community.

§ 9.5 Systems Development. By using the systems and forms suggested in this chapter and adding others, the lawyer can devise a step-by-step system for management of each matter involving medical questions. Checklists, progress reports and docket monitoring should assure efficient progression toward successful termination of each matter. The assistant should be involved in developing, expanding and refining the systems. Detailed written instructions, schedules and forms should be prepared for each routine task. See generally the discussions in chapter 1 and the other chapters in this volume concerning systems development.

§ 9.5.1 Use of Word Processing and Forms. The entire system should be designed to use whatever automated word processing and computer equipment or services the law firm has. Forms and form letters save time and are efficient work organizers. They are also excellent public relations tools. For examples, see the personal injury and labor cases flow charts shown at Forms 9:3 and 9:4.

§ 9.6 Task Analysis. Analysis of usual legal assistant tasks reveals six major areas. These will be discussed in order of frequency.

§ 9.6.1 Recordkeeping Functions. Recordkeeping functions include organizing files, preparing reports, obtaining medical bills, computing special damages and wage loss, recording costs, monitoring calendar and followup, and medical library maintenance functions.

§ 9.6.1.1 Suggested Methods of Organizing Files — Medical Reports Storage and Indexing: The Medical Portion of the Personal Injury File. The legal assistant should organize a separate subfile for "Medical Evidence," with a tabbed folder. It should contain, in chronological order, all medical reports from physicians, copies of hospital records and other evidence. These should be filed on the right side of the file. The lawyer's and assistant's notes, copies of medical-related correspondence and the medical reports index should be filed on the left side in chronological order. A manila envelope fastened to the inner file folder on the right side under the medical reports is a convenient place to store all small photographs and other items which may be introduced in evidence. Contents should be listed on the outside of the envelope. All large items should be stored in a separate, safe area and also be listed in the file both as to item and location. An example might be a large envelope of X-ray film.

§ 9.6.1.2 Special Damages, Wage Loss Computation and Settlement Notes. There should be a separate subfile for this category with a tabbed folder. The folder should contain, on the left, carefully dated chronological notes on each conference and telephone discussion regarding settlement. On top (and kept on top by removing it when filing anything on the left side) should be the loss of wages and profits summary shown at Form 9:5. The assistant should maintain the form on a current basis.

A manila envelope attached to the inner file folder on the right side is a convenient place to store all bills, invoices and receipts for medical expense and losses that can be claimed as special damages. All correspondence related to expenses and special damages should be filed on top of it in chronological order. The topmost item on the right side should be the special damages summary sheet shown at Form 9:6. The legal assistant should also keep this form current. In computing a client's special damages when negotiating settlement, the lawyer can thus simply add the total out-of-pocket loss to the client.

§ 9.6.1.2.1 Details in Recording Medical Expenses and Special Damages. Completing the form in pencil facilitates correcting errors in preliminary stages and keeping the figures current. Where treatment is prolonged, with many charges, the legal assistant must ensure that bills run consecutively, *i.e.*, that all statements are included so that the ending balance of one coincides with the starting balance of the next. If necessary, the assistant should request from the medical creditor an itemized statement omitting any reference to insurance payments or costs added for preparing reports for the firm.

The lawyer should caution the assistant not to disclose any information from the summary sheet without express permission and not to release any original bills. When directed by the lawyer to give copies to opposing counsel or an insurance adjuster, the assistant should make photocopies and keep the original bills.

§ 9.6.1.2.2 Items of Special Damages. Special damages may include, but are not limited to, those listed on the items of special damages form shown at Form 9:6. The list is included only as a guide for the assistant. The supervising lawyer will doubtless add to it as necessary.

§ 9.6.1.3 Preparing the Summary. Prior to any deposition, settlement conference, pretrial conference, hearing or trial, the legal assistant should review the bill folder to ensure that there is accurate written evidence of every charge entered on the special damages sheets.

§ 9.6.1.4 Recording Office Costs and the Legal Assistant Expense Account. An effective system must be developed to ensure that costs incurred in acquiring medical data are promptly paid and routinely posted to client ledgers. For example, the firm should arrange for prompt payment of copying costs incurred in duplicating medical and hospital records. If possible, the assistant should have cash available to pay the costs encountered in investigation and the authority to spend limited amounts without having to seek specific permission each time the need arises. Whatever method is adopted, the legal assistant should be given clear directions in its use.

§ 9.6.1.5 Calendar Monitoring and Followup. The lawyer and the legal assistant together should devise a reminder system so that deadlines are met and work progress is evaluated regularly. This system must connect with or be a part of the firm's general docket control and reminder system. Ample time must be allowed in advance of deadlines so the lawyer can prepare documents or perform whatever function is necessary based upon the completed data submitted by the assistant. For examples of such calendaring systems see §§ 8.6 and 13.4.4.

§ 9.6.1.6 Medical Library Maintenance Functions. The legal assistant should regularly spend some time on library maintenance. The time could be used to review medical and forensic publications; to preview trial aids such as charts, models and graphs; to examine audiovisual materials; and to make recommendations for additions and deletions to the firm's library. For suggested medical reference books see the bibliography at § 9.9.

The legal assistant should be taught to use the firm's retrieval system for its work product and research materials. See § 13.3.3. A close working relationship with the person responsible for library organization and maintenance is also helpful.

§ 9.6.2 Interviewing. This includes oral discussions and written communication between the legal assistant and clients, witnesses and medical agencies.

§ 9.6.2.1 Preliminary Interview.
The legal assistant may interview the client before he or she meets the lawyer. This permits the assistant to complete the preliminary client data sheet shown at Form 9:7, to summarize it quickly, and to present it to the lawyer. The lawyer then has a written set of facts as an aid in deciding whether or not to take the case. For those lawyers who prefer to conduct the initial client interview personally, the format can be easily changed. If the lawyer presents the assistant to the client as a specialized medical team member, good client rapport is usually established and a great deal of lawyer time can be saved in future client conferences and questions.

§ 9.6.2.2 Documenting Pain, Suffering and Disability.
The legal assistant should be taught to conduct detailed interviews with clients to document medical history, pain and disability. See the pain, suffering and disability chart shown at Form 9:8.

§ 9.6.2.3 Witness Interviews.
Witness interviews may be conducted by the legal assistant. See generally the discussion at § 5.6.

§ 9.6.2.4 Interviewing Medical Agencies.
From information on the client data sheet, the lawyer can direct or instruct the legal assistant to obtain health records from government or private medical facilities, hospitals, clinics, insurance companies, employers, pharmacies, prosthetic suppliers or other health care providers. See Form 9:9.

§ 9.6.2.5 Authorization to Release Medical Information.
A specific written release of information form signed by the patient or parent/guardian is required to obtain medical records and other data. See Form 9:10. The release should specify what records may be seen, the treatment dates to be included and should be reasonably current. The client may be asked to sign either several undated general or specific authorizations or a blank one which the lawyer or assistant can complete as needed. Many institutions will accept a photocopied release even though the dates are inserted afterward. It is advisable, however, to include the wording "A photocopy of this authorization shall be considered as valid as the original."

§ 9.6.3 Interpretation of Medical Reports.
An assistant who has extensive background and knowledge of medical terms is a major timesaver for the lawyer. When the firm receives a written report or copy of a medical record it should be sent to the assistant for analysis.

§ 9.6.3.1 Further Research.
If the lawyer requires further exploration of any medical-related facet of the client matter, the legal assistant can research, report and digest the problem, using both office search tools and outside library sources.

§ 9.6.3.2 Audiovisual Graphs, Charts and Trial Aids.
The responsibility for designing and preparing any required graphs, transparencies, charts and trial aids should be shared by the lawyer and the legal assistant. The assistant should also work with any artists employed to produce such materials to ensure both that they are accurate and that they convey effectively the information desired.

§ 9.6.4 Investigation, Research and Communication with Outside Medical Facility Personnel.
If additional research is to be done at the lawyer's direction, especially in state and federal agency files such as worker's compensation and Veterans Administration, it is essential to have the correctly executed authority from the client.

§ 9.6.5 Litigation Documents. The legal assistant should be able to aid in preparing interrogatories involving medical questions. The assistant also can aid clients in answering medical questions, answering interrogatories, checking treatment dates, etc.

§ 9.6.6 Assistance at Hearings and Trials. Preparation of a properly indexed hearing or trial notebook with the medical testimony in logical sequence is most helpful to the trial lawyer. See generally the discussion at § 7.2. Obtaining and copying of medical exhibits can be performed by the legal assistant. If medical records or X-ray films are entered into evidence at trial, the assistant should include a reminder in the firm's docket system to prepare a motion to release the exhibits at the close of testimony so the medical facility can have its files returned. The assistant must first determine whether the medical record is on microfilm and, if so, be sure to arrange for a microfilm reader-projector for courtroom use.

§ 9.6.7 Continuing Education and Systems Development. The lawyers and legal assistants in a firm will need to discuss, analyze and improve the medical information delivery system regularly. The assistant can also aid in teaching relief or replacement personnel to perform necessary medical-related functions.

§ 9.6.7.1 Further References for Form Development. In developing further forms and methods, an excellent reference is S. Hornwood, Systematic Settlements (Bancroft-Whitney, 1979). With little revision, a legal assistant could use these forms and checklists for many medical problems in personal injury litigation. Trial preparation, medical releases and fee agreements are also covered in detail. The forms lend themselves to an automated word processing system.

§ 9.7 Worker's Compensation. An example of developing such a system for worker's compensation cases is the labor cases flow chart shown at Form 9:4. Some other forms included in this chapter apply equally to personal injury tort litigation and industrial accident matters. Since state laws and regulations differ widely, the details of industrial injury case management are beyond this chapter's scope. Procedures, forms and checklists must be developed separately for each state.

§ 9.8 Suggested Additional Forms. The firm will doubtless wish to develop additional forms either instead of or in addition to those shown here. Such forms might include the following: Medical creditor guarantee letter, letter to client regarding settlement, covenant not to sue form, form letter regarding interrogatories, form letter setting up medical deposition, form letter to medical creditors to confirm amount owed, form letter to witness requesting interview, and payout form for client fund disbursal on judgment or settlement.

§ 9.9 Bibliography.
AMA Guide to the Evaluation of Permanent Impairment (A.M.A., 1971).
Anatomy & Physiology (Health Education Aids, 1972).
R. Blanchard, Litigation and Trial Practice (West Publishing Co., 1978).
F. Cole, Guide to Medical Reports (Med. Exam. Pub. Co., 1973).
W. Curran, Law and Medicine (Little, Brown and Co., 1960).
Dorland's Medical Dictionary (W. B. Saunders Co., 25th ed., 1974).
A. Frenay, Understanding Medical Terminology (Catholic Hospital Foundation, 1973).
H. Gray, Gray's Anatomy of the Human Body (Lea & Fiberger, 1973).
S. Hornwood, Systematic Settlements (Bancroft-Whitney, 1979).

M. Houts & L. Marmor, Proving Medical Diagnosis and Prognosis (Matthew Bender Co., 1977).

H. McCormick, Social Security Claims and Procedures (West Publishing Co., 2d ed., 1978).

Medical Terminology, an Individualized Approach (Westinghouse Learning Process, 1975).

A. Mosier, Medical Records Technology (Bobbs-Merrill, 1975).

Physicians' Desk Reference (Medical Economics Co., 34th ed., 1980).

G. Smith & P. Davis, Medical Terminology, a Programmed Text (John Wiley & Sons, Inc., 1976).

A. Soukhanov & J. Haverty, Webster's Medical Office Handbook (G. & C. Merriam Co., 1979).

Form 9:1 — Checklist of Legal Assistant Duties in Medical Litigation.
Text — § 9.1.

1. Interview clients regarding medical history, disability, etc.
2. Develop interview checklists.
3. Obtain medical reports.
4. Extract data from medical reports and annotate them.
5. Do research on medical terms; interpret medical vocabulary.
6. Maintain followup system for medical reports.
7. Interpret, annotate and digest insurance reports.
8. Keep disability and/or pain and suffering log, or assist client in doing so.
9. Keep itemized records of medical expenses and related items of special damages.
10. Keep records and compute loss of wages and related benefits.
11. Prepare "medical creditor guarantee" letters as necessary; compile payout data if creditors are to be paid from settlement.
12. Summarize and digest medical depositions.
13. Prepare interrogatories.
14. Assist client with answers to interrogatories.
15. Work with attorneys in evaluating disability, longevity, etc.
16. Attend hearings, with lawyer supervision.
17. Arrange appointment for lawyer with physician and send followup letter.
18. Set up physician's deposition.
19. Take photographs.
20. Investigate and make client aware of public assistance, rehabilitation and disability pension aid.
21. Prepare forms and papers to assist client at Social Security hearings.
22. Prepare exhibits for trial: X-rays, medical models, charts, reports, bills, prosthetic devices, etc.
23. Make subfile for medical evidence.
24. Help client compile dates and data needed for trial testimony.

Form 9:2 — Training Courses and Texts.
Text — § 9.2.3.

Course of Study	Suggested Text
Medical Terminology and Anatomy-Physiology	*Medical Terminology, a Programmed Text* (with Audio-cassettes), G. Smith & P. Davis; John Wiley & Sons, NY (1976)
	Medical Terminology: An Individualized Approach (film strip materials with instruction booklets and tests), Westinghouse Learning Press, Sunnyvale, CA (1975)
	Anatomy & Physiology Health Education Aids, Goddard, KS (1972)
Medical Diagnosis, Evidence and Evaluation of Disability	*Law and Medicine* W. Curran, Little, Brown & Co., Boston/Toronto (1960)
	AMA Guide to the Evaluation of Permanent Impairment American Medical Association, Chicago (1971)
Medical Records, Hospitals, Insurance, Medical Office Practice	*Medical Records Technology* A. Mosier; Bobbs-Merrill, Indianapolis (1975)
	Webster's Medical Office Handbook A. Soukhanov and J. Haverty; G. & C. Merriam Co., Springfield, MS (1979)
Civil Procedure, Litigation, Investigation and Discovery	Federal and state rules of civil procedure
	Litigation and Trial Practice (part of paralegal series) R. Blanchard; West Publishing, St. Paul (1978)
Interviewing and Reporting Forms	*Systematic Settlements* S. Hornwood; Bancroft-Whitney, San Francisco (1979)
Worker's Compensation	Local and state handbook and rules

Form 9:3 — Personal Injury Flow Chart.

Text — § 9.5.1.

CASE NAME: _____ v. _____ FILE NO. _____

DATE OPENED: _____ MANAGING ATTORNEY: _____

Personal Injury Flow Chart: Client/Attorney/Legal Assistant
Check off items as completed.

CLIENT'S FIRST VISIT

1. Receptionist gets basic data.

2. Legal assistant assists client in completing interview form. Form to attorney with comment.

3. Client confers with attorney. If no case, end of matter, and close file. If case has all elements necessary, go on to Item 4.

4. Back to assistant for in-depth interview. Assistant requests following reports: wage slips, state and federal tax returns, insurance claim forms, medical reports, bills. Assistant obtains signed releases; takes photos of injuries. Assistant makes date for client to bring or send in data. Client instructed on use of log sheet (Form 9:8).

   Meanwhile, secretary prepares fee contract. Client and attorney sign fee contract.

5. Tickler followup made.

6. Photocopy of interview sheet to secretary or file manager for opening file.

7. Attorney-legal assistant conference. Assistant directed to get medical reports and digest and to get hospital records copied and digest.

FOLLOWUP

8. As medical reports arrive, analyze, summarize and route to attorney. Read directions at § 9.6 before starting.

9. Start MEDICAL REPORTS section of file. See Medical Report Index.

10. Start SPECIAL DAMAGES WORKSHEET. Read directions at § 9.6.1.2 before starting.

11. Start WAGE LOSS WORKSHEET. Read directions at § 9.6.1.2 before starting.

12. Send reminder letters for delinquent medical reports.

13. Send requests for itemized bills.

14. Attorney-assistant conference.

    A. If not ready to settle or sue, assistant instructed to keep in touch with client, keep records current, continue investigation, arrange medical exams, etc., as necessary.

Form 9:3 *Continued*

    B. If complaint is to be filed, whether drafted by the assistant and approved by the lawyer, or prepared by the lawyer, do the following:

        Provide a list of special damages to date;
        Provide up-to-date summary of disability, with specific diagnosis;
        Provide, if possible, an estimate of permanent disability;
        Summarize client's log sheet on loss of function and pain and suffering.

Form 9:4 — Labor Cases Flow Chart.

Text — § 9.5.1.

INITIAL VISIT

1. Short legal assistant interview with client regarding:
   a. Client's work and personal history
   b. Injuries
   c. Treatment
   d. Disability
   e. Prior hearings/compensation received/offers to settle, etc.

2. Client conference with attorney (if attorney refuses case, close matter here; if attorney takes case, go on to Item 3).

3. Secretary prepares fee agreement and releases for both medical and work history data.

4. Client back to assistant for:
   a. In-depth interview
   b. Client signs releases
   c. Client signs fee contract

DISCOVERY & INTERIM MATTERS

5. Calendar:
   a. All deadlines
   b. Tickler notes to get client medically examined, if necessary.
   c. Other reminders

6. Medical reports requested (follow up for receipt) (see Form 9:10).

7. Worker's compensation carrier file ordered (follow up for receipt).

8. Request permission for examination by doctor of attorney's choice, if necessary — confer with client.

9. Arrangement for medical examination:
   a. Client form letter
   b. Physician form letter outlining problem

10. Medical reports come in.
    Digest, annotate and give to attorney.

11. Confer with client re progress and prepare disability checklist.

12. Do Social Security wage freeze if pertinent to case.

13. Compute wage loss and put on Form 9:6.

14. Confer with lawyer and arrange deposition of physician if necessary.

Form 9:4 *Continued*

GETTING READY FOR HEARING	15. If ready to do so — 　　a. Lawyer will negotiate 　　b. Have assistant set hearing or 　　c. Both of the above. 16. Prepare documents and organize file. 17. Have legal secretary make travel arrangements, if necessary, for client, attorney and medical witnesses.
HEARING	18. Hearing held — attorney/client attend. 19. (Follow up for) receipt of settlement or rejection of claim.
SETTLEMENT, APPEAL OR CLOSE (IF LOSE)	20. Calendar for appeal time. 21. Appeal or close. 　　a. If appealed — draft notice, complaint, or petition, depending on state's court system. 　　b. If win — 　　　1. Compute settlement and fee. 　　　2. Prepare attorney fee petition and order, if court approval required. 22. Settlement draft received. 23. To accounting department for disbursal. 24. Close file and return exhibits.

Working With Legal Assistants

Form 9:5 — Loss of Wages and Profits Summary.
Text — § 9.6.1.2.

CLIENT: Name: _____ CASE NAME _____ v. _____

Address: _____ Case No. _____ Managing Attorney _____

Telephone: _____ DATE OF ACCIDENT _____ S/Lim. _____

Name of injured person (if other   Suit Filed _____ Court _____

than client) _____ Employer _____

Occupation _____ Date employed _____

Include all time lost because of injury and time loss for trips to doctor or therapist, if wages reduced thereby.

Wage Loss

Inclusive Dates Unable to Work	Number Days or Hours Missed ×	Monthly, Daily or Hourly Pay Rate $_____	Usual No. Hours Worked Per Shift	Lost Wages
From To				

Total $ _____
Lost
Wages

LIST HERE: Any pay raises that would have gone into effect per union contract, etc., if they have not been included under the "Wage" column. If there has been any decrease in pay, explain.

Form 9:5 *Continued*

If your employment has terminated, state facts here:

If you have taken a different job, state the name and address of new employer, job description, pay rate and date employed.

LIST HERE: Items of value, such as uniforms, work clothes, safety equipment, laundry allowance, free meals, paid health insurance, etc. that were furnished by your employer. Give dollar value.

ITEM	EXPLANATION	DOLLAR AMOUNT
	Total	$
	Total Wage Loss (from preceding page)	$
	Total Loss to Date	$

Form 9:6 — Special Damages Summary Sheet.

Text — § 9.6.1.2.

DIRECTIONS: Fill in with pencil. Keep totals current.

File No. ____ Client: _____ Date of accident _____
(if not injured party, specify) Birth date _____
Case: _____ v. _____
Managing attorney _____ Age at D/A _____

Medical Expense

Date of Bill	Have Bill	Name & Address of Provider of Services	Date & Itemized Chg.	Total to Date	Grand Total to Date	cc to Opp. Counsel (Date)

Nonmedical losses: (Specify) _____
_____
_____ Total $ _____

Medical Travel Costs

Date	From	To	& Return	Miles	Cost	Purpose of Visit

Total $ _____

Total of all expenses, $ _____
losses and costs

Form 9:6 *Continued*

ITEMS
OF
SPECIAL DAMAGES

Special damages may include, but are not limited to, the following:

1. Costs of examination, surgery, care, treatment or evaluation by physicians, dentists, chiropractors, osteopaths, hospitals, extended care facilities, psychologists or physical therapists.

2. Drugs prescribed by a licensed practitioner.

3. Prosthetic devices, including limbs, artificial eyes, and cosmetic replacement items.

4. Orthopedic appliances including crutches, braces, trusses and special shoes.

5. Equipment purchase or rental including wheelchairs, hospital beds, commodes, special auto equipment or other items recommended by the practitioner.

6. Nonprescription injury-related items purchased at practitioner's suggestion including heating pads, hearing aids, batteries, ointments, vitamins, lotions, disposable gloves, sanitary pads, waterproof pants, shields and sheets for the incontinent paraplegic patient, and other items as applicable.

    The client should be instructed to save all drugstore slips for such items and to keep boxtops or other proof of purchase, taping the sales slip to the item. When making such purchases, the client should ask to have such items rung up separately.

7. Cost of attendant, when necessary, if patient is nonambulatory and requires care.

8. Mileage to and from all medical facilities at the current IRS-recognized cost per mile; or bus, plane, rail or cab fare if applicable.

Working With Legal Assistants

Form 9:7 — Preliminary Client Data Sheet. Auto Accident.
Text — § 9.6.2.1.

                                                                         Date of Accident _____

Directions: Fill in every blank. If inapplicable, write "N/A".

FULL LEGAL NAME _____ Other names used in lifetime _____
Nickname _____ Birth Date _____ Age ____ Age at D/A ____
Social Security No. _____ Marital status _____ Name of Spouse ____
ADDRESS   Telephone: _____
(street) _____ Veteran? ____ If so give number _____
(box no.) _____
city ____ state ____ zipcode ____ U.S. citizen? ____ If not, what country? ____

Children: give names, ages and addresses: (use back if additional space required)

_____ _____ _____

_____ _____ _____

_____ _____ _____

Parent or guardian if client a minor: _____ Address _____

Other family information:

_____

_____

_____

Who referred you to us? _____

EMPLOYMENT:
Were you employed at time of accident? _____
                                      (Employer)   (Address)
Employer's telephone number: _____
Name of supervisor or foreman: _____
Length of employment: _____ Past employment _____
Present occupation: _____
If not working, last date worked _____
Reason: 1. Disability? ____ (a) From illness ____ (b) From injury ____
          2. Termination? ____ (a) From layoff? ____ (b) Quit? ____
          (c) Discharged? ____
Explain any details here:

_____

_____

Form 9:7 *Continued*

What training did you have for this job? _____
Hours regularly worked? _____ per _____ Union contract? _____
Fringe benefits? _____
Wages: $_____ per _____
         (hour/week/month/year)

Dates/hours you missed from work because of accident:
    (Use back if necessary)

Did you file state income tax returns for the last 3 years?_____ If so, where?_____

Did you file federal income tax returns for the last 3 years?_____ If so, where?_____

Do you have copies of these returns you could bring in to us?_____

Do you now or did you at the time of the accident
have other employment (hold a second job)? _____ If so, specify _____

If self-employed, give details here:

The accident: Date _____ Hour _____ Location _____
_____

Full name of opposing party/
defendant: _____ Address: _____

Was anyone else injured? _____ If so, give name and address _____
Other interested parties: _____
Defendant's insurance carrier, if known _____
Police interview? _____ Citation issued? _____
Defendant's car:
Make of auto _____ Was owner driving? _____

Witnesses: Name   Address
_____
_____

Ambulance? _____
              (Name)   (Address)

175

Form 9:7 *Continued*

Explain in your own words what happened:
_____
_____
_____
_____
_____

What caused the accident?

Parties at fault and why?

How could accident have been avoided?

Was alcohol involved? _____ If so, explain.

Your car:
Make and model _____ Serial no. _____

Your driver's
license no. _____ valid? _____   Your insurance carrier _____
Estimated cost of repairing   Address _____
your automobile $_____   Telephone _____

Totalled out?   _____ _____
                 yes   no

Repaired by:

Were photos taken at the scene? _____ (If so, describe)

Did you give a written or oral statement to anyone? _____ If so, specify:

List here any other information you think is pertinent.

Form 9:7 Continued

Injuries: Describe your injuries.

Describe any remaining disability from the accident.

Give names and addresses of all medical facilities at which you were treated. Provide itemized bills for such treatment. Estimated total cost of treatment to date is $ ____

Did you have any hospitalization or surgery as a result of the injury? _____
Explain:

Do you anticipate having any hospitalization or surgery in the future as a result of the injury? _____ Explain:

Are you still under treatment? _____ If so, by whom _____

Has defendant's insurance company offered to settle with you? _____ If so, give details.

Form 9:8 — Pain, Suffering and Disability Chart.

Text — § 9.6.2.2.

Directions for use — Interview client monthly and fill in one of these forms on each visit. After the initial visit, prior history portion will contain only additional items not previously mentioned.

File No. ____ Client: _____ Date of accident _____

Case: _____ v. _____ Birth date _____

Age at D/A

Managing attorney _____ Type of acc: _____

Summary of injuries _____

DIRECTIONS: Put a check mark in appropriate column regarding the following activities: ACTIVITIES (Some activities are designed primarily for females and some for males. Add others to fit your circumstances.)	Did before accident	Can't do	Can do — extreme pain	Can do — moderate pain	Can do — slight pain	Can do now — no pain
Lift heavy objects						
Drive an automobile/truck/motorcycle						
Ride a bicycle						
Work on auto						
Shovel snow						
Mow lawn						
Kneel down						
Squat down						
Walk/jog/run						
Dance						
Do exercises						
Enjoy sexual intercourse						
Do same work as before injury						
Do home repairs						
Saw wood						
Chop						
Do wallpapering						
Paint walls/ceilings						
Lift children						

Form 9:8 *Continued*

ACTIVITIES	Did before accident	Can't do	Can do — extreme pain	Can do — moderate pain	Can do — slight pain	Can do now — no pain
Do grocery shopping						
Make beds						
Scrub floors						
Sweep						
Run vacuum cleaner						
Use lower shelf of cupboards and bottom drawers						
Use higher shelf of cupboards and upper-reach areas						
Do cooking						
Do dusting and cleaning						
Sew						
Wear high-heeled shoes						
Turn head to look behind when driving						
Put chin on chest; hold phone with shoulder						
Garden						
Sit in bathtub with legs outstretched						
Sit on floor/grass/low furniture						
Play tennis/baseball/football/ basketball/golf						
Do laundry						
Hunt/fish/climb mountains/ride horseback						
Snow/water ski						
Swim						

APPEARANCE: Mark all those that apply

____ Weight gain (in pounds) _____ Weight loss (in pounds) _____
____ Limp-Right side _____ Left side _____ Use cane or crutch? _____
____ Posture change?   Wear brace or cast? _____ (explain)
____ Abdominal "flab"?
____ Scars? specify and give location, size and whether permanent.
   Arms _____ Legs _____ Hands _____ Feet _____
   Head _____ Face _____ Teeth _____ Neck _____
   Chin _____ Back _____ Abdomen/chest/hips _____

Form 9:8 *Continued*

Describe any of above here:

Other disfigurement:

Have the above caused any of the following? If so, explain.

1. Change in how you dress.

2. Change in how you believe others perceive you?

3. Change in your image of yourself?

EMOTIONS: Check any that apply, and supply others that may be pertinent. Check only those you believe may be related to your injury — not those that are the same as pre-injury.

Are you:	Tearful ___ Angry ___ "Blue" ___ Tired ___ Happy ___
Explain frequency, etc., if you deem these serious problems.	Sleepy ___ Forgetful ___ Anxious ___ Insomniac ___ Bored ___ Discouraged ___ Hopeful ___ Afraid ___ Alert ___ Lonesome ___ Enthusiastic ___ Specify others here:

PAIN AND HEALTH PROBLEMS: Mark any that apply.

Headaches ___ Fainting ___ Blackouts ___ Dizziness ___ Nausea ___ Ringing in ears ___
Mark if pain in any of following areas: Ears ___ Eyes ___ Head ___ Neck ___ Shoulder L R ___ Back ___ Arm L R ___ Chest ___ Hands L R ___ Fingers (which ones?) ___ Toes (which ones?) ___ Leg L R ___ Hip L R ___ Buttocks ___ Knee L R ___ Abdomen ___ Other: _____

Reactions to medicines? Anesthetics? Hormone imbalance? List any allergy, hives, diarrhea, vomiting, swelling/edema, loss of hair, dry skin/nails, constipation, anorexia, frequent urination, or other medical problem here.

PRIOR HISTORY:
   List below: All prior accidents in your lifetime, giving extent of injury, date it occurred, who treated you and the outcome.

Form 9:8 *Continued*

List here all prior illnesses and conditions you have had requiring medical treatment. Give name of physician who treated you, whether hospitalized, and dates of such treatment and hospitalization.

List here all surgeries you have had in your lifetime. Give name and address of operating physician, whether hospitalized and dates of such surgery; list outcome.

Trauma: List here any traumatic accidents and what treatment you have had prior to the accident in question. If you have had X-rays or other tests list them, the dates they were done and who performed them.

Do you believe your present accident has aggravated an old injury? ____ Explain.

Did you suffer from any chronic pain prior to the present accident? ____ If so, list and give details of any treatment or remedies you have used for such pain.

List here all medications you were taking within one year prior to the accident.

Working With Legal Assistants

Form 9:8 *Continued*

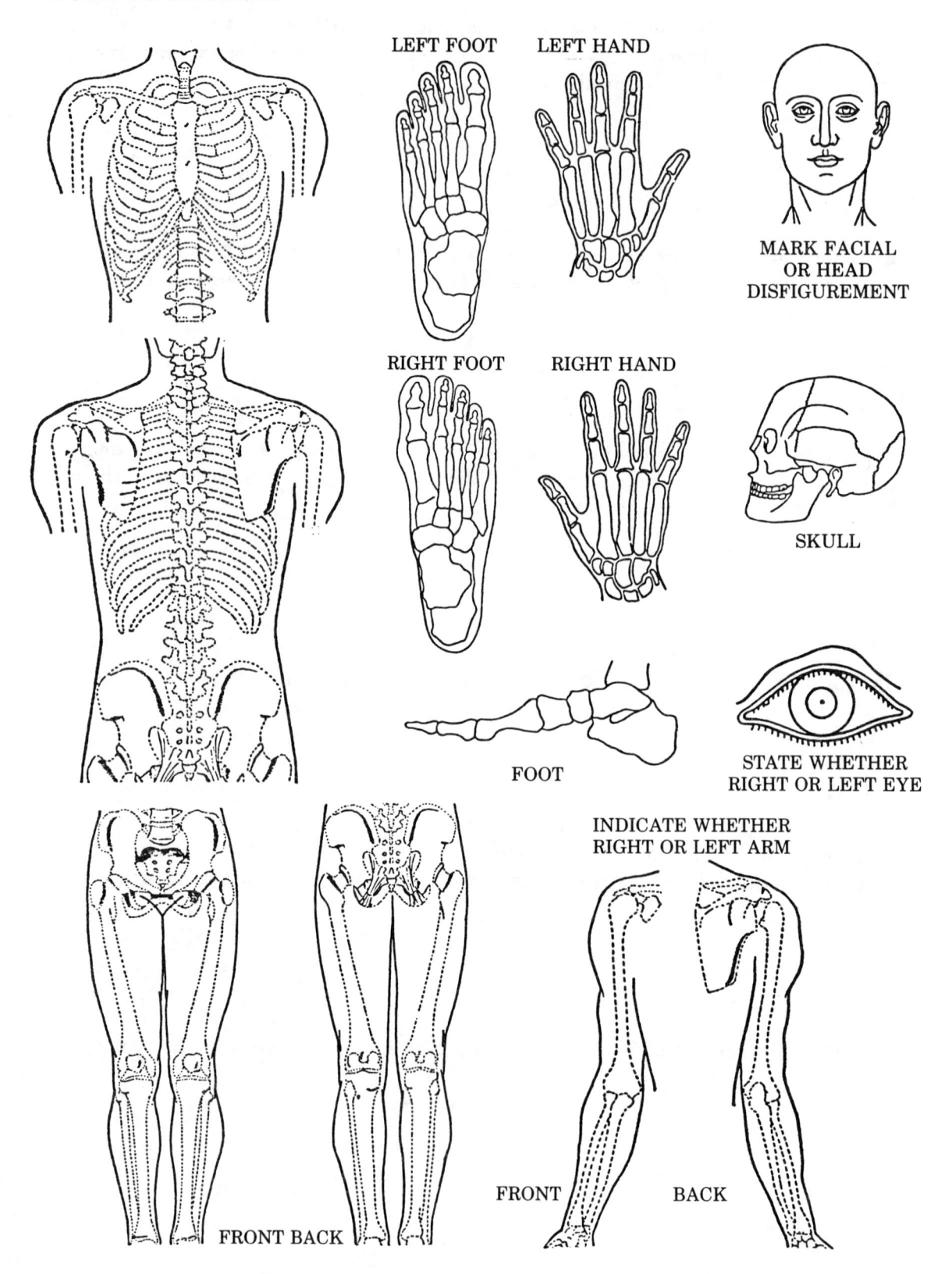

LEFT FOOT   LEFT HAND

MARK FACIAL OR HEAD DISFIGUREMENT

RIGHT FOOT   RIGHT HAND

SKULL

FOOT

STATE WHETHER RIGHT OR LEFT EYE

INDICATE WHETHER RIGHT OR LEFT ARM

FRONT BACK

FRONT   BACK

Form 9:9 — Form Letter to Physicians.

Text — § 9.6.2.5.

Re: _____
    (name of client–patient)

_____
of (address)

Age _____ Injured (Date) _____

Dear _____

We represent your patient, (name of client), in (his/her) claim for injuries as a result of (nature of accident, *i.e.,* auto or other) accident occurring on (date).

In order to evaluate the claim and handle this matter, we need a detailed medical report from you.

Would you please supply the following information in narrative report form:

1. Date(s) patient seen.
2. History of injury.
3. A report of each of your examinations, findings, and results of laboratory and radiological studies.
4. Diagnosis.
5. Treatment rendered, hospitalization and surgery, if any; prescriptions given.
6. Prognosis and recommendations.
7. Estimate of disability, if condition has stabilized; if not, please explain.

Please also send an itemized bill for services to the patient thus far.

We enclose the patient's signed authorization requesting you to give us this information.

If there is a charge for this report, please enclose a separate statement for it and we will remit promptly. The charges should not be included with the charges for treatment, however.

Your cooperation will be of benefit in resolving your patient's legal problems. We appreciate your help.

                        Sincerely,

                        (Law Firm)

                        By _____

Form 9:10 — Authorization for Release of Medical Information.

Text — § 9.6.2.5.

To (Medical Facility):

(Date)

Re: (Patient's name)

Date of accident:

  This will authorize (name of law firm) to examine, inspect and make photostatic copies of all medical reports, records, charts, notes, X-rays, and other data, including correspondence and documents in your possession, pertaining to the undersigned or any child of the undersigned. A photocopy of this authorization shall be as valid as the original.

  You are further authorized to mail to the above law firm, upon request, all medical reports which may be requested and all itemizations of charges for services rendered by you to the undersigned or to any child of the undersigned. You are not authorized to release any information to anyone else without obtaining permission in writing from me or my attorney(s).

Dated: _____

_____
(Client's name)

_____
(Client's address)

10

BANKRUPTCY PRACTICE

H. Rey Stroube III[*]

§ **10.1 This Chapter's Scope.** Employing legal assistants in a bankruptcy practice can be invaluable to the lawyer, both in time conservation and income production. This chapter discusses such employment in relation to the new Bankruptcy Code, 11 U.S.C. § 101 *et seq.* (1978). It will consider three areas: (1) representation of a debtor under Chapter 7 and to some extent Chapter 13 of the Bankruptcy Code; (2) performance of a bankruptcy trustee's duties; and (3) creditor representation under the Code. The functions and duties described in the specific topics will also have some limited applicability in debt reorganization and debt adjustment cases under Chapters 11 and 13. The degree of applicability will in most instances depend on the complexity of the case and the lawyer's preferences.

§ **10.2 The Legal Assistant's Role in Bankruptcy Practice.** The legal assistant's role in bankruptcy practice can best be understood by considering the relationship between the lawyer and the assistant. The primary goal should be maximum use of the lawyer's analytic skills and abilities on the client's behalf, with the minimum time expenditure necessary. An assistant can aid the efficient handling of a client's problem in a bankruptcy practice by relieving the lawyer from having to compile and assimilate empirical data and from handling the many detailed administrative matters that arise. The assistant's most significant responsibilities in a bankruptcy practice are thus gathering and assimilating facts, reviewing them with the lawyer and then aiding the lawyer in taking the necessary actions after the facts have been analyzed.

§ **10.3 Debtor Relief Under the Bankruptcy Code.**

§ **10.3.1 Initial Client Conference.** In most situations the initial conference is crucial to determining the path that a client having significant debt problems and contemplating relief under the Bankruptcy Code should follow through that labyrinth. Initial conferences should not be conducted by a legal assistant alone. It is most important for the lawyer to understand the basic facts surrounding the client's debt problems, make a first impression analysis of the best course of action under the Bankruptcy Code, view the client's demeanor, and analyze the client's desires and ability to deal with debt problems under one of the three basic Bankruptcy Code chapters providing debtor relief. For example, in the case of an individual debtor who is a sole proprietor of a business, an initial factual review and analysis is very important to determine whether it would be in that client's best interest to proceed under either Chapter 7 or Chapter 13 of the Bankruptcy Code. Each of these two chapters provides different forms of relief and places entirely different requirements and demands upon the debtor.

---

[*] Partner, Sheinfeld, Maley & Kay, Houston, Texas.

The legal assistant should attend the initial conference, take notes concerning the relevant facts as described by the client, and learn the client's personality and state of mind to deal better with future financial and emotional conditions. In the ordinary debtor relief case the assistant should have the most significant amount of contact with the client in preparing the case for filing.

§ 10.3.2 Gathering and Assimilating the Facts.

Preparing and filing three basic documents — the original petition, the schedule of assets and liabilities, and the statement of affairs — are essential in any case under the Bankruptcy Code. In a Chapter 13 case the last two documents are combined in the "Chapter 13 Statement." The information contained in these documents will determine whether a case should be filed under the Bankruptcy Code and, if so, under what chapter relief should be pursued. The forms for the documents are found in the official forms published with the Rules of Bankruptcy Procedure. They are also generally available from commercial legal stationery concerns.

§ 10.3.2.1 Completing the Bankruptcy Information Form.

At the conclusion of the initial conference, the lawyer or legal assistant should provide the client a questionnaire to obtain answers to all formal questions pertinent to a filing under any relief chapter of the Code and to provide the data necessary for the preparation of the statements and schedules of assets and liabilities. Form 10:1 is suggested for this purpose. Such a questionnaire contains questions in simplified form. It should provide all data required for a filing under any chapter of the Code. Unless there is a crucial timing problem, the client should be asked to complete and return the questionnaire within a week to ten days. The legal assistant should establish a date for an interview with the client to review the questionnaire.

The purpose of the questionnaire is two-fold. First, its answers provide the legal assistant with the raw data necessary for the preparation of the petition, the schedules and the statement of affairs. They also provide the assistant with information indicating the client's understanding of his debt problems. Equally important, the file must contain a document prepared by the client which states all assets and, most particularly, liabilities to the best of the client's knowledge. After filing a petition for relief, a client may on occasion be confronted with a nondischargeable debt owed a creditor not listed in the schedule of liabilities. The questionnaire signed by the client is the best response to any claim that the lawyer or assistant was told of the existence of such creditor and that it was the lawyer's fault that the indebtedness was not properly scheduled.

The legal assistant should be the one contacted by the client to discuss any problem areas that may arise in preparing answers to the questionnaire. In conferring with the client the assistant must at all times be aware of the absolute necessity for full disclosure of facts and details required in the statement and schedules.

§ 10.3.2.2 Reviewing and Verifying the Client's Answers.

When the questionnaire is completed, the legal assistant should conduct an exhaustive interview of the client, reviewing the questionnaire and making sure that the client has both fully understood and fully answered each and every question. The assistant must ensure that the questionnaire contains a *complete* list of all debts outstanding, either current or in arrears, regardless of their age or delinquency. Contingent and unliquidated claims should be estimated and scheduled. Any indebtedness incurred either out of state or out of the country must also be included. It is not uncommon for a debtor to have left one geographic location to obtain a fresh financial start and then learn to his chagrin that both his debts and the creditors seeking to collect them are highly mobile.

After being satisfied with the completeness of the information, the legal assistant should, as discreetly as possible, confirm the information concerning the amounts of indebtedness. Even though it is not an absolute necessity that the amounts of indebtedness be accurate to the penny, avoiding disputes over those amounts will permit the case to be handled more efficiently and expeditiously. If the amount indicated by a creditor differs significantly from the amount listed by the client, the client should be consulted. If the client has a legal basis for disputing the creditor's claimed amount, the amount asserted by the creditor should be scheduled, with a notation that the amount claimed is disputed by the debtor. A statement as to the nature of the dispute will further aid future conduct of the case.

§ 10.3.2.3 Preparing the Schedule of Liabilities.

The schedule of liabilities requires a distinction between secured and unsecured debts. In the event a debtor has granted a creditor a security interest in or given a lien on a portion of his assets, the legal assistant should confirm the secured claim's existence, the nature of the secured creditor's interest and the assets pledged to secure the debt. In most jurisdictions the information necessary can usually be obtained by requesting a check of the Uniform Commercial Code filings at either the central place of filing (usually the secretary of state's office), the county clerk's office and, in the case of a real property lien, in the real property records of the county in which the real property is located. Also, in certain circumstances, if additional or supplemental confirming documentation is necessary, the creditor holding the interest and collateral can be required to provide the pertinent documentation and recording data.

Another category of special indebtedness to be verified by the legal assistant is taxes owed to any governmental unit. Tax indebtedness may be either secured, priority unsecured or general unsecured indebtedness. The legal assistant should inquire of the appropriate taxing authority as to the status of the tax owing and should confirm its status by checking with the jurisdiction's appropriate agency for recordation, particularly if there is a claim that a tax lien exists.

§ 10.3.2.4 Listing Claims for Exempt Property.

In compiling information concerning the client's property, the legal assistant should be aware of and consult with the client regarding any claims for exempt property allowable under the Bankruptcy Code. The Code provides the debtor with an election of either state or federal exemptions. The facts of each case will determine which exemption provisions are most beneficial. The client and the legal assistant should categorize items of property, *e.g.*, homestead, other real property, home furnishings, tools of trade, etc.; divide these categories into detailed itemization and stated value; and communicate this factual data and the client's desires to the lawyer.

§ 10.3.2.5 Preparing the Formal Petition, Statement and Schedule of Assets and Liabilities.

Upon completing the client interview on the bankruptcy questionnaire, the legal assistant should review the questionnaire with the lawyer. The lawyer should analyze any new information concerning dischargeability of debts, preferences or fraudulent transfers, and questions concerning exemption of property. The assistant should then draft the formal petition, the statement, and the schedule of assets and liabilities, using the information from the bankruptcy questionnaire, the other sources previously discussed and further consultation with the client. After all the information has been verified and confirmed by the client the formal pleadings should be prepared for filing. One procedure might be to mail the draft of the petition, schedule and statement to the client for review, initialing and return. However, this can be time-consuming and often cause delays. It may be easier to prepare the pleadings and then to arrange for an office conference with the client as a final check. If any minor changes or corrections are necessary, they can usually be made immediately without any serious delays or problems. Once approved, the schedules and the statement should be signed by the client and notarized. The client need not sign the original petition.

§ **10.3.3 Creditor Contacts.** Debtor representatives often must deal with and answer questions from creditors. Debtor clients will often desire assistance in responding to such contacts. The legal assistant should become responsible for day-to-day creditor contacts. In most instances a general letter stating that the law firm has been retained to assist with the client's debt problems is helpful. However, no reference to bankruptcy should be made until the petition is ready for filing. Client harassment, action against the client's assets or both may be encountered if premature reference is made to a bankruptcy filing.

Once a case under the Bankruptcy Code has been filed there are circumstances in which creditors should be informed of the filing either by letter or by telegram. This is particularly true if immediate notification of the effectiveness of the automatic stay under § 362 of the Bankruptcy Code must be provided. The statutory automatic stay prevents a creditor from commencing or continuing a lawsuit against the debtor, enforcing a judgment against the debtor or taking any action against the debtor's property. Immediate notification to particular creditors thus may be essential. In most circumstances the bankruptcy court clerk will prepare and mail notices to all creditors of the filing and the stay order. However, this does not occur until there has been a time lapse from date of filing. Section 342 of the Bankruptcy Code provides that "there shall be given such notice as is appropriate." Suggested Interim Bankruptcy Rule 2003 requires that "the court shall call a meeting of creditors to be held not less than 20 nor more than 40 days after the order for relief."

§ **10.3.4 First Meeting of Creditors.** A notice of the date for the first meeting of creditors is included within the court's notice of the filing and of the automatic stay. Under the Bankruptcy Code the bankruptcy judge does not conduct the first meeting of creditors. It will instead be scheduled and conducted by the clerk, a court-appointed trustee or, if in a pilot district, by a United States Trustee or his appointed representative. The legal assistant should inform the debtor of the first meeting of creditors and ensure the debtor's attendance. The debtor's appearance at the first meeting is required by § 343 of the Bankruptcy Code.

At the first meeting, the trustee or examiner and any creditor may examine the debtor. The purpose of this examination is to enable creditors and the trustee to determine if assets have improperly been disposed of or concealed or if there are grounds for objection to discharge. Generally, the scope of the examination under § 343 will be governed by the Rules of Bankruptcy Procedure. These rules provide that only the debtor's acts, conduct or property, or any matter that may affect the administration of the estate or the debtor's right to a discharge are subject to inquiry at the first meeting. Both the lawyer and the legal assistant should consult with and prepare the client for this examination. The lawyer should advise the client regarding his testimony and structure the client's testimony by direct examination.

In some districts, upon the filing of an original petition the debtor and his counsel are given a questionnaire that must be completed and filed with the clerk at the time of the first meeting of creditors. In most instances, this questionnaire repeats substantially all of the questions contained in the statement. It is intended to provide any updated information and to reaffirm the validity of the schedules and statement as of the date of the first meeting of creditors. If, in assisting the client in answering this questionnaire, the legal assistant discovers that additional information has been obtained or a modification of information already submitted with the schedules and statement is required, the assistant should draft an amendment to the appropriate pleading for filing at the first meeting. Thereafter, the assistant should continue to review the facts to determine whether any further amendment to the schedules or the statement may be required.

§ 10.3.5 Post-Filing Matters. Subsequent to the filing of a Chapter 7 case, its administration and the liquidation of assets become the bankruptcy trustee's responsibility. Section 521 of the Bankruptcy Code states the debtor's other required duties. In addition to filing the schedules and the statement of affairs, and appearing at the first meeting of creditors, § 521 requires the debtor to "cooperate with the trustee as necessary to enable the trustee to perform the trustee's duties under this title" and to "surrender to the trustee all property of the estate and any recorded information including books, documents, records and papers relating to property of the estate." 11 U.S.C. §§ 521 (2), (3). The "recorded information" should include all financial data obtained by the legal assistant during the preparation of the schedules and the statement of affairs, except the firm's own work product. Included within this definition are all evidences of debt; evidences of payment; and financial records of any nature kept by the debtor, including bank statements, check registers, check books, ledgers, etc. All such items should be made available to the trustee immediately. Hopefully, the trustee's primary contact will be with the assistant and will be directed toward obtaining "cooperation" and information from the debtor. Efficient initial organization and updating of the file will improve the client's and the firm's ability to comply with the trustee's requests.

§ 10.3.6 Chapter 13 Plans. Chapter 13 of the Bankruptcy Code is designed to adjust the debts of an individual having regular income either from a salary or noncorporate business operation. This contemplated adjustment is accomplished by filing a plan proposing the terms and conditions of debt payment. The details of a Chapter 13 plan are stated in § 1322 of the Code.

One of the mandatory provisions of § 1322 is that "all or such portion of future earning or other income of the debtor" must be submitted in order to enable the execution of the plan. The other significant mandatory requirement is that § 507 priority debts must be paid in full either at confirmation or by deferred cash payment. See §§ 1322(a)(1) and (2).

The Chapter 13 plan does not require that the debtor's assets be liquidated. But the debtor must agree to pay to his unsecured creditors under his plan an amount not less than the creditors would have received if the property of the debtor had been liquidated. This amount can be paid in a lump sum or by deferred payments up to five years in duration. See §§ 1322(c) and 1325(4). An evaluation of the debtor's earning capacity and his non-exempt asset value thus is critical in formulating a Chapter 13 plan. A legal assistant can provide significant benefit by conducting the necessary financial compilations and analysis. The actual details and strategy of a Chapter 13 plan, however, should be decided by the lawyer.

§ 10.3.7 Discharge. The primary goal of any bankruptcy filing is the discharge of indebtedness. The discharge as such is covered by § 727 of the Bankruptcy Code. That section clearly illustrates why it is most important for the legal assistant to aid the debtor with the full disclosure of information, preservation of the debtor's assets, and compliance with the debtor's duties and responsibilities to the court, the creditors and the trustee. For example, if the debtor transfers, removes, destroys or conceals property within one year before the date of the filing of the petition or the estate's property after the petition is filed, with an intent to hinder, delay or defraud a creditor or officer of the estate, the debtor's discharge may be forever barred. Similarly, if the debtor has concealed, destroyed, mutilated, falsified or failed to keep or preserve any recorded information from which the debtor's financial condition might be ascertained (unless such act or failure to act was justified under all the circumstances of the case) the discharge may be barred.

§ 10.3.8 Discharge Hearing. The final, formal, statutory act which must involve the debtor is the discharge hearing. Section 524 (d) of the Bankruptcy Code provides that "in a case concerning an individual, when the Court has determined whether to grant or not to grant a discharge . . . the Court shall hold a hearing at which the debtor shall appear in person. At such hearing the Court shall inform the debtor that a discharge has been granted or the reason why a discharge has not been granted." The hearing also provides an opportunity for the court to review any agreements intended to ratify or reaffirm pre-petition indebtedness that may have been agreed to by the debtor subsequent to the filing of the bankruptcy. Any such agreement or desires to make such an agreement must be disclosed to the court. The court must then inform the debtor that the agreement is not required by law and of the legal effect and consequences of such an agreement, including the consequences of default under the agreement. Finally, the court will determine whether the agreement complies with the mandatory provisions of the Code. 11 U.S.C. § 524 (c), (d). The legal assistant should keep informed of any of the debtor's contacts with creditors. The assistant should also consult with but not advise the client concerning any proposed debt reaffirmation agreement. The assistant should then contact the creditor involved and request that the creditor channel all such proposals and inquiries through the law firm so that an analysis may be made concerning the propriety of any reaffirmation agreement.

If the bankruptcy involves debts which may be nondischargeable if sufficient asset value is not realized to pay them, the legal assistant should monitor and assist in liquidating the estate's assets. For example, if sufficient funds are not obtained to satisfy the tax priority under § 507 of the Bankruptcy Code, the bankruptcy will have no effect on such taxes and they will continue to be the debtor's obligations. Therefore, it is obviously in the client's best interest to ensure that the liquidation of assets generates sufficient funds to pay a portion or all of such debts whenever possible.

This discussion of the legal assistant's role in a debtor relief case suggests that such a filing is often a great financial and emotional burden on the client. The assistant's role in bankruptcy matters is important and requires meticulous and skillful handling of both facts and personalities. Following the guidelines suggested in this chapter should aid the assistant in successfully preparing, filing and completing a case under the Bankruptcy Code.

§ 10.4 The Trustee in Bankruptcy.

§ 10.4.1 The Trustee's Responsibilities. As previously stated, once a bankruptcy is filed, its administration, the analysis of its problems, the recovery of the estate's assets, the actual liquidation of assets and the payment of the claims filed are the bankruptcy trustee's duties. The following discussion describes the functions that can be performed by a legal assistant employed by a lawyer or non-lawyer professional who serves as a bankruptcy trustee.

The bankruptcy trustee's first obligation is to collect the estate's assets and to reduce them to money. The trustee's legal assistant may participate in and conduct a number of the activities related to this general duty. For example, upon receipt of the debtor's schedules and statement of affairs, the assistant should thoroughly review and analyze the facts stated. The assistant should then collect all cash and cash deposits held by the debtor or any other third party. More specifically, the assistant should prepare and transmit demand letters to banks, utility companies and landlords notifying them of the filing of the debtor's bankruptcy, of the appointment of the trustee, and of the rights of the trustee to the funds held by each entity. The letter should conclude with a polite demand that the monies be turned over to the trustee forthwith.

Similarly, the legal assistant should initiate the demands for turnover of property where appropriate. Section 542 of the Bankruptcy Code generally states that the bankruptcy estate's property shall be delivered to the trustee. After consulting with the debtor and reviewing the facts, demands should be made upon any entity that does not comply with the requirements of §§ 542 or 543 where the entity in possession is a custodian as defined by the Code.

§ 10.4.2 Avoiding Transfers of Property. The legal assistant should note any transfers of property or expenditures of funds that have occurred within the statutory periods defined by the preferential and fraudulent transfer provisions of the Bankruptcy Code, 11 U.S.C. §§ 547 and 548. The assistant should also note any facts indicating that any transfers of property of the debtor, debtor's obligations or the attachment of statutory liens have occurred within the period that would allow the bankruptcy trustee to rescind such transfers, obligations or liens under 11 U.S.C. §§ 544 and 545. If any facts exist that might justify invoking the powers of the trustee, the assistant should summarize those facts and discuss them with the trustee or his attorney so that any necessary action can be undertaken. Once such action is determined, the assistant should prepare the appropriate pleadings to recover the property and to rescind the transfer, obligation or lien.

Actions designed to exercise these powers of the trustee are considered adversary proceedings. The procedures to be followed in such proceedings are contained in the Rules of Bankruptcy Procedure and the Suggested Interim Bankruptcy Rules. Under the Bankruptcy Code all such causes of action are appropriately filed in the United States bankruptcy court. There is no longer any dichotomy of jurisdiction between the bankruptcy court, the United States district court or a state trial court. Under the Code the United States bankruptcy court has original but not exclusive jurisdiction over causes of action to recover money or property and to rescind transfers or liens.

§ 10.4.3 Liquidating Property. Once the debtor's property is discovered, recovered and assembled it is the trustee's duty to reduce that property to money either by private or public sale. The legal assistant should analyze each type of such property and the logistics involved in disposing of it. If it is economically more feasible for the property to be sold by private sale, the assistant should prepare the advertisements, place them in appropriate trade or local publications and communicate with potential buyers. In some instances it will be most appropriate that the property be sold at public auction. The assistant should then be responsible for obtaining appointment of the auctioneer by means of an application to and order of the bankruptcy court and should help the liquidator inventory the assets. An appraisal of the property should be obtained in conjunction with either a public or a private sale to support the trustee's obligation to sell the property for the best price obtainable and at a price that corresponds as closely as possible with the appraised market value. Regardless of the method of sale, applications authorizing and approving sales must be submitted to the bankruptcy court. The assistant should be responsible for such tasks.

§ 10.4.4 Preparing Accountings. On completing the sale of the estate's property, the legal assistant should prepare a full accounting of each asset disposed of and the price received. This accounting must be submitted to the bankruptcy court, since the trustee is required to be accountable for all property received and sold. A continuous and detailed accounting of how the estate's property is distributed, the conduct of the liquidation, and the estate's administration is necessary to enable the assistant to prepare a final report and accounting of the estate's administration. This final report and accounting is the trustee's mandatory statutory duty in concluding a bankruptcy case.

§ 10.4.5 Paying Creditors' Claims. After the debtor's estate has been liquidated, creditors' claims must be paid in order of their priority and to the extent funds are available. Priorities are determined in accordance with § 507 of the Code. In bankruptcy estates where funds are available for distribution to creditors, § 704 of the Code requires the trustee to examine proofs of claim and object to the allowance of any improper claim. The legal assistant should review all claims filed by the creditors, note any claims or amounts of claims that are different from those stated in the debtor's schedules, books or records; determine the reasons for those differences; and, where possible, establish the basis for the dispute of any such claim prior to payment. After consulting with the trustee or the trustee's attorney, appropriate pleadings then should be prepared disputing the status or amount of the claim.

§ 10.4.6 Opposing Discharges. The bankruptcy trustee is also required by statute to oppose the discharge of the debtor when appropriate. Because the legal assistant will have the most direct contact with the facts concerning the financial condition, the financial affairs and records, and the conduct of the debtor, the trustee or the trustee's attorney should be immediately notified upon the discovery of any facts supporting the bar to discharge. The categories of facts which may bar a debtor's discharge are stated in § 727 of the Bankruptcy Code. The assistant must become familiar with this section. Determining whether the debtor's indebtedness should be discharged is the final and crucial element of any bankruptcy case. If discharge is barred and the debtor's assets have been completely liquidated, the debtor will not have achieved a full discharge and satisfaction of his debt. An action to bar discharge is not one to be taken lightly or pursued frivolously.

§ 10.4.7 Handling Contested Matters and Adversary Proceedings. Many of the matters previously discussed may become contested matters or adversary proceedings. Adversary proceedings are those stated in Rule 701, Rules of Bankruptcy Procedure. A contested matter is any other issue raised in the course of a bankruptcy over which a dispute has arisen that must be resolved by the bankruptcy court. In virtually all circumstances, the trustee's attorney should handle contested matters or adversary proceedings.

The trustee's attorney is appointed by order of the bankruptcy court. The authorization and criteria for the appointment for a lawyer or other professional person to represent the trustee are stated in § 327 of the Bankruptcy Code. In those cases whose contested matters require the services of a trustee's attorney, the lawyer's role is similar to that of a trial lawyer in any litigated matter. The types of representation are potentially without limit. More often than not, the representation will arise in connection with the pursuit of matters created under the Bankruptcy Code, such as preferences, fraudulent transfers, avoidance of security interests or liens and turnover of property to the bankruptcy estate. The legal assistant employed by an attorney for a bankruptcy trustee as a practical matter should have responsibilities identical to those of an assistant aiding a lawyer in a litigated matter. See generally the discussions in chapters 5, 6 and 7.

§ 10.5 Creditor Representation. The principal objectives of a lawyer representing a creditor in bankruptcy are to see that the client's interests as a creditor are protected and preserved, and that the lawyer's efforts result in payment of the client's claim to the greatest possible extent. A lawyer representing a creditor can also employ a legal assistant to achieve these objectives efficiently. For the most part the assistant's role involves obtaining, evaluating and reporting the essential facts.

§ 10.5.1 Preparing Creditors' Claims. In order to receive payment of all or a part of the amount a creditor believes is owed, a creditor's claim generally must be filed in the bankruptcy. This is done by filing a formal proof of claim with the bankruptcy clerk. The forms for a proof of claim are generally circulated with the notice of the filing of a bankruptcy. They are also available from the office of each United States bankruptcy clerk. The information necessary to complete the form can usually be gathered by the legal assistant. The assistant should also prepare the formal proof of claim in final form.

In circumstances where some complexity is involved in the creditor's claim, the legal assistant may be required to review the client's documents and other business records thoroughly to ascertain or confirm the amount of the claim and its potential status under the Code. In determining the status of a claim the assistant should be aware of the categories of priority unsecured claims that are set forth in § 507 of the Code. The assistant should be aware of the elements necessary to determine whether the indebtedness owed to the creditor can be classified as a secured claim.

§ 10.5.2 Secured Creditors. In the event the firm represents a secured creditor, additional duties should be assigned to the legal assistant. The first is to determine the status of any collateral. All security and mortgage documents should be formally reviewed to determine what property the creditor can claim as collateral to secure the payment of its indebtedness. This can involve review of security agreements, loan agreements, mortgages, deeds of trusts, abstracts of judgment or financing statements to determine the existence of a secured claim. The client's documents should also be reviewed to determine whether the secured status has been properly perfected as required by applicable law concerning the particular type of collateral.

The legal assistant next should determine who is in actual physical possession and control of the collateral. Depending on the type of collateral involved, physical inspection of the property should be made if at all possible. Where items of property such as accounts receivable are involved as collateral the debtor should be asked to produce sufficient books and records to enable the assistant to evaluate and determine such matters as the existence, the amount, the maturity, and aging of accounts receivable and contract rights. The assistant should then inform the lawyer and client of the condition of the collateral and should be authorized, where appropriate, to have it evaluated. In situations involving real property collateral the legal assistant may be called upon to work closely and coordinate facts with a real estate appraiser retained by the creditor client to provide an estimate of its fair market value.

Having a legal assistant perform each of these generally described responsibilities will aid the lawyer and creditor client in obtaining the facts necessary to evaluate the status of the secured claim and to determine what action, if any, should be taken with respect to the status of the collateral. For example, such facts must be considered in determining whether action should be taken to obtain relief from the automatic stay under § 362 of the Code in order to foreclose on the collateral. They are also necessary to determine whether the secured creditor should act under § 363 of the Code to prohibit or condition the continued use of its collateral in the ordinary course of a debtor's business operations. If the bankruptcy is filed under either Chapter 11 or Chapter 13, the lawyer should consider assigning an assistant to monitor the business's continued operation by reviewing its monthly operation reports or by other appropriate methods, as well as reviewing the condition and status of a secured creditor's collateral.

§ 10.6 Summary and Conclusion. Legal assistants should be heavily involved in bankruptcy cases. Obtaining and analyzing sometimes voluminous facts are necessary to prepare, file and administer bankruptcy matters efficiently. Informed contacts with both debtors and creditors are essential parts of the assistant's role. When necessary, that role also should include preparing and filing various pleadings and reports. For these tasks to be performed expeditiously and efficiently, the assistant should have a working knowledge of the Rules of Bankruptcy Procedure and of the pertinent statutory provisions. Having assistants perform the tasks described in this chapter in a professional manner will significantly benefit the lawyer, client and the bankruptcy estate generally.

Bankruptcy Practice — Forms

Form 10:1 — Bankruptcy Information Form.

Text — § 10.3.2.1.

Although we are asking questions about all of your property, it does not mean that you will lose it by filing for bankruptcy.

Complete all questions fully and completely based on all information available to you. If you do not have the information available, make your best effort to obtain the information from all sources.

1. **NAME AND RESIDENCE INFORMATION:**

   A. Full name: _____

   B. Marital status (if married and separated from your spouse, please state "Separated" or if divorced state "Divorced"): _____

   Your spouse's name: _____

   C. Social Security number: _____

   Your spouse's Social Security number: _____

   D. List any other names used by you or your spouse (including maiden name) in the last six years: _____
   _____
   _____

   E. Current address: _____
       Street   City   County   Zip

   F. Telephone number: _____
       Home   Work

   (1) List spouse's current address and telephone number, if different than above:
   _____
   _____

   G. List all addresses you have had in the last six years. If husband and wife are both filing bankruptcy, list addresses for each for the last six years: (Include street, town and zip code)
   _____
   _____
   _____
   _____

2. **OCCUPATION AND INCOME:**

   A. Usual type of work you do: _____

   B. Name and address of CURRENT employer: _____
   _____

   C. Spouse's usual type of work: _____
   _____

Form 10:1 *Continued*

    D. Name and address of spouse's CURRENT employer: _____

    E. How long were each of you at your current job: _____

       If not employed by present employer for at least one year, state the names of the prior employers of either of you and nature of your job
_____
_____

    F. When do you receive payment of your salary (weekly, twice monthly, monthly, etc.)? _____

    G. Have you or your spouse been in business by yourself or with others during the last six years? Yes ____ No ____ If yes, give the name of the business, its address, and the names of others in business with you or your spouse.
_____
_____
_____

    H. Amount of wages that you and your spouse received for last year:

       Your wages: _____

       Your spouse's wages: _____

       Amount of wages that you and your spouse received for the year before last:
Your wages: _____

       Your spouse's wages: _____

       Amount and type of payroll deductions:
_____
_____

       Amount of any other income received by you and your spouse last year (specify source such as welfare, child support, unemployment compensation, etc.):
_____

       Amount of any other income received by you and your spouse for the year before last (specify source): _____

       Amount of income which you and your spouse believe you will receive during the next twelve months:
_____
_____

       Is your employment or your spouse's employment subject to seasonal change or variation?
_____

Form 10:1 *Continued*

3. **TAX RETURNS AND REFUNDS:** (Bring a copy of your income tax returns with you to our office.)

   A. Did you file a federal income tax return during the last three years? _____
   Which year or years? _____

   Did you file a state income tax return during the last three years? _____
   Which year or years? _____

   B. Where did you send tax returns for the last two years? Give city and state to which each form was mailed.

   State: _____
   Federal: _____
   State: _____
   Federal: _____

   C. Have you received any income tax refunds this year? Yes ____ No ____

   Amount: State $_____ Federal $_____

   D. What income tax refunds do you expect to receive this year? _____

   Amount: State $_____ Federal $_____

4. **BANK ACCOUNTS AND SAFE DEPOSIT BOXES:**

   A. Name and address of each bank in which you have had any account (checking, savings, etc.) during the past two years. Include every name on the account and the name of **every** person authorized to make withdrawals:
   _____
   _____

   B. Name and address of each bank you had any safe deposit box in during the past two years. Include name and address of all persons with a right to open the box, describe the contents of the box, and if given up, when:
   _____
   _____

   C. Are you a member of a credit union? Yes ____ No ____ If yes, give its name and address and how much you have saved there:
   _____ $_____
   Name   Address   Amount

5. **BOOKS AND RECORDS**

   A. Have you kept books of accounts or records of any nature or type whether formal or informal which relate to your finances during the last 2 years? Yes ____ No ____ If yes, where are these books or records now (Give names and addresses and include information about check books, bank statements, invoices, statements of accounts, etc.)?
   _____
   _____
   _____

Form 10:1 *Continued*

    B. If any of the records of your financial affairs have been lost or destroyed during the past two years, tell when and how:

    _____
    _____
    _____

6. **PROPERTY HELD FOR ANOTHER PERSON:** Do you have in your possession any property, furniture, etc. that belongs to another person? Yes ____ No ____ If yes, what is the property, who owns it and what is it worth? Include name and address of the owners:

Type of Property	Value	Owned by	Address	Relative Yes or No

7. **PRIOR BANKRUPTCY:** Were you ever involved in any prior bankruptcy action? Yes ____ No ____ If yes, bring **all** papers relating to the action to our office.

8. **RECEIVERS AND ASSIGNEES:**

   A. Is a receiver or trustee holding any of your property? (Generally, a receiver is a person appointed by a court to receive and preserve the property or funds involved in a legal proceeding. A trustee is generally a person appointed by the court who is required by law to care for property and administer its disposition). Yes ____ No ____ . If yes, bring in all papers relating to the property and the person's appointment.

Trustee's Name	Address

   B. Did you give, transfer, deliver, pledge or assign for any reason whatsoever any of your property (including wages) to a creditor within the past year? Yes ____ No ____ If yes, describe the property, its worth and give the name and address of the person you gave it to:

Type of Property	Value	Name and Address of Person Who Has It

9. **PROPERTY HELD BY ANOTHER PERSON:** Does anyone have anything of value that belongs to you? For example, have you loaned any of your property to another person or does a person other than a creditor hold any of your property for any reason? Yes ____ No ____ If yes, who has the article, what is that person's address and what is the article worth:

Form 10:1 *Continued*

Article   Who Has the Article/Address   Value

10. **LAWSUITS AND ATTACHMENTS:**

    A. Have you been a party to a lawsuit of any kind during the past 12 months? Yes ____ No ____ If yes, bring in all papers pertaining to any lawsuits in which you have ever been involved.

    B. Are you suing anyone, or do you have any possible reason for suing someone, for injuries to yourself or other members of your family? Yes ____ No ____ If yes, who are you suing, for how much are you asking and why are you suing?

    C. To your knowledge, does anyone have any reason for suing you (*e.g.*, car accident)? _____

    D. Have you had any property sold in a sheriff's sale or seized by a creditor or creditor's representative during the last 4 months? Yes ____ No ____ If yes, bring any papers concerning those actions. Below, give a description of the property and the names and addresses of any creditors involved, as well as the dates involved.

    E. Has your bank account or paycheck been garnished in the last 4 months? Yes ____ No ____ If yes, give the following:

    Who Received the Money   Amount Taken   Dates: From To

11. **LOANS REPAID:**

    A. If you have made any payments within the last 12 months to creditors from whom you have a loan of any type whether secured or unsecured (not medical bills, charge accounts or other open accounts), give the name of the creditor, the dates of the payments and the amount of the payments:

    Creditor   Payment Dates   Amount of Payment

Form 10:1 *Continued*

    B. Have you paid off any loans in full in the last 12 months? Yes ____ No ____
       If yes, give the following:

Creditor	Address	Date Paid	Amount Paid	Relative Yes or No

12. **PROPERTY TRANSFERS:**

    A. Describe any gifts other than ordinary and usual presents to family members and charities during the past one year. Include the date of transfer and name and address of who received the gift:

    B. Describe any sales or other transfers of any of your property during the past one year. Include the date of the transfer and the names and addresses of the people who received the property:

Property	Amount Received For It	Date	Person It Was Sold to/Address

    C. State the amount of money you actually received for the sale or transfer of any of the property you listed in A and B above:

13. **REPOSSESSIONS AND RETURNS:** If any property was repossessed (taken by a creditor) or returned during the past one year, give the following:

Description of Property	Date of Return or Repossession	Creditor	Address	Value

14. **LOSSES:**

    A. If any property was lost in the past one year due to fire, theft or gambling, describe the property and its value, give the date of the loss and identify all persons involved.

Form 10:1 *Continued*

    B. Did insurance pay for any part of the loss? Yes ____ No ____ If yes, give date of payment _____ and amount paid _____

15. **PAYMENTS OR TRANSFERS TO ATTORNEYS:**

    A. Give the date, name and address of any attorney you consulted during the past one year:

    _____
    _____

    B. Give the reason for which you consulted an attorney during the past year:

    _____
    _____

    C. Give the date and amount you have paid an attorney or any property you have transferred to any attorney:

    _____
    _____

    D. If you have promised to pay an attorney within the past year, give the amount and terms of the agreement:

    _____
    _____

16. **BUSINESS:** If you are in business, list the names of all the partners in your business, or if your business is a corporation, the names of all of the officers, directors and stockholders of the corporation:

    _____
    _____
    _____
    _____

17. **DEPENDENTS:**

    Does either spouse pay or receive alimony, maintenance or child support?

    Husband: _____ How much? _____
    Wife: _____ How much? _____

    If support received, for whose benefit is it received? _____
    _____

    List all dependents other than present spouse for whose support either spouse is responsible. Also state their relation to you. _____
    _____
    _____

18. **BUDGET:**

    A. Please estimate what you believe will be you and your spouse's average future monthly income for the next 12 months:

Form 10:1 *Continued*

    Others (describe) _____ Amount _____
                                            _____ Amount _____

C. If there is a co-signer or guarantor for any of your debts, give co-signer's or guarantor's name and which debt he or she co-signed for or guaranteed:

_____
_____
_____
_____

D. Have you ever been a co-signer or guarantor for someone else's debts? Yes ____ No ____ If yes, give the following:

Creditor	Address	Amount Owed	Date You Co-signed	Person You Co-signed For

ASSET LISTING

1. **REAL PROPERTY:**

Do you own real estate? Yes ____ No ____ Describe and give the location of all real property (lot, house, burial plot, etc.) in which you hold an interest: (if you have the deed or mortgage bring them with you to our offices)

_____
_____
_____

Outstanding mortgage balance: _____

Name of mortgage company: _____

Purchase price: _____ Year purchased: _____

Address: _____

Present value of your house: _____

Is there a second mortgage? Yes ____ No ____ If yes, give the name and address of the company:

_____

2. **PERSONAL PROPERTY:**

A. Cash on hand: _____

B. Do you have any deposits of money in banks, savings and loan associations, credit unions, utility companies, or with landlords or others? If yes, list the name and address of the company and the amount of deposit:

_____
_____
_____

Form 10:1 *Continued*

Husband: _____ (take home pay)
Wife: _____ (take home pay)

    B. Please set out the estimated average amount of the following monthly expenses you believe will be incurred over the next 12 months

       (1) Rent or mortgage: _____

       (2) Utilities: _____
       _____
       _____
       _____

       (3) Food: _____
       (4) Clothing: _____

       (5) Laundry and cleaning: _____

       (6) Newspapers, periodicals, etc: _____

       (7) Medical and drug expenses: _____

       (8) Insurance (not deducted from wages): _____

       (9) Transportation: car loans: _____
                           other: _____

     (10) Entertainment and recreation: _____

     (11) Dues (if not deducted from wages): _____

     (12) Taxes not deducted from wages and not included in mortgage payment:
     _____

     (13) Alimony, maintenance or support: _____

     (14) Other support of dependents not at home: _____

     (15) Other (specify): _____
     _____
     _____
     _____

CREDITORS

1. **SPECIAL CREDITORS:**

    A. Do you owe wages to anybody? Yes ____ No ____
       To whom? _____
       Address: _____
       How much: _____

    B. Do you owe taxes to anybody? Yes ____ No ____ If so, to whom and how much:
       U.S.A. _____ Amount _____ State _____ Amount _____
       County _____ Amount _____

Form 10:1 *Continued*

    C. List your major personal property items such as furniture, tools, appliances, stove, refrigerator, T.V., sewing machine, etc., giving approximate age and value (what you think you could get for it if you sold it). Itemize as completely as possible:

Item	Approximate Age	Value (what you could get for it if you sold it)

If any of the above items are being financed through a company, list the item and the name and address of the company below and bring the financing papers to our offices:

_____
_____
_____

Give an estimate of the value (what you could get for it if you sold it) of the following:

All your furniture: _____ All your clothing: _____

All minor appliances: _____ All your jewelry: _____

All your other household goods (such as dishes, utensils, food, etc.): _____

    D. CARS, MOBILE HOMES, TRAILERS AND BOATS:

        1. Do you have any cars? Yes ___ No ___ If so, give the year, make, model, value and who is financing it: (Also give the amount owed and to what company or bank it is owed)

_____
_____
_____

Form 10:1 *Continued*

    2. Do you have any mobile homes, trailers, and/or boats? Yes ____ No ____ If so, give brand, year, value and who is financing it: (Also give amount owed)

    _____
    _____
    _____

E. **ACCESSORIES:**

    1. Do you own any life insurance policies? Yes ____ No ____

    Company/Address: _____

    How long have you had the policy? _____

    Cash surrender value: _____

    2. Do you own any stocks? Yes ____ No ____ Value of stocks: _____

    3. Do you own any bonds? Yes ____ No ____ Value of bonds: _____

    4. Do you have any interest in or own any machinery, tools or fixtures used in your business or work? Yes ____ No ____ If yes, describe and state what you could sell it for:

    _____
    _____

    5. Do you have any books, prints or pictures of substantial value? Yes ____ No ____ If so, estimate the value of them:

    _____

    6. Do you have any stocks, bonds, certificates of deposit or the like? Yes ____ No ____ If so, estimate the value of them:

    _____

    7. Do you own or claim any other property not mentioned above? (Include livestock or animals other than family pets). Yes ____ No ____ If so, what:

    _____

    Value: _____

    Have you had any previous marriages? Yes ____ No ____

    If so, what is the name of your former spouse? _____

    8. Does anybody owe you any money, alimony or child support?
    Yes ___ No ___ Who: _____

    How much: _____

    9. Do you owe any alimony or child support? Yes ____ No ____ If so, how much and to whom: _____

    _____

    10. Have you been involved in any automobile accidents in the past two years? Yes ____ No ____

    11. Do you expect to inherit any money within the next six months? Yes ____ No ____

Form 10:1 *Continued*

12. Do you expect to receive any settlements from any insurance companies? Yes _____ No _____ Amount: _____

F. **BUSINESS:**

1. If you own or operate a business, does the business have any equipment or furniture of any type used in the business? Yes _____ No _____ If so, list all items and their estimated value:
   _____
   _____

2. Does the business have any outstanding and unpaid accounts receivable? Yes _____ No _____ If so, list the name and address of each person owing money to the company and the amount owed:
   _____
   _____

3. Does the company have any inventory of finished or unfinished goods or merchandise for sale? Yes _____ No _____ If so, list and give your best estimate of value:
   _____
   _____

4. Do you or does your business own or have an interest in any type of property about which we have not asked? Yes _____ No _____ Please describe the property and the value you would give it:
   _____
   _____

I certify that the information contained in this application is true and correct to the best of my knowledge.
Dated: _____   _____
                                           Applicant(s)

Form 10:1 *Continued*

IT IS IMPORTANT TO ANSWER EACH OF THESE QUESTIONS ABOUT EACH OF YOUR CREDITORS. WE CANNOT FILE YOUR BANKRUPTCY WITHOUT THIS INFORMATION

FULL NAME OF CREDITOR AND FULL ADDRESS, INCLUDING ZIP CODE	WHEN DID YOU FIRST OWE THE MONEY? GIVE MONTH & YEAR	DID YOU BORROW MONEY OR BUY ON TIME? IN EITHER CASE, WHAT WAS PURCHASED? OR, WAS THE DEBT FOR A SERVICE, *e.g.* MEDICAL, REPAIR, ETC.	HOW MUCH DO YOU NOW OWE, INCLUDING INTEREST FEES AND LATE CHARGES?	WHERE ARE THE PURCHASED GOODS NOW LOCATED?	DO YOU DENY OWING THE DEBT OR PART OF IT?	NAME AND ADDRESS OF THE COLLECTION AGENCY AND ATTORNEYS WHO ARE TRYING TO COLLECT THE DEBT.

Please ask us for more pages if you need them.

11

DOMESTIC AND FAMILY LAW PRACTICE

Donn C. Fullenweider*

§ 11.1 The Unique Problems in Family Law Practice. The family law matter is unique because of its emotional impact on the client throughout the litigation. A second significant difference from other litigation is the client's usual lack of sophistication in dealing with legal problems, lawyers, conflicts and the court process. The legal assistant can play a significant role in dealing with problems in both these areas.

Though the divorce, custody, support and property division issues facing the client are legal problems, the client often only considers the underlying emotional loss that such problems bring. Often the client permits such considerations to cloud the objectivity needed to begin the rational problem-solving required at any particular time. The divorcing process has been described by scholars as similar to the mourning process. Perfectly simple and logical legal answers are often misunderstood by clients. They are unable to cope with the situation because of their emotions.

§ 11.2 Locating the Appropriate Legal Assistant. Family law lends itself very well to using non-lawyer personnel to assist in "hand-holding," sensitive fact gathering, solving daily problems in the early stages, keeping the client informed, and keeping the lawyer current in a concise fashion as to the emotional and psychological problems that confront such clients. Essential criteria for a legal assistant in the family law field include the ability to accomplish these tasks, relating to the client's emotions and having a sincere interest in such problem solving. Some degree of formal training or interest in areas such as sociology or psychology is very helpful to the assistant in this field. Since the family law assistant often provides a role model as an emotionally stable presence, he or she should have an above average degree of maturity, emotional stability and objectivity. The assistant should be more interested in solving client problems and projecting that interest to the client than in merely performing any required secretarial or clerical tasks.

Some degree of formal training or working knowledge of the family law field is also very useful. Some lawyers believe that the assistant who has been through a divorce and has handled the experience well can be very helpful in identifying with the client and offering a helping hand through the entire frightening process. That background or training can be very useful in explaining basic questions of law first introduced by the lawyer, thereby reducing the emotional trauma connected with the client's lack of understanding of the legal processes and the attendant anxiety brought on by the high-pressure situation into which the client is thrust. Such assistance reduces the client's costs and conserves the lawyer's time for planning, discovery, strategy, settlement negotiations and preparation of legal memoranda.

---

* Shareholder, Haynes & Fullenweider, Houston, Texas.

The average family law case may be handled on the basis of two-thirds legal assistant time and one-third lawyer time. Having a legal assistant in whom the client can place his or her confidence can expedite the fact-gathering and paperwork from the initial telephone interview through the property settlement agreement and judgment of divorce or dissolution. Beyond providing such technical assistance, the assistant is a resource person available to clients who may see small annoyances or details very much out of proportion to the overall picture.

§ 11.3 Stages of the Developing Family Law Case and the Legal Assistant's Role. Most family law cases develop through four stages. First is the decision stage. Here the client is faced with the decisions of whether to file for divorce, seek custody, respond to an action for divorce, and then locate and employ a competent lawyer. Second is maintenance of the status quo. After the decisions have been made to proceed or respond, the client must maintain the status quo with reference to support, custody and possession of certain properties such as the house, car, bank accounts and financial records. Most court rules encourage settling such matters preliminarily at this phase. It is often only concluded by a formal court order affecting the parties during the pendency of an action. The third stage is discovery. This involves locating the information to determine support needs, the ability to support, and the nature and extent of divisible property. These are to be gathered for the lawyer's use in trial or settlement during this stage of the case. Fourth, often directly related to discovery, but essential as a completely separate stage, is the final evaluation stage, in which the lawyer and client evaluate the nature and extent of the properties to be considered by the court, the scope of support needs and the availability of funds. This final stage includes decisions as to settlement or trial. Planning for the final evaluation stage is based on the information acquired during each of the prior stages. The assistant should have an important role throughout this process.

§ 11.4 The Decision Stage. Using a systems approach is as helpful in family law cases as in the other types of law practice discussed throughout this volume. Generally, the client's first office contact will be with the legal assistant. Regardless of whether the office prefers to secure an interview with each caller or is using selective screening by assistants to avoid unnecessary, inappropriate and time-wasting interviews, an assistant can perform well in either capacity. Time-saving information can frequently be obtained during an initial telephone interview. This interview can be handled successfully by an assistant selected for his or her overall judgment and sensitivity to the needs of this particular kind of client.

To determine proper lawyer assignment, the initial telephone interview should obtain such information as names and addresses of parties, other lawyers involved, and the nature and extent of the parties' property. The assistant should be able to form some opinion about the nature of the case, and be able to advise the lawyer as to the client's most pressing needs and any extenuating circumstances. The assistant therefore must be sensitive enough to the potential client's needs to obtain as much information as possible without upsetting the client and to ease any initial problems the client faces. The assistant may advise the client of the hourly fee for consultation and any other particular information with regard to fees or retainers that the client might wish to know in advance. A suggested client telephone interview form is shown at Form 11:1.

When the initial interview occurs, the legal assistant should greet the client, provide refreshments and give the client a detailed information form to complete, explaining that the lawyer would like as much information as possible to assist in the initial interview. During this consultation, the lawyer should not only be concerned about building appropriate rapport with the client, but also with laying the groundwork for rapport between the assistant and the client. The explanation at this session of how the assistant will work with the lawyer and the client throughout the development of the case is important. The lawyer should inform the client about the assistant's position, skills and background, to instill confidence in the assistant's ability. The client should feel free to contact the assistant when the lawyer is not available or to seek help in sorting out problems that may appear larger than they really are. This is a crucial stage; the client should be instructed as to how calls and problems are to be handled during the course of the case. The use of an assistant as an important communicating tool between the lawyer and client cannot be overemphasized. The groundwork for this relationship should be established during the initial consultation.

During the initial interview, the lawyer also should outline the basis for fees, have the client sign a form of fee agreement, obtain an initial retainer or deposit, or instruct the assistant to prepare the fee agreement. Where future periodic payments are expected from the client, the assistant's role in obtaining and collecting money for the firm should also be identified and explained. If the assistant is used in the firm's collection effort at a future date, the client should not be surprised or shocked that the assistant is reminding him or her of a past-due bill. Emotional anxiety can be diminished at this point by making sure the client understands that although the lawyer is busy and may often be unavailable, there will always be a competent person available who can either answer the client's questions, reassure the client that the case is developing as it should or, in more urgent circumstances, contact a lawyer to remedy an emergency situation.

Once the lawyer has concluded the initial consultation, the legal assistant should use the form completed by the client to prepare the original petition or answer, whichever is applicable. See Form 11:2. The lawyer by this time should have determined and instructed the assistant as to what temporary relief, if any, is needed. The assistant should prepare the pleadings and submit them to the lawyer for final review and signing. The assistant should also open the file and determine what subfiles will be needed in each particular case. The property or custody situations involved should be considered. The filing system will vary with each office and case. The assistant's primary responsibility and value, apart from assisting the client directly, is to prepare documents and to organize the file to permit ready document retrieval.

After preparing the petition or answer the legal assistant should complete the steps of filing, serving notice on the opposing attorney or obtaining service on the adversary. Where permitted, obtaining court settings for temporary hearings can be most efficiently handled by the assistant having knowledge of the client's and the lawyer's schedules. Directions to process servers based on information furnished by the client can effectively reduce the time required for serving process. The assistant should then create a tickler system to note all important dates.

§ 11.5 The Status Quo Stage. The lawyers representing the parties will be making important early decisions to maintain the status quo. Often, time is most important. An assistant can reduce the anxieties incident to this stage. It usually will be completed by a court hearing for support and maintenance of status quo. After consulting with the client, the lawyer must determine which assets the client desires or needs to have during the pendency of the action, and what financial information will have to be secured from the client or the opposing party, and then prepare for the hearing. Decisions on such issues as support, custody, visitation and liabilities are crucial. Often this stage calls for practical and common sense solutions to the client's day-to-day problems. Matters such as aiding the client in changing locks, physically dividing clothing and personal effects, arranging visitation schedules, transferring insurance records and obtaining credit can all be handled by the assistant.

When the temporary hearing is scheduled in the more complex case, subpoenas for financial information should be prepared by the assistant at the lawyer's direction. Once the basic plan is made for the temporary hearing and the necessary relief is determined, the assistant should work with the client to gather all financial information with regard to the parties' property and the standard of living to which they have been accustomed. See Form 11:3. When the wife is the client, a temporary support figure must be established. Where possible the check spread, explained below, can be helpful. The assistant and the client should list the client's checks for the past year or more, dividing expenses into categories. The spread sheet provides an overall picture of the amounts spent in each category for the court's information in determining the amount of temporary support and alimony to be awarded.

The spread sheets shown at Form 11:4 are useful in helping the client understand his or her financial picture. This may well be a new experience for the client. Its most valuable aspect is in preparing the client to testify knowledgeably concerning his or her needs during the pendency of the divorce. The assistant can offer advice and reassurance to the client, especially to one who has little knowledge of his or her real financial needs. Some lawyers also use video or audio tapes such as "Preparing the Client to Testify or for Deposition." The assistant should arrange for the client to view or hear the tape.

During this process the assistant should also give the client forms to aid in preparing the estate's inventory and appraisal required in most jurisdictions. Although this may not have to be filed before the temporary hearing, its early completion will better enable the client to discuss the parties' property with the assistant so a complete inventory can be prepared.

The emotional impact of the temporary hearing can be reduced by having the legal assistant attend, explain its processes to the client, answer any questions and reassure the client, especially when there is a delay in the hearing and the lawyer is discussing the matter with opposing counsel or the judge. If the file is organized properly in advance of the hearing the lawyer should be able to rely on the documentary exhibits prepared by the client and the assistant. If the assistant attends the hearing he or she can help the lawyer with exhibit retrieval and will be better able to prepare the temporary order. If not, the lawyer should outline the judge's order and then have the assistant prepare a formal order for the lawyer's review and the judge's approval.

§ 11.6 Discovery. Whether or not the client will be responding to discovery from the opposing party, the legal assistant performs an important task in obtaining information and in organizing, categorizing and determining its completeness. The property pathfinder form shown at Form 11:5 can be useful in helping the client organize financial information. For greatest accuracy, prior financial records should not be the exclusive source of information. The assistant should interview the client using a checklist of this sort to ensure that all assets and liabilities are disclosed. When information is to be furnished by the opposing party, the legal assistant can follow up with informal requests for documentation and by scheduling accountants' and other experts' interviews.

In more complex proceedings, the assistant should arrange oral depositions, as well as subpoenas duces tecum for depositions and hearings. Through the use of form written interrogatories, the assistant can obtain information with little direction from the attorney except as to the information desired and the source to be checked. The filing deadline for motions for compelling answers and production should be logged in the assistant's calendar system. Assistants with financial or bookkeeping backgrounds can be helpful in analyzing and summarizing information of this nature obtained during the discovery stage.

One aid in organizing the information furnished during the evaluation stage, settlement negotiations and trial is a notebook or organizational file analyzing the information obtained during discovery. In preparing a notebook, the assistant should index each major piece of property according to the numbers assigned in the property pathfinder form. A summary should be prepared for the lawyer's review once the client's inventory is completed.

The client and lawyer should determine what type of settlement would be desirable as soon as possible. To aid these decisions, the legal assistant should prepare ledger sheets from the property pathfinder, asking the client to list property with net values and arranging it in columns according to who should receive it. Doing so can save hours of lawyer time in trying to learn the client's needs and expectations. The assistant's experience in this area can also aid in giving the client general ideas of what to expect. Once the inventory and listings are finished, the lawyer should determine whether additional discovery will be necessary.

§ 11.7 Evaluation. Either during or after discovery the assistant can contact appraisers at the lawyer's direction, and furnish them property descriptions and other background information. The assistant should know what information will be required by the appraisers, obtain the information, schedule appointments with the client and appraiser or with adversaries to allow opportunity for examinations, and inform the lawyer if information is being refused by the other party so that appropriate court orders may be obtained. Any necessary reminders to appraisers for reports and evaluations should be prepared by the assistant. Once all necessary appraisals and evaluations have been received, the final working trial and negotiation inventories should be prepared for the lawyer's use in the final stages of the case.

§ 11.8 The Concluding Stages. The legal assistant can be most helpful in updating the property list and informing the lawyer of any changes during the critical negotiation of support or property settlements. The effect on the parties of various proposals can be obtained from other experts. Income tax pro forma statements can be prepared by an assistant or obtained from accountants or a tax expert for use in presenting settlement proposals to the client.

If settlement negotiations are unsuccessful and the case will be tried on any issue, the legal assistant can aid as in any other kind of litigation through the preparation of proposed stipulations; issuance of subpoenas; preparation of witnesses for testimony; organization and obtaining of transportation and scheduling of witnesses; directing final investigation; and, in appropriate cases, presence during the trial with the lawyer for note taking, location of documents and assisting with witnesses. See the discussions in chapters 6 and 7. The assistant can also gather briefs from brief files for use in preparing trial memoranda or oral arguments. Again, the client rapport and contact at this stage can be very helpful, particularly when the lawyer is involved in conferences with the judge, negotiations with other lawyers or preparation of other witnesses. Often the client is left alone in unhappy surroundings. The friend who has helped the client through many troubled stages in the past is able to provide assurance and confidence at a very crucial time.

§ 11.9 The Custody Case. Custody issues present unusual challenges for the use of legal assistants. In such a case the emotional level of the client is even more intensified. Preparation for testimony, analysis of the home situation and obtaining witnesses are much more crucial and perhaps time consuming than in the ordinary divorce case. Daily contacts with the client concerning important issues such as the names of witnesses and obtaining documentation should be handled by the assistant. Often custody cases are resolved in a short period. The lawyer should ask the assistant to do as much of the preparation and location of key witnesses for the hearing as possible.

§ 11.10 General Responsibilities. Throughout the case, the legal assistant should maintain rapport with the client by keeping the client fully informed as to the case's status. This can be done primarily by furnishing the client with all documents filed in the case and the information obtained through discovery. Often, office meetings between the assistant and the client can save the lawyer considerable time, particularly if the assistant reviews with the client documents obtained through discovery. Time records should be kept by the assistant throughout the case to form the basis for interim and final billings. These also can be used by the lawyer testifying on the attorneys' fee issue at trial and in preparing statements to the client for legal services.

§ 11.11 Summary and Conclusion. Because of the unique nature of the emotional problems facing the client in the family law case and the customary lack of client sophistication, a legal assistant can be most effective. As described in this chapter, the gaps between the client's practical and emotional needs, the legal solution and the lawyer's advocacy skills can be bridged most satisfactorily by a legal assistant.

Domestic and Family Law Practice — Forms

Form 11:1 — Potential Client Telephone Interview Form.
 Text — § 11.4.

Date _____ Appointment Date _____ Time _____
Name _____
Phone (h)_____ (o)_____ Type of case _____
Referred by _____ Consultation fee _____
Basic information: no. years married _____ Ages, H ____ W _____
Children, names, ages _____
Custody an issue? _____
Employment and/or income (H) _____

Employment and/or income (W) _____

Business interests or property that you are particularly concerned about? _____
_____
Other information _____
_____

Remarks by legal assistant _____
_____

Other attorneys involved? _____
Suit already filed _____
Hearings scheduled? _____ Taken place? _____
What court? _____ General result _____
Remarks by attorney _____
_____
_____

215

Form 11:2 — Client Information Form.

Text — § 11.4.

PERSONAL AND CONFIDENTIAL

Use additional sheets of paper or the reverse side of this form if necessary.

_____

1. Your full name _____
                   First   Middle   Last   (Maiden)
2. Your present address _____
                   Street   City   State   Zip
3. Home phone _____ 4. Age ____ 5. Birth date _____
6. How long in state _____
7. If you wish mail from this office sent to a different address, please furnish the desired address here _____
8. Employer _____ 9. Business phone _____
10. Business address _____
11. Job title _____ 12. Salary/income _____
13. How did you happen to contact this office? _____
_____

SPOUSE

1. Full name _____
               First   Middle   Last   (Maiden)
2. Address _____
             Street   City   State   Zip
3. Home phone _____ 4. Age ____ 5. Birth date _____
6. How long in state _____
7. Employer _____ 8. Business phone _____
9. Business address _____
10. Job title _____ 11. Salary/income _____

CHILDREN

1. How many children do you have of this marriage? _____
2. How many children do you have of prior marriages? _____ Self _____ Spouse
3. Please list names, ages and birthdates of all children living with you.

_____
_____
_____
_____

Form 11:2 *Continued*

MARRIAGE
1. Are you separated at this time? _____ 2. Date of separation _____
3. If so, how are you supporting your children? _____
_____
4. Date of marriage _____ 5. Place of marriage _____
6. Any prior separations or divorce actions between you and your spouse?
_____
7. Are you considering divorce? _____ Yes _____ No
8. If so, will spouse contest your action? _____ Yes _____ No
9. Is your spouse considering divorce? _____ Yes _____ No _____ Not sure
10. Do you think your spouse will be agreeable as to custody of the children?
_____
11. Has your spouse ever threatened to seek custody of the children?
_____
12. Have you sought personal or marital counseling as a result of marital problems? If so, please state the counselors, number of visits, whether you attended with spouse and status.
_____
_____
_____

13. Do you anticipate any particular problems in this matter with your spouse? Please explain.
_____
_____
_____

14. Do you think your spouse has hidden property from you or may hide property in the future?
_____
_____

15. Here are some problems that can exist in a marriage. Please check any that may apply to your case.
    Finances _____ In-laws _____ Sex _____ Immaturity _____
    Raising children _____ Drinking _____ Drugs _____ Gambling _____
    Another man _____ woman _____
    Physical abuse _____ Mental abuse _____
    No communication _____ Excessive absence _____
    Personality change in spouse _____ in myself _____ other _____
16. What is the condition of your mental and physical health?
_____
_____

17. Is there any danger of extreme violence? Please explain.
_____
_____

18. Are you concerned about being seen coming to or leaving this office?
_____

Form 11:2 *Continued*

19. Please number this list in order of priority to you at this time. Your greatest concern should be numbered "1", and continue on through number "7".

    _____ Knowing my legal rights
    _____ The effects on the children
    _____ Not being taken advantage of
    _____ The total cost of all this
    _____ How can I save the marriage
    _____ Finding someone to help me get through this
    _____ Getting this over as quickly as possible

PROPERTY

1. Who has the best financial information?
    Me _____   Spouse _____   About equal _____
2. Can you give current values or estimates to any of the following:

Present value of home	_____	Current debts	_____
Present balance of mortgage	_____	Bank debts	_____
Property in the home	_____	Charge card debts	_____
Jewelry, collections antiques	_____	Do you have life insurance	_____
My car	_____	Does your spouse have life insurance	_____
Spouse's car	_____	Does your spouse have pension, retirement, or profit sharing plans	_____
Cash on hand	_____		
Cash in savings	_____		
Stocks	_____		
Land	_____		
Other	_____		

Form 11:3 — Financial Information Form.

Text — § 11.5.

	Amount	Who Makes Pymt.	Is Pymt. Made Weekly, Mthly?	Non-Applicable	Applicable
I. Shelter					
A. Rent	_____	_____	_____	_____	_____
B. House payment	_____	_____	_____	_____	_____
C. Utilities					
1. Gas	_____	_____	_____	_____	_____
2. Electricity	_____	_____	_____	_____	_____
3. Water	_____	_____	_____	_____	_____
D. Furniture	_____	_____	_____	_____	_____
E. Maintenance fees	_____	_____	_____	_____	_____
1. Yardman	_____	_____	_____	_____	_____
2. Maid	_____	_____	_____	_____	_____
F. Home insurance (Fire, theft, etc.)	_____	_____	_____	_____	_____
G. Repairs and upkeep	_____	_____	_____	_____	_____
H. Miscellaneous (curtains, carpets, etc.)	_____	_____	_____	_____	_____
I. Appliance payments	_____	_____	_____	_____	_____
J. Telephone bills	_____	_____	_____	_____	_____
II. Food					
A. Household supplies	_____	_____	_____	_____	_____
B. Pet supplies	_____	_____	_____	_____	_____
C. Children's lunches	_____	_____	_____	_____	_____
D. Beverages	_____	_____	_____	_____	_____
E. Family groceries	_____	_____	_____	_____	_____
III. Clothing					
A. Cleaning bills	_____	_____	_____	_____	_____
B. Laundry bills	_____	_____	_____	_____	_____

Form 11:3 *Continued*

Text — § 11.5.

	Amount	Who Makes Pymt.	Is Pymt. Made Weekly, Mthly?	Non-Applicable	Applicable
C. Children's clothing					
1. School clothes	_____	_____	_____	_____	_____
2. Summer clothes	_____	_____	_____	_____	_____
3. Play clothes	_____	_____	_____	_____	_____
4. Shoes	_____	_____	_____	_____	_____
D. Individual clothing					
1. Work clothes	_____	_____	_____	_____	_____
2. Play clothes	_____	_____	_____	_____	_____
3. Under clothes	_____	_____	_____	_____	_____
4. Shoes and hosiery	_____	_____	_____	_____	_____
IV. Automobiles					
A. Liability Insurance	_____	_____	_____	_____	_____
B. Collision Insurance	_____	_____	_____	_____	_____
C. Car payments	_____	_____	_____	_____	_____
D. Gas and oil	_____	_____	_____	_____	_____
E. Repairs	_____	_____	_____	_____	_____
F. Other transportation	_____	_____	_____	_____	_____
V. Doctors					
A. Children	_____	_____	_____	_____	_____
B. Individual	_____	_____	_____	_____	_____
VI. Dentists					
A. Children	_____	_____	_____	_____	_____
B. Individual	_____	_____	_____	_____	_____
VII. Drugs					
A. Children	_____	_____	_____	_____	_____
B. Individual	_____	_____	_____	_____	_____
VIII. Insurance					
A. Life	_____	_____	_____	_____	_____
B. Hospitalization	_____	_____	_____	_____	_____
C. Other	_____	_____	_____	_____	_____

Form 11:3 *Continued*

Text — § 11.5.

	Amount	Who Makes Pymt.	Is Pymt. Made Weekly, Mthly?	Non-Applicable	Applicable
IX. Miscellaneous					
A. Taxes	_____	_____	_____	_____	_____
B. Entertainment	_____	_____	_____	_____	_____
C. Gifts	_____	_____	_____	_____	_____
D. Child care	_____	_____	_____	_____	_____
E. Newspapers or magazines	_____	_____	_____	_____	_____
F. Hair and personal care	_____	_____	_____	_____	_____
G. Church	_____	_____	_____	_____	_____
H. Investments (such as land, etc.)	_____	_____	_____	_____	_____
I. School costs for children (tuition, supplies, etc.)	_____	_____	_____	_____	_____
X. Other	_____	_____	_____	_____	_____

1. How much money does wife take home? _____ How often paid? _____
2. How much money does husband take home? _____ How often paid? _____
3. Do either of these salaries include hospitalization benefits, retirement funds, etc.? _____

Form 11:4 — Financial Spread Sheets.

Checks cleared bank statement   Bank name _____
Period from _____ to _____

Check #	Payee	Amount	Clothing	Cash	Auto	Home Mortgage

Form 11:4 *Continued*

Account # _____

Utilities			Cash	Net Deposit	Miscellaneous Description	Amount

Form 11:4 *Continued*

Deposits cleared bank statement   Bank Name _____
Period from _____ to _____

Date	Source	Amount	Net Salary	Interest	Dividends	Rent

Form 11:4 *Continued*

Account # _____

Transfers			Cash	Net Deposit	Miscellaneous description	Amount

Form 11:5 — Family Law Property Pathfinder.
Text — § 11.6.

Client: _____

File # _____

1. Do you own your home? (If yes, complete "home owned" form.) _____
2. How many other pieces of real estate does the family own?* _____
3. How many motor vehicles does the family own? _____
4. How many checking accounts in family? _____
5. How many savings accounts in family? _____
6. How many certificates of deposit in family? _____
7. How many bonds does family own? _____
8. In how many corporations does family own stock? _____
9. How many debts are owed to family members? _____
10. How many charge card accounts does family hold? _____
11. How many charge accounts without credit cards? _____
12. How many bank loans in family? _____
13. How many finance company loans in family? _____
14. How many pension, profit sharing or retirement plans of which family members are beneficiaries? _____
15. How many safety deposit boxes in family? _____
16. How many partnerships in family? _____
17. How many joint ventures in family? _____
18. How many life insurance policies on members of family? _____
19. How many health and accident insurance policies covering members of family? _____
20. How many auto liability insurance policies now in effect on members of family? _____
21. Did you bring any personal or real property into marriage? _____
22. Did your spouse bring any property into marriage? _____
23. Did you inherit any property during marriage? _____
24. Did your spouse inherit any property during marriage? _____
25. Have you been given anything during marriage by anyone? _____
26. Has your spouse been given anything during marriage by anyone? _____

*Answers to each question are to be supplemented by using forms comparable to "Home Owned" form shown on next page.

Form 11:5 *Continued*

"HOME OWNED" FORM

Client _____
File # _____
Address of home _____
Legal description _____
_____

General description of house _____
_____

Date acquired _____
Total cost _____
Title company _____
Down payment _____
Source of down payment _____
First lien holder _____
Amount of payment _____ Due date _____ Interest rate _____
Second lien holder _____
Address _____
Phone _____
Amount of payment _____ Due date _____ Interest rate _____
Does payment include taxes & insurance? _____
Who lives in home now? _____
Do you wish to live in house during divorce proceedings? _____
Do you wish to live in house after divorce? _____

ATTORNEY USE ONLY: Date _____ Attorney _____
_____ Com., _____ H. Sep., _____ W. Sep., Bec. _____

Right of Reimbursement to _____ Com., _____ H. Sep. _____
_____ W. Sep. $ _____ Bec. _____
_____

12

THE CORPORATE SETTING

Melvin S. Merzon[*]

§ 12.1 This Chapter's Scope. This chapter concerns the use of legal assistants in corporate law departments. It describes the various roles they can perform and how they can be used most effectively in the corporate environment.

The assistant's roles described in this chapter are not exclusive to corporate law practice. Many large law firms can — and do — use legal assistants in much the same manner. What is perhaps different, however, is the approach taken by the corporate law department. This approach is required by the characteristics unique to the corporation that are discussed in the next section.

This discussion does not describe the functions of legal assistants who aid in conducting the business of the corporation itself, *e.g.*, scheduling meetings, completing corporate business forms, transmitting waivers and notices to stockholders, and keeping minute books. These duties are primarily proprietary in nature, in contrast with those performed in law practice. Similarly, this discussion also does not deal with the use of assistants as law librarians.

§ 12.2 Introduction. Increasingly, corporations — even relatively small ones — are relying less upon outside counsel and more upon legal services provided by their own law departments. The practice of sending all legal work to outside counsel has been changed in favor of establishing an internal legal staff to handle as many matters as possible.

At least three characteristics typify corporate law practice. First, the "client" is the corporation itself, even though particular divisions or units may have specialized needs for legal representation. As a result, the corporate lawyer in many instances has a closer client relationship than does the private practitioner. The corporate lawyer may also be more fully aware of particular situations from direct contacts with the actual information sources than would an outside lawyer obtaining information from a client with whom there had been no prior relationship.

Secondly, particularly in large corporations, there is a tendency toward narrow areas of specialization. Although not limited to corporate law practice, this tendency is encouraged by the corporation's structure as a compartmentalized entity.

Finally, corporate law departments must in many instances rely upon outside counsel, particularly in litigation. The corporate lawyer's role then tends to become supervisory. Corporate lawyers often can appear in court on the company's behalf. However, the importance of knowing a particular jurisdiction's statutes, case law and local procedure, as well as the distance involved, usually results in dependence in varying degrees upon local counsel.

---

[*]Attorney, International Harvester Co., Chicago, Illinois.

The corporate use of legal assistants also reflects these characteristics. The kinds of services assistants can perform and the extent of their participation, however, will be determined — as in private law practice — by the attitude and philosophy toward their employment held by corporate officials and staff lawyers.

§ 12.3 The Litigation Assistant Discovery Specialist. The use of legal assistants in litigation practice is not unique to the corporation. In both public and private sectors, in small firms and large ones, including corporate law departments, assistants can aid in every phase of litigation, from the initial claim stage to judgment, post-trial motions and the appellate process. See, *e.g.*, the discussions at chapters 3, 5, 6, 7 and 13. The use of a legal assistant as a "discovery specialist", however, readily lends itself to the corporate setting. In bringing a case to trial, local counsel will work closely with the corporate lawyer. In preparing that lawsuit, the discovery specialist becomes an important member of that team.

§ 12.3.1 Reviewing and Responding to Claims. While a matter which may ultimately lead to litigation is still in the claim stage, the corporate lawyer may review the claim with the legal assistant, discussing its factual basis, the various legal grounds upon which it may be founded and the alternative responsive approaches the company can take. Once such initial determinations have been made, the assistant can establish a file, add it to the company's filing/index system and obtain the necessary data to permit an informed response. Often, based on the assistant's findings, the lawyer can dispose of the claim by rejection or settlement.

§ 12.3.2 Working with Local Counsel. If a claim develops into a lawsuit or if the first notice of claim is the filing of a lawsuit, the legal assistant can assume a major role, working closely with outside counsel and the corporate lawyer. If, for example, the lawsuit has been filed in a jurisdiction distant from the corporate offices, the assistant's first obligation is to ensure that the company's interests are fully protected. Establishing contact with the company's insurance carrier to comply with its notice requirements, promptly retaining local counsel and filing timely responsive pleadings are the first items requiring attention. The extent to which these responsibilities can be delegated to an assistant depends upon the education and experience of the individual involved. The experienced assistant can act as a communications link between outside counsel and the corporate lawyer to ensure that deadlines are met, discovery is progressing and the file is kept current. The assistant accordingly should assume considerable responsibility for the day-to-day details of file control. See the discussion at § 6.4.

§ 12.3.3 Investigating Claims and Obtaining Background Information. Through discovery, the legal assistant can initiate an investigation of the incident causing the claim. The assistant also can become an investigator, establishing appropriate contacts, both within the company and locally, to carry out the investigation, using company personnel or hiring outside investigators as needed. On occasion, the assistant may personally conduct the investigation. This might include locating and interviewing witnesses, collecting reports and statements, and arranging for photographs, sketches, diagrams and accident reconstruction assistance. The assistant can also be responsible for locating and retrieving company-generated documents, such as contracts, purchase orders, bulletins, correspondence and technical reports. Although prompt retrieval of such documents can be time-consuming, it may be vital to defending the litigation. The investigative role places considerable responsibility upon the assistant for sharing the lawyer's discovery burden. It also allows both the corporate lawyer and outside counsel to concentrate on the legal aspects of the matter.

Where the incident is not recent or occurred far from corporate headquarters, the legal assistant may not be able to become as fully involved. Nonetheless, the investigative role remains important. The assistant can coordinate the efforts of others in obtaining documents and materials, statements and reports, particularly any available police, medical or fire department reports. Equally essential is determining whether there were any witnesses to the occurrence, then locating them and making arrangements through local counsel for taking statements.

§ 12.3.4 Indexing Information for Future Reference. In gathering materials for a single lawsuit, the assistant may appear to be spending excessive time in developing company and outside sources of information and expertise. However, having the assistant consistently record and index sources facilitates their later retrieval and saves time and energy if subsequent lawsuits based upon the same or similar allegations require similar data. With the ideas and suggestions of various local counsel, as well as those of the corporate lawyers and assistants, a current index can be a source of vital information and a useful tool available to everyone involved in litigation.

§ 12.3.5 Preparing and Responding to Interrogatories and Requests for Production. Although either local counsel or the corporate lawyer will have final responsibility for submitting interrogatories, the legal assistant can be used to great advantage in preparing them. The assistant will have worked with lawyers throughout the country, each with an individual style and approach and perhaps familiar only with his or her own "territory." By compiling interrogatories from these diverse sources and acting as a clearinghouse, the assistant can identify and recommend specific questions that have proved to be most fruitful in prior use. Collecting and assembling interrogatories and then indexing them for later retrieval for a similar situation is thus an important responsibility. In some instances, the situation presented may be somewhat unfamiliar to local counsel, but not to the assistant. The assistant should be able to determine other instances in which the situation occurred and suggest appropriate interrogatories.

The use of legal assistants is of equal importance in supplying answers to interrogatories and in responding to requests for production. It may often be preferable for initial draft responses to be prepared by local counsel more fully familiar with local requirements. The assistant, however, with ready access to sources of information throughout the company, having established rapport with other company personnel, and having identified company people as sources for specific kinds of information, may be in the best position to furnish the substance of the required responses.

The more interrogatories propounded and the greater the scope of requests for production, the greater should be the legal assistant's involvement. The assistant can, if necessary, spend considerable time in searching for appropriate data, reviewing it to determine the extent to which it may be responsive, and presenting outside counsel with alternative responses for consideration.

On occasion, the company may be bombarded with dozens of boilerplate interrogatories and "shotgun" requests for production which are no more than "fishing expeditions" attempting to uncover enough information to sustain the burden of proof.

In many instances, such interrogatories and requests will have been copied from commercially published form books or interrogatory banks without regard to their specific applicability. The legal assistant may well have encountered similar interrogatories and requests from various jurisdictions around the country and have seen the diverse responses prepared by local counsel. From prior experience with such interrogatories, requests and prior responses, the assistant should be in an excellent position to suggest appropriate approaches for local counsel's use.

Finally, a legal assistant can be responsible for preparing summaries of answers to interrogatories. This will provide both a convenient, time-saving review of discovery material and a factual springboard for taking depositions.

§ 12.3.6 Depositions. Prior to a deposition, the assistant can, working from the previously gathered discovery material, suggest questions to be asked of the witness, facts which only that individual can supply or corroborate, and any areas of exploration to be undertaken. If the deponent is an expert, the assistant should prepare a dossier including the witness's academic background, areas of expertise, citations to lawsuits in which the expert has previously testified and substantive summaries of such prior testimony obtained from the company's transcript collection. That collection can be assembled and indexed by an assistant. An assistant can also digest deposition transcripts for that collection.

At the deposition itself, the legal assistant can be of considerable help. By listening to the testimony and being familiar with the file, the assistant can suggest to the deposing lawyer where additional factual data may be needed and suggest appropriate questions. Any particular responses that do not "ring true" should also be noted for the lawyer's consideration.

Following the deposition, the assistant can provide feedback, sharing thoughts and reactions with the lawyer and acting as a sounding board. This can be done either immediately or later when, with only a cold transcript available, the lawyer wants to recall the deponent's demeanor at the time or his reactions to the questions asked.When the deposition transcript has been furnished, the legal assistant can summarize the pertinent responses. All discrepancies and contradictions should be noted. Depending upon the lawyer's particular needs, the testimony should be digested, abstracted and indexed. See the discussion at § 6.3.2 and Forms 6:3, 6:4 and 6:5.

§ 12.3.7 File Maintenance and Control. The legal assistant can maintain control of the file by reviewing and updating it periodically, adding discovery material and investigative information. This information may be obtained from local counsel, collected from personal efforts, or gathered from various sources both inside and outside the company. By continuously monitoring the file and maintaining open lines of communications between local counsel and the corporate lawyer, the assistant can provide any needed information and alert the lawyer to any developments requiring attention. This will ensure that expeditious progress is made toward trial.

Although not permanently fixed, procedures for the legal assistant's handling of a claim and lawsuit can be systematized and applied to most litigation sections in a corporate law department. There are, of course, aspects of the litigation process which can be handled only by a lawyer. However, much of the litigation work presently handled by corporate lawyers can be easily and properly delegated to assistants.

§ 12.4 The Labor Relations Legal Assistant.

§ 12.4.1 Employment Claims.
When a laid-off, discharged or retired employee applies for compensatory benefits based upon an alleged wrongful or unfair practice by the corporation, there is generally a hearing before a state commission. When the claim is first made against the corporation, the legal assistant can establish the file and conduct an investigation. The complainant's employment records, including any medical data and disciplinary reports, should be obtained from the company's personnel department and a file established. This should be followed by interviews, conversations and discussions with management personnel. From this information and after consulting with the corporate lawyer, the legal assistant can prepare a detailed analysis of the claim for the lawyer in preparation for the hearing.

At the hearing, the lawyer usually presents the company's case. Some states permit representation by nonlawyers; if so, the legal assistant may respond on the company's behalf. The assistant can also attend not only to assist the lawyer in conducting the hearing but also, if an adverse decision is later rendered, to be able better to assist on appeal. Knowing the facts developed at the hearing, the assistant can better conduct any necessary legal research and prepare a legal memorandum supporting the company's position. If necessary, the legal assistant can also assist in drafting the pleadings necessary to perfect the appeal after consulting with the lawyer.

§ 12.4.2 Fair Employment Practices.
When an employee charges the company with employment discrimination, *e.g.*, concerning claimed racial, religious, sex or age discrimination, an administrative hearing generally follows. In preparation for this hearing the legal assistant can obtain the complainant's records and any other relevant background information, create a file and make an investigation. Through conversations and interviews with involved persons, the assistant can provide the corporate lawyer with a complete dossier and report concerning the employee. The assistant can also perform preliminary legal research and prepare a memorandum concerning the legal issues involved. In preparation for the hearing, the assistant's role is the same as outlined for litigation assistants. See the discussion at § 12.3.

Because of the usual complexity of legal issues involved in employment discrimination claims, the company should be represented by a lawyer. An assistant, however, can aid the lawyer in presenting the company's position at the hearing. The assistant's summaries and observations at the hearing can aid in determining any factual and legal issues for appeal. If an appeal is taken, the assistant can then aid in performing any necessary legal research and in drafting the brief.

§ 12.4.3 Worker's Disability Cases.
When an employee or former employee claims worker's compensation for a job-related illness or injury, the legal assistant can establish a file; gather all necessary background data, including all employment information, plant records, and reports of company and other treating physicians; and summarize and digest medical depositions. In these early stages, the assistant can communicate directly with the claimant's attorney and, based upon the information obtained and an evaluation of the circumstances, recommend an appropriate disposition. See generally the discussion in chapter 9.

Where a compensation commission hearing ensues, the legal assistant can aid in drafting pleadings and subpoenas and see that they are properly served. If local practice calls for pre-hearing conferences, the assistant can arrange for them, assume responsibility for handling all administrative matters and provide any needed support to the corporate lawyer. If local practice permits, an experienced assistant may represent the company at that conference. If the conference cannot resolve the dispute, the assistant can prepare the matter for further proceedings in much the same manner as a litigation assistant.

§ 12.5 Creditors' Rights Matters. If an employee falls behind in his personal financial obligations, a supplier becomes insolvent or the corporation is holding property belonging to another, it may become a garnishee defendant in an attachment proceeding brought by a creditor of that principal obligor. In such situations, the legal assistant can, under the lawyer's direction, review the pleadings served on the company to determine if service was proper and if the documents comply with applicable law and local court rules.

The principal defendant's identity, whether an employee or supplier of the company to whom monies are owed or an outside firm which has property in the company's custody, is not always apparent from the garnishment pleadings. These may be the company's first notice of the matter. Accordingly, the legal assistant should gather all available factual data regarding the principal defendant, including his identity, his relationship to the company, the extent to which the company has a monetary obligation to him and the scope of that obligation. If the defendant is an employee, employment, personnel and payroll records should be obtained. If the defendant is a supplier or entity whose property is in the company's custody, the assistant should determine the nature of the property, its location, the terms of the agreement leading to the situation and all other details regarding the transaction. With the corporate lawyer's approval, the assistant can issue instructions to the appropriate offices to withhold payment of funds and inform the court if any amounts are owed to the principal defendant.

If a corporation conducts operations at various locations, considerable coordination of efforts by the assistant may be necessary to determine whether money is owed or property is in fact in its custody. If so, the assistant can prepare any necessary disclosures and authorize payment of funds or release of property when appropriate, again with the corporate lawyer's approval.

§ 12.6 Residential Real Estate Transactions. When an employee is transferred for the corporation's convenience from one location to another, the company may assist in selling the employee's former residence and in acquiring a new one. Depending upon local property law, a legal assistant can be used in this area as well.

Working with the company's realty office, the assistant can aid in the disposition or acquisition of a home by coordinating the company's activities with brokers, title insurance companies and lawyers. After obtaining market appraisals, applying for title searches, reviewing abstracts of title and title documents, and noting for the lawyer's review any impediments to clear title, the assistant can draft preliminary opinion letters, contracts and deeds for the corporate lawyer's review and approval. When the transaction is to be completed, the legal assistant can prepare for the closing by making sure all necessary documents are in order, by determining and allocating funds, fees and taxes, and, at the lawyer's discretion, attending the closing.

§ 12.7 Property Taxes. Corporations must, of course, file property tax returns for each state in which the company has property. The legal assistant can retain property ownership records, updating them as sales or purchases are made; make deeds and descriptions available when needed; check on tax rates and maintain records of assessed valuations; analyze tax assessments and statements for correctness; alert the supervising attorney when an assessed valuation is adjusted; and assist in drafting the company's response to such adjustment. In addition, an assistant can continuously monitor proposed tax legislation affecting the company.

Each state has its individual requirements for tax returns and unique forms and procedures which must be followed. A legal assistant can obtain and compile all necessary information and support data for computing taxes, and assist in completing the tax returns.

Deadlines for tax return filings vary among jurisdictions. The legal assistant can maintain a progress log for each taxing authority in every state with which the company is concerned, recording the progress toward filing. This log should note the dates on which the forms are received, when all information must be obtained from the field, when the return is to be completed and the date when it is to be filed. The assistant thus can ensure expeditious handling of tax information and timely compliance with filing dates.

§ 12.8 Transportation. A corporation dealing in commercial products or consumer goods purchases materials and components for processing, then ships its products or goods to the wholesaler, distributor or consumer. A transportation system is thus an integral part of the company's operations. Depending on the mode of transportation required — road, rail, air or water, or a combination of these — and the destination — intra- or interstate — the company will need to be aware of all applicable federal, state and international transportation law.

A legal assistant aiding the lawyers responsible for advising the company's transportation office can daily review government publications, particularly the Federal Register and specialized reporters, for applicable legislation, rulings and case law. By reviewing and summarizing applicable rules and laws as specifically interpreted, the assistant under the corporate lawyer's supervision can bring any applicable rules to the attention of those with transportation responsibility. The assistant also can provide day-to-day operational guidelines by preparing a useful handbook and maintaining a current index for ready access to such materials.

Working with the transportation office or the company division with transportation needs, the legal assistant can prepare drafts of transportation contracts with carriers for the lawyer's review. In addition, where contract proposals are made by carriers to the company, an assistant can review and summarize them.

An assistant can also aid in processing claims for losses sustained while goods are in the carrier's possession. When damage or loss claims are to be made on the company's behalf or are presented to the company by the consignee, the assistant can initially review the claim and contact all those who have been involved with or have information regarding the shipment. Drafting necessary reports and preparing advisory memoranda for the corporate lawyer as to whether the claim should be negotiated, rejected or paid is another task the assistant can perform.

Finally, a legal assistant can enter into preliminary settlement negotiations with the involved parties on the company's behalf for claims under transportation contracts. If there is no settlement and litigation ensues, the assistant can aid in providing material for its defense.

§ 12.9 Document Reviewer/Analyst. Each year, large corporations generate billions of words in countless documents for myriad purposes. To some degree, all such documents have legal import. Consumer material, advertising, instruction books, warranty statements, repair manuals, insurance policies and retail installment purchase contracts, to name a few, must all be reviewed prior to their release to ensure complete and appropriate disclosure, as well as full compliance with all applicable state and federal laws and regulations concerning content, language and appearance.

A legal assistant can become responsible for initially reviewing such printed materials. Acting as part of the legal staff and responsible to a corporate lawyer, but available to any section of the company requiring review of materials, the assistant can examine draft copies of proposed publications. Checking for legal adequacy of content and propriety of language, the assistant can recommend changes or additions.

A legal assistant can also be employed to simplify contract language and substitute "plain language" for "legalese" in an insurance policy or a contract. Examining warranty statements and other types of consumer-related documents to ensure compliance with the Magnuson-Moss Act and the Uniform Commercial Code is another task for the assistant. Reviewing proposed advertising copy submitted by the company's agencies to evaluate its acceptibility in terms of corporate standards and conformity with state and federal truth-in-advertising requirements can be an additional responsibility.

State and federal regulations or local ordinances may require specific packaging or labeling of products as to quality, content or use, including warnings dealing with hazardous contents. A legal assistant can review any applicable provisions of the Code of Federal Regulations (CFR), rules of the federal Consumer Product Safety Commission, "consensus standards," and guidelines published by representative groups, *e.g.*, the American Society of Testing Materials (ASTM), to determine whether any such requirements exist as to particular products.

Whenever a corporation deals in words addressed to others, the legal implications of such language require the involvement of a reviewing lawyer. A legal assistant, however, can help the lawyer greatly in meeting this responsibility.

§ 12.10 Patents. Much of the work accomplished by a lawyer in obtaining a patent can be delegated to a legal assistant having the necessary technical background. An assistant can confer initially with the company employee who believes his invention may be patentable. From that discussion, the assistant can make some initial assessments regarding the obviousness or novelty of the invention.

If, after consultation with the corporate lawyer, a decision is made to attempt to patent the invention, the assistant should order a novelty search. If the results of the search are promising, the assistant should confer further with the inventor and draft a patent application. After determining that the specifications, *i.e.*, the background, summary, description, claims and abstract, have been properly framed, and upon obtaining lawyer approval, the assistant can see that the application is filed. When an official response, often negative, has been received from the Patent Office, the assistant can review the action and, working further with the inventor and the supervising attorney, draft appropriate amendments for submission. These may ultimately result in the application's acceptance and the issuance of a patent.

Thus, at every step of the processing of a patent application the legal assistant can provide the analytical skill, drafting ability and technical expertise which will result in a successful application. With appropriate education and adequate experience under the direction of a supervising lawyer, the assistant may qualify as a patent agent.

§ 12.11 Antitrust. In today's political and economic climate, a large corporation desiring to expand its business by acquisition or joint venture faces the possibility of a government antitrust investigation. To comply fully with all FTC requests for information, the corporation can use legal assistants to gather, compile and organize necessary statistical information and technical data, and to search for, collect, organize and index relevant documents. As a researcher, the assistant can also digest and abstract voluminous records and lengthy documents.

Should antitrust litigation ensue, the legal assistant can work closely with the supervising lawyer in preparing the company's defense. Such litigation, by its very nature, can initially require production of a staggering number of documents. The responsibility for searching company files in anticipation of or in response to requests for production can easily be assigned to an assistant.

As the search is undertaken, the legal assistant can analyze and catalog each item for later retrieval. A summary of each document should be made to permit easy access and make possible its production when requests to produce are filed. The assistant should also prepare a detailed index to the files to permit their prompt retrieval, acting as a search and reference "librarian" in a collection of tens of thousands of documents. Educated in the fundamentals of antitrust law and conversant with the applicable rules of discovery, the assistant can work with the supervising lawyer to determine whether the assembled materials are discoverable.

The corporate legal assistant in an antitrust case can also compile company witness files in anticipation of depositions. After initial interviews with prospective deponents, the assistant can attend the deposition and assist the supervising lawyer. Summaries of and indexes to the deposition transcript should then be prepared.

In responding to interrogatories propounded to the company, the legal assistant can obtain necessary responsive information and prepare draft answers. The assistant can also become involved in research concerning specific legal issues, Shepardizing, and checking citations for completeness and accuracy.

The antitrust legal assistant should become responsible for the care and control of the mass of information which must be compiled for an investigation and litigation. The assistant should be able to meet the corporate lawyer's needs in locating all documents which must be produced, in providing necessary indexes, abstracts and summaries, and in preparing for trial.

§ 12.12 Legislative Assistant. By doing business in many states, larger corporations subject themselves in varying degrees to their statutes and to regulation by their administrative agencies. The company should be fully aware not only of presently applicable rules and regulations but of proposed legislation and regulations as well, together with their possible effect on the company's operations. The company must be prepared to respond in appropriate and timely fashion. A legal assistant, skilled in statutory analysis, and able to review legislation and the rules of regulatory agencies under the corporate lawyer's direction, can help the company deal with situations and problems, potential or actual, arising from proposed or newly enacted legislation.

The legislative assistant can review each piece of proposed or enacted legislation and trace its legislative history, comparing it with prior versions, reading legislative committee reports and determining its similarity to other versions of the legislation. Working with the supervising attorney, the assistant can note the impact of the legislation on the company; *e.g.*, contract language, limitations or extensions upon product liability, changes in tax liabilities and tax structuring, or changes in product packaging or labeling.

The legal assistant can also determine the existence of regulatory enactments, trace their legislative history and summarize their provisions as they affect the company's operations. Under the corporate lawyer's direction the assistant can, for example, determine whether or to what extent the company's rates for utility services are affected, how workers' disability claims and administrative hearings are to be conducted, in what categories of business operations disclosures must be made or what changes in production must be effected. In fulfilling these responsibilities, the assistant should examine language usage, note various possible interpretations in content based upon any expressed legislative intent, point out ambiguities and unclear expressions, note technical uses and definitions, and suggest the possible impact the enactment might have on the company. Through frequent discussion with and analytical reports from the assistant, the corporate lawyer is better able to keep the company aware of its legal position within each state and to be informed of the need for any changes in the corporation's business.

§ 12.13 **Office Manager/Administrative Assistant.** Like any other business, a law practice requires a manager for its business operations. A corporate law department also must be concerned with efficiently operating within its budget as it provides legal services to the company. An administrative assistant can accomplish a number of important law department administrative duties. For example, the assistant can maintain a central docket system and supervise overall file control when required; maintain, abstract and index for ready retrieval all the company's legal memoranda and briefs; and compile a periodic summary of important events, such as important trials, hearings and deadlines. The assistant can receive inquiries for legal assistance from other company offices and operations and after determining their nature, direct them to the appropriate responsible attorney. The assistant also can compile information about the department's legal activities, *e.g.*, number of trials and hearings and their results; litigation settlements and other compromises; and tabulate and summarize any information on such activities required for the company's annual report to its stockholders.

The assistant can arrange the introductions of newly hired lawyers and provide other help lawyers may require during their first days on the job. The assistant can also handle the logistics of assigning summer law clerks to different lawyers. For a more complete discussion of the legal administrator's role, see the discussion in chapter 2.

§ 12.14 **Summary and Conclusion.** This discussion is not intended to be exhaustive. Rather, it suggests diverse kinds of legal assistance, a composite description based on the author's experiences and discussions with professional and paraprofessional acquaintances and colleagues. Of the various tasks performed, many are, with variation or modification, performed in the private sector as well. This chapter has concentrated its discussion on those legal assistant functions more prevalent in the corporate setting.

The role fulfilled by a corporate legal assistant and the degree of responsibility assigned depends on the nature of the matter and the complexity of applicable law, together with the knowledge, expertise and experience of the individual assistant and the extent to which the corporate lawyer is willing and able to delegate responsibility. Given the proper circumstances, however, there are few limitations on the tasks to which an assistant can be assigned.

13

APPELLATE PRACTICE

Paul G. Ulrich*

§ 13.1 This Chapter's Scope. This chapter concerns employing legal assistants as part of a positively managed appellate practice. It discusses the assistant's role in preparing and presenting individual appeals. It also describes how to employ an assistant in managing the firm's appellate practice generally.

§ 13.2 The Importance, Need and Benefits of Managing Litigation and Appellate Practice. The appellate process is the continuation of litigation begun elsewhere. The facts, procedural background and legal issues involved in an appeal are almost always the result of prior work at the trial level. Even the best appellate brief usually cannot present factual matters not previously included in the record or raise legal or procedural issues not previously presented for consideration.

Contingency preparation for an appeal should thus be begun at the very early stages of the trial level activity. The litigator's obvious primary objective is to resolve a dispute successfully at the trial level. However, should the litigation not be concluded at that stage, a record should have been made that best presents the factual, procedural and legal issues involved either to sustain or overturn the trial level result. Other chapters in this volume describe in detail how to employ legal assistants effectively throughout the trial court process. See chapters 6 through 12. Doing so should substantially improve the quality of trial practice. Thoughtfully managed trial preparation and presentation also should materially increase the likelihood of success in the event of a later appeal.

§ 13.3 Use of Legal Assistants in the Appellate Process.

§ 13.3.1 Preparing Findings of Fact, Conclusions of Law and Judgments. The legal assistant's trial notes can be the starting point for preparing or objecting to any proposed findings of fact, conclusions of law and judgment. Often the trial transcript is not available soon enough to be of assistance. Having concentrated on presenting witnesses and exhibits, the trial lawyer often may not be able to record or to recall sufficiently the necessary details of testimony and other evidence. An assistant can assume those responsibilities. See the discussions at §§ 6.4.3 and 7.9. The assistant's trial notes also provide a quick reference as to whether all necessary testimony and exhibits have been offered in evidence and whether all objections or motions have been made that may be necessary to preserve an issue for later appellate review.

Whether findings of fact are actually supported by the record and conclusions of law correctly stated and dispositive of the issues presented is often central to the appellate court's determination of the correctness of the trial court's judgment. In preparing for or objecting to proposed findings of fact or conclusions of law and judg-

---

* Partner, Lewis and Roca, Phoenix, Arizona. Copyright © 1980 by Paul G. Ulrich. All rights reserved.

ments, consideration should be given for appellate purposes to how the evidence actually relates to the legal theories alleged in the pleadings. An assistant preparing proposed findings of fact and conclusions of law should verify whether all necessary facts have actually been presented and whether they are sufficient to support a legal claim or defense. Similarly, proposed conclusions of law should be reviewed to verify that they follow from and are supported by the facts as found, and are at least arguably correct statements of legal principles. Once an appeal has been taken, it's usually far too late to seek to amend the trial court's findings of fact, conclusions of law and judgment with the benefit of hindsight. Those documents and the underlying record have by then largely become carved in stone.

§ 13.3.2 **Organizing the Record for Appeal.** Once a decision has been made to appeal, an immediate determination should be made as to what should be included in the appellate record and how it should be prepared for proper consideration by the appellate court. The lawyers responsible for the appeal should by then have decided what issues are to be raised in the appeal, how to present the facts and legal arguments concerning them, and how best to delegate responsibility to assistants as the appeal progresses. The details of record designation and preparation will vary according to the particular jurisdiction's rules of procedure. In some instances, it may not be possible or desirable to transmit the entire trial court record or to have all the trial proceedings transcribed. Assistants can participate in deciding on the portions of the record that should be included by reviewing the testimony, exhibits and pleadings in relation to the factual, legal and procedural issues involved in the appeal.

A legal assistant can also be responsible for preparing a designation of record to be transmitted by the trial court and for organizing and assembling the firm's copy of that record. Any necessary deposition or trial transcript summarizing should be completed. The firm's own record should be fully organized, summarized and indexed to permit briefing to begin by the time the record has been transmitted to the appellate court and the date for filing the opening brief has been established.

§ 13.3.3 **Preparing Briefs.** The lawyers responsible for the appeal should discuss its factual, procedural and legal issues with the legal assistants who will be working on it at the earliest possible stage. The lawyers should decide on the best general approach, method of presentation and issues to be emphasized. Following orientation discussions with the assistant, they can delegate substantial portions of the factual and legal research and writing. In drafting a brief, the assistant should be able to use the previously prepared transcript summaries and legal memoranda, or materials from the firm's information retrieval system prepared in similar cases. An assistant can also perform much of any necessary independent legal research under the lawyer's supervision concerning either issues not previously presented or issues that need to be reconsidered or expanded. For discussions of legal research retrieval systems see, *e.g.*, P. Ulrich, *Organizing and Preserving Our Work Product*, 21 LOEM 215 (1980); P. Ulrich, *Developing Information Retrieval and Other Law Firm Management Systems*, Legal Economics, Summer 1978, at 19; M. Wallace, *Designing a Manual System for Legal Research Memoranda*, Legal Economics, Mar./Apr. 1980, at 27. Discussion of appellate advocacy techniques is beyond this chapter's scope. For articles concerning appellate advocacy, see the bibliography at § 13.5.

The keys to success in legal assistant involvement in preparing briefs or appellate memoranda are clear direction, communication and control by the lawyer responsible for the appeal, and organized procedures for delegation, supervision and review as the work progresses. The assistant's responsibilities must be stated clearly and organized properly from the beginning so the task does not seem too large or complex and so the brief can be prepared in an organized, section-by-section manner.

Legal assistants can also substantively cite-check and critically analyze an opponent's brief. An opponent may occasionally indulge in wishful thinking on whether particular testimony was given or legal authority actually supports his position. Assistants can be most helpful in identifying such errors and suggesting any necessary corrections or responses. To aid in this process, they should be sufficiently familiar with the record to be aware of significant facts, issues or arguments the opponent may have overlooked, ignored or misstated.

§ 13.3.4 **Participation in Oral Argument.** A legal assistant who has participated in the trial, record organization and briefing processes described in this chapter should also be able to aid the lawyer during oral argument. By having worked extensively with the record, the assistant may be able quickly to identify record references in response to questions from the court or arguments by opposing counsel. The lawyer arguing the appeal, of course, should be fully prepared concerning the facts and issues involved and for likely questions or opposing arguments. Having a "moot court" argument before each actual argument is most helpful in such preparation. If, however, the assistant is also fully familiar with the facts, their significance and where they exist in the record, the lawyer can concentrate on the larger picture of the legal issues in relation to the most important facts to make the appellate argument most effective. Having two persons fully familiar with the record substantially increases the likelihood of making the most of the appellate argument opportunity.

§ 13.3.5 **Preparation of Motions for Rehearing, Responses or Applications for Further Review.** When the appellate court has issued its decision, a motion for rehearing, objection to such motion or application for further review by a higher appellate court may be necessary. The considerations previously stated suggest that a legal assistant also can be helpful in preparing such documents. For example, either the court's opinion or the opposing party's motion for rehearing may reflect misunderstanding or misstatement of the applicable facts, procedural background or legal issues. A legal assistant should be able to identify the correct information and present it accurately. Similarly, any petition or application for further review before a higher appellate court also involves defining, analyzing and stating the applicable facts, procedural issues and legal arguments as they have become refined in the appellate process. An assistant also can prepare drafts of such documents under the lawyer's supervision.

§ 13.3.6 **Summary and Conclusion.** The approach to involving legal assistants in appellate practice described in this chapter assumes both that the assistant has become fully familiar with the case and that the lawyer responsible for the appeal is able and willing to organize, supervise and review to encourage maximum delegation of responsibility at each stage of the appellate process. This is by no means an abdication of the lawyer's responsibility. Instead, those responsibilities also include teaching, training, developing and reviewing the assistants' work to increase their skills and ability. For more detailed discussions of such matters see chapters 1 and 2.

Some assistants may well have more aptitude for appellate work than others. Intellectual ability, research, analytical and writing skills, and aptitude must all be carefully considered and developed before making such assignments. Proper use of assistants, however, can substantially improve the quality of a firm's appellate practice, reduce the amount of lawyer time involved for the more routine and time-consuming aspects of factual and legal research and drafting, and thus lower the appeal's cost to the client. Use of assistants should also result in a more organized, methodical approach to appellate practice, substantially improving the quality and clarity of both written and oral presentations.

§ 13.4 Use of Legal Assistants in Managing an Appellate Practice. This chapter's discussion has thus far concerned the legal assistant's role in preparing and presenting particular cases on appeal. In a larger firm, a number of litigation assistants might perform such tasks as part of their general litigation responsibilities. Litigation assistants should be encouraged to follow their cases into the appellate process when required so that their knowledge of them can continue to be used efficiently. In addition, however, there is another distinct role — the appellate assistant — which may be either a full-time or part-time assignment. Those activities should be supervised and directed by one or more lawyers responsible for handling the firm's appeals. The following discussion describes an appellate management system involving both lawyers and legal assistants that can be used in any firm, regardless of its size. The responsibilities discussed may either be divided between a single lawyer and assistant-secretary or among a number of lawyers, assistants and secretaries.

§ 13.4.1 Basic Roles. The basic roles in an appellate management system include those of the appellate lawyer, the trial lawyer and the appellate assistant. The appellate lawyer should be responsible for all matters relating to appellate procedure and for the quality of all written and oral presentations. As examples, the appeal must be properly initiated. Remaining trial level proceedings must be stabilized to the extent necessary while the appeal is pending. All procedural steps must be accomplished efficiently, systematically and on time. All briefs, motions and other appellate papers must be well-written, well-argued and technically accurate. All oral arguments must be organized and presented persuasively. Any necessary rehearing, review and further trial level procedures must then be accomplished.

Even though the appellate lawyer may be in charge of the case while it is on appeal, the trial lawyer should continue to be consulted and involved as the appeal progresses. Often, the trial lawyer has had the primary client contact and desires to retain general responsibility for the appeal. The appellate lawyer's role in such instances may thus be more limited and specialized, oriented toward procedure and quality control.

The trial and appellate lawyers should agree on how their responsibilities will be divided before the appeal is initiated. There should also be discussions concerning whether to take the appeal at all, the likelihood of success in relation to the client's situation and objectives, and the issues involved and record required to present the appeal most effectively. These discussions should communicate the trial lawyer's knowledge and perspective of the case, provide the appellate lawyer an opportunity to review it substantively as early as possible, and facilitate the process of organizing and delegating the tasks required to prepare and present the appeal.

Management of both the substantive and procedural aspects of the firm's appellate practice should be centered in one or more designated appellate lawyers for greatest efficiency and quality control. The more routine, detailed appellate management tasks, however, should be delegated to one or more specially trained appellate assistants working under the appellate lawyers' supervision. This person may be a full-time appellate assistant or may also have responsibilities as a litigation docket clerk, legal assistant or secretary. The appellate assistant's responsibilities include working closely with the appellate lawyers in monitoring the status and meeting the procedural requirements of all the firm's appeals. The appellate assistant may also assist in preparing appellate records, briefs and procedural motions.

§ 13.4.2 **The Appellate Assistant's Responsibilities.** The appellate assistant should maintain a comprehensive docketing and calendaring system, and prepare or review, docket and file all appellate papers under the appellate lawyer's supervision. The assistant should also be responsible for the technical accuracy of all record references and citations in briefs and memoranda. The assistant should verify that the record transmitted to the appellate court is complete, that all necessary fees are timely paid and that the appeal is properly docketed by the appellate court clerk. The assistant should also be responsible for preparing and filing any required abstract, excerpt of record or appendix.

Another portion of the appellate assistant's duties should include developing, organizing and maintaining under the appellate lawyer's supervision a complete file of appellate forms, checklists and procedures. Maximum benefit can thus be obtained from prior experience and each recurring appellate situation can be dealt with properly. A number of state court appellate practice texts are beginning to appear. See, *e.g.*, Arizona Appellate Handbook (State Bar of Arizona 1978); Appellate Procedure in Texas (Texas Bar Foundation, 2d ed. 1979); Washington Appellate Practice Handbook (Washington State Bar Ass'n 1979). To the extent they are available, such texts increase lawyers' awareness of appellate practice and greatly facilitate training of appellate assistants. Should one not exist in a particular state, the firm's appellate lawyers and assistants should together develop and maintain their own procedural guides, checklists and forms.

§ 13.4.3 **Elements of an Appellate Management System.** The appellate assistant should maintain a master appellate docketing and calendaring system under an appellate lawyer's supervision. This system consists of checklists and time sequence summaries for all appellate filing deadlines, status sheets for each appeal, a dockets file showing all forthcoming deadlines both for the firm and its opponent, a monthly appellate calendar and quarterly reports concerning the status of all pending appeals. For an example of a civil appeals time sequence adapted from the *Arizona Appellate Handbook* see Form 13:1.

The importance of preparing time sequence summaries cannot be overemphasized. They enable the appellate assistant quickly to determine each appeal's status at any time in relation to all applicable forthcoming deadlines or events. If no such summary is available, preparing one under an appellate lawyer's supervision should be one of the appellate assistant's first assignments.

A sample appeal status sheet appears at Form 13:2. Each status sheet should contain the caption and list the firm's lawyers and opposing counsel, the parties, a brief summary of the issues, and the dates on which all documents are due, filed, transmitted or received. The status sheet permits reviewing the history and status of each appeal quickly without having to retrieve and examine each file individually.

The appellate assistant's dockets file is a tickler calendar system maintained and reviewed in addition to the individual status sheets. A card is maintained for each appeal by date order in perpetual calendar fashion showing the deadline for the next action to occur, whether by the firm or the opponent. A sample of such a card appears at Form 13:3.

The appellate assistant should also prepare and distribute an appellate calendar twice each month. An example of such a calendar appears at Form 13:4. The appellate calendar shows all entries in the dockets file for the next 30 days. The calendar makes it possible for all lawyers involved to become aware of and plan to meet all forthcoming deadlines. Opponents' filing deadlines should also be recorded and carefully monitored to confirm timely filings and to plan for preparing any necessary responsive documents. The appellate assistant can also be delegated responsibility for preparing any necessary motions to dismiss should opponent's papers not be timely filed. The appellate docket can be maintained as a portion of the firm's general litigation docketing system. Maintaining both an appellate docketing system and a general litigation docketing system, however, provides a double safeguard. In any event, a separate appellate calendar is essential. General litigation calendars often report only immediate deadlines, not those up to thirty days in the future. The longer lead time is necessary to plan for preparing and filing briefs and other papers on time without last-minute crisis or confusion.

The appellate assistant should also prepare a quarterly status report on the existence and status of all the firm's appeals. This report, the firm's appellate inventory, reminds all lawyers involved of those appeals, even though they may not be active currently. See Form 13:5.

The purpose of these forms and procedures is to provide a system sufficiently redundant so that it is virtually impossible for any appeal to be forgotten or for any deadline to be missed. The system, however, is only as reliable as the people responsible for its operation.

§ 13.4.4 Docketing and Routing Systems. An appellate management system will be successful only when the appellate assistant promptly receives copies of every appellate document prepared or received by the firm. If this does not occur, papers may easily become lost, misplaced or filed without being docketed. Such an omission may well be fatal if the appellate assistant and the appellate lawyers involved are not aware that the document exists.

Every document received must be docketed by the appellate assistant and reviewed by the appellate lawyer as soon as possible. The assistant should enter its receipt and the next action date on the appeal status sheet and the docket file card. The document should then be circulated with a routing slip to all lawyers concerned. The routing slip also should indicate the next relevant deadline and confirm that all necessary persons have reviewed the document before it is filed. The appellate assistant and the responsible appellate lawyer should also review all of the firm's outgoing appellate documents before they are filed to ensure that all technical requirements have been met and that all documents are in proper form. The appellate assistant should be responsible for docketing all such papers.

Another most important rule is that no one should retain a document in his or her office without first having it docketed and circulated. If someone feels compelled to retain the document, another copy should be made for docketing and circulation. Under no circumstances should a document simply remain with the lawyer receiving it without the knowledge of the appellate assistant and appellate lawyer. If this occurs, the likelihood of missing the deadline for the next step is substantially increased.

§ 13.4.5 Other Appellate Responsibilities. The appellate assistant's role should be defined in relation to the roles of other legal assistants also participating in particular cases as discussed at § 13.3. The appellate assistant may also become involved in the substantive aspects of a particular appeal. Regardless of whether this occurs, however, the appellate assistant should ensure that all briefs and other appellate papers are in proper form, that they have been thoroughly cite-checked and Shepardized, and that they are timely filed. The appellate assistant should also see that the firm's copy of the record on appeal is current, complete and correct.

Regardless of who actually prepares the briefs on appeal, the trial lawyer should remain involved in reviewing, analyzing and discussing them. The trial lawyer's participation is most helpful in ensuring that no errors have been made concerning what occurred at trial, that the appeal is argued as well as possible and that the trial lawyer's perspective of the issues has been respected. A part of the review process for each brief and in each stage of the appellate process should include conferences for these purposes involving the appellate lawyer, the trial lawyer, the appellate assistant and any other lawyers or assistants working on the appeal.

Related responsibilities for the appellate assistant can include indexing briefs and appellate memoranda for the firm's internal information retrieval system, being responsible for maintaining the information retrieval system generally, and reviewing recent decisions to note any appellate procedure issues that should be called to the lawyers' attention or included in the firm's appellate management system. The appellate assistant should also be responsible for the preparation of briefs by outside printers or by the firm, including proofreading final draft manuscript and page proofs. Standard formats for briefs required by the applicable rules of procedure should be developed, distributed and followed consistently throughout the firm.

The appellate assistant should be also responsible for preparing and filing any required request for oral argument. The appellate lawyer should then see that supplementary research is completed shortly before oral argument and that any necessary supplemental briefs, memoranda or authorities are filed. The appellate assistant may also become involved in conducting the supplementary research and preparing such documents.

Once the appellate court has issued its decision, the appellate assistant should prepare a timely statement of costs on appeal. The assistant should also review opponents' cost statements for timeliness and reasonableness, and prepare any necessary objections under the appellate lawyer's supervision. The appellate assistant may also participate in preparing and filing motions for rehearing or any responses or objections to such motions, or any petition or other application for review by higher appellate courts.

Once the appellate process has been completed, the case will probably be returned to the trial lawyer for any further required proceedings. The appellate lawyer and assistant, however, may retain responsibility for obtaining an entry of formal judgment, conducting further proceedings in accordance with the appellate court mandate, obtaining payment of costs on appeal, filing a cost statement at the trial level or handling any matters stayed at the trial level while the appeal was pending.

§ 13.4.6 Summary and Conclusion. Appellate procedures are highly structured and specialized. Regardless of the variations in detail from one jurisdiction to another or the firm's volume of appeals, a complete, comprehensive appellate management system is essential. It need not be elaborate or expensive. It is most effective when operating as an extension of the firm's existing litigation management system. The appellate assistant has a most important function in such a plan.

Operating without any appellate management system, however informal, may well create situations where missed deadlines and last-minute crises can jeopardize clients' interests and lawyers' peace of mind. There is no justification for permitting such situations to occur when an organized, systematic approach to appellate practice management can be implemented to meet the firm's professional responsibilities to its clients and to the courts.

§ 13.5 Bibliography. The following materials are representative of the literature available on how to write a good brief:

J. Appleman, Approved Appellate Briefs (1958).
M. Pittoni, Brief Writing and Argumentation (3d ed. 1967).
R. Stern and E. Gressman, Supreme Court Practice §§ 13.6-13.13 (5th ed. 1978).
H. Weihofen, Legal Writing Style (1961).
F. Wiener, Briefing and Arguing Federal Appeals §§ 20-90, at 37-274 (1967).

Reference works on writing style include:

G. Rossman, Advocacy and the King's English (1960).
G. Miller, *On Legal Style*, 43 Ky. L. J. 235 (1955), including Appendix B (a bibliography on English and jurisprudence reference works).
W. Strunk, Jr. and E. B. White, The Elements of Style (2d ed. 1972).

References concerning appellate oral argument include:

S. Abrahamson, *Some Thoughts About Appellate Argument*, Wis. Bar. Bull., Feb. 1979, at 41.
M. Closen and M. Ginsberg, *Preparation and Presentation of The Oral Argument in a Court of Review*, 13 New Eng. L. Rev. 265 (1977).
J. Davis, *The Argument of an Appeal* (delivered to the Association of the Bar of the City of New York, October 22, 1940).
E. Devitt, *The Search for Improved Advocacy in the Federal Courts*, 13 Gonz. L. Rev. 897 (1978).
W. Erickson, *Effective Appellate Advocacy*, Colo. Law., September 1978, at 1548.
J. Godbold, *Twenty Pages and Twenty Minutes — Effective Advocacy on Appeal*, 30 Sw. L. J. 801 (1976).
J. Harlan, *What Part Does the Oral Argument Play in the Conduct of an Appeal?*, 41 Cornell L. Q. 6 (1955).
R. Jackson, *Advocacy Before the Supreme Court: Suggestions For Effective Case Presentations*, 37 A.B.A.J. 801 (1951).
I. Kaufman, *Appellate Advocacy in the Federal Courts*, 79 F.R.D. 165 (1978).
J. Napoli, *Forceful Brief Writing and Oral Argument*, 12 Trial Law. Q. 82 (1977).
A. Reilly, *Courtroom Advocacy*, 8 Cap. U. L. Rev. 185 (1978).
R. Simons, *Effective Appellate Advocacy*, N.Y. St. B.J., January 1976, at 18.
R. Stern and E. Gressman, Supreme Court Practice, ch. 14 (5th ed. 1978).
J. Wallace, *Wanted: Advocates Who Can Argue in Writing*, 67 Ky. L. J. 375 (1978-79).

F. Wiener, Briefing and Arguing Federal Appeals (1967).

R. Wydick, *Plain English for Lawyers*, 66 Calif. L. Rev. 727 (1978).

See generally the Winter 1978 issue of *Litigation*, devoted generally to appellate topics.

Working With Legal Assistants

Form 13:1 — Outline of Procedural Steps and Time Limits.
Text — § 13.4.3.

After an appealable judgment or order has been entered in superior court, the following steps, set forth in the normal order of their filing, are usually necessary in the Arizona state court system to ensure that a civil appeal will be considered on its merits.

1. Notice of appeal and bond or authorized substitute filed.

    A. Appellant files both within 30 days after entry of the judgment or order. ARCAP 9(a), 10(a).

    B. If an ARCAP 9(b) post-judgment motion is filed, appellant files a notice of appeal from both the judgment and the order disposing of the motion, and a bond or substitute within 30 days after formal order is entered. ARCAP 9(b), 10(a).

    C. Cross-appellants file both within 20 days after the notice of appeal is filed. ARCAP 9(a), 10(a).

    D. Appellants who appeal pursuant to statutes with special appeal limitations must file both within specified statutory time periods. ARCAP 9(a), 10(a).

    E. Appellants exempt from bond requirements file notice of appeal only within 30 days after entry of the judgment or order. ARCAP 10(d).

2. Preparation fee to superior court paid.
    Appellant pays when notice of appeal filed and appellee pays if and when notice of cross-appeal filed. See Fee Schedule.

3. Transcript of proceedings ordered and designated.

    A. Appellant orders within 10 days after notice of appeal filed, and files within the same 10-day period a designation of transcript portions and statement of issues to be presented if partial transcript is ordered. ARCAP 11(b).

    B. Appellee files supplemental designation of partial transcript, if any, within 10 days after service of appellant's designation. ARCAP 11(b).

    C. Appellant notifies appellee within 5 days if he refuses to order additional transcript. Appellee may then order additional transcript or apply to superior court for order compelling appellant to do so. ARCAP 11(b).

    D. Party ordering transcript files notice of satisfactory arrangements for payment of court reporter within period allowed for ordering. ARCAP 11(c).

4. Indexing and transmittal of record on appeal including reporter's transcript of evidence.
    Superior court clerk numbers, indexes and transmits record within 40 days after notice of appeal filed unless extension is timely ordered, and serves copy of index on all parties. ARCAP 11 (a).

5. Appellate court fees paid.

Form 13:1 *Continued*

    A. Appellant pays within 30 days after clerk's notification of receipt of record on appeal.

    B. Appellee (and cross-appellant) pays within 30 days after clerk's notification that record on appeal is filed and appeal docketed (date appellant pays fees). See Fee Schedule.

6. Briefs filed.

    A. Appellant's opening brief filed within 30 days after clerk's notification of filing of the record and docketing of the appeal. ARCAP 15(a).

    B. Appellee's answering brief filed within 30 days after service of appellant's opening brief. ARCAP 15(a).

    C. Appellant's reply brief, if any, filed within 15 days after service of answering brief. ARCAP 15(a).

7. Petition for transfer to supreme court.
Filed by any party, if at all, within 10 days after last brief is filed or time for filing it has expired. ARCAP 19(a).

8. Request for oral argument.
Filed by any party, if at all, within 10 days after last brief is filed or time for filing it has expired. ARCAP 18.

9. Oral argument, if requested, and disposition of appeal.

10. Statement of costs on appeal.

    A. Filed by prevailing party on appeal within 10 days after notice of appellate disposition mailed by clerk. ARCAP 21(a).

    B. Objections to statement of costs filed, if at all, within 5 days after service of statement. ARCAP 21(a).

    C. Reply to objections filed, if at all, within 5 days after service of objections. ARCAP 21(a).

11. Motion for rehearing in court of appeals.

    A. Losing party on appeal files, if at all, within 15 days after notice of appellate disposition mailed by clerk. ARCAP 22(a).

    B. Prevailing party files objections to motion for rehearing within 15 days after service of the motion. ARCAP 22(a).

12. Petition for review by supreme court.
Losing party on appeal files in court of appeals, if at all, within 15 days after denial of motion for rehearing. ARCAP 23.

13. If petition for review is granted.

    A. Parties file four additional copies of the briefs with clerk of the supreme court. ARCAP 23.

Form 13:1 *Continued*

    B. Petitioner pays filing fee to the supreme court clerk within 15 days after notice.

    C. Prevailing party files statement of costs on appeal within 10 days after notice of supreme court disposition mailed by clerk. ARCAP 21(a).

14. Motion for rehearing in supreme court.

    A. Losing party on appeal files, if at all, within 15 days after notice of appellate disposition mailed by clerk. ARCAP 22(b).

    B. Prevailing party files objections to motion for rehearing within 15 days after service of the motion. ARCAP 22(b).

15. Appellate court mandate.
    The appellate court issues its mandate at the conclusion of all appellate proceedings. The record on appeal is then returned to the superior court for any further proceedings necessary.

Appellate Practice — Forms

Form 13:2 — Appellate Status Sheet.
Text — § 13.4.3.

File No. 15066-999
Budgeted fee $ _____

IN THE
COURT OF APPEALS
STATE OF ARIZONA
DIVISION ONE

WILLIAM F. RANDOLPH,	No. 1 CA-CIV 5432
Plaintiff-Appellant,	
vs.	MARICOPA County Superior Court No. C-633999
ALEXANDER JOHNSON, JR.,	
Defendant-Appellee.	

OUR CLIENT: Randolph, Appellant

APPEAL LAWYER: Anderson   TRIAL COURT LAWYER: Thompson

ASSOCIATE WORKING ON APPEAL: Meyers

OPPOSING COUNSEL: Herbert Ellis, Ellis & Whitley,
    234 North Central, 85003

APPEAL FROM JUDGMENT OF 12-5-__

ISSUES INVOLVED: Contract dispute

STAGE AT PRESENT:

1-2-__   Filed our notice of appeal, cost bond, transcript designation. Our record due (40 days up) 2-13-__

2-10-__   Ct. of appeals received record.
    Our filing fee ($25) due 3-13-__

3-13-__   Our fee paid.
    Their fee ($15) due; our opening brief due 4-12-__

4-12-__   Filed our opening brief. (delivered)
    Their answering brief due 5-12-__

5-12-__   Filed their answering brief. (delivered)
    Our reply brief due 5-29-__

5-29-__   Filed our reply brief. (delivered)
    Our request for oral argument due 6-8-__

Form 13:3 — Appellate Docket File Card.

      Text — § 13.4.3.

Randolph v. Johnson   15066-999   Anderson
1 CA-CIV 5432 (C-633999)   Meyers

  1-2-__   Filed our notice of appeal, cost bond, transcript designation.
             Our record due (40 days up) 2-13-__

  2-10-__ Ct. of appeals received record.
             Our filing fee ($25) due 3-13-__

  3-13-__ Our fee paid.
             Their fee ($15) due; our opening brief due 4-12-__

  4-12-__ Filed our opening brief. (delivered)
             Their answering brief due 5-12-__

  5-12-__ Filed their answering brief. (delivered)
             Our reply brief due 5-29-__

  5-29-__ Filed our reply brief. (delivered)
             Our request for oral argument due 6-8-__

Appellate Practice — Forms

Form 13:4 — Appeals Calendar.

Text — § 13.4.3.

APPEALS CALENDAR
February 1 – February 28

DELINQUENT?
1-26   Anderson*   Wayne v. Brinkman, *National Title* (99999-066)
        Jones   Their opening brief due.

___

2-1   Fields*   Bailey v. IC, Janus Properties, *Univ. Ins.* (11111-022)
        Worth   Our answering brief due.

2-3   Fields   Jefferson v. *Lincoln* (56789-123)
        Johnson   Their opening brief due.

2-4   Williams*   *Adams* v. Collingwood (99999-023)
        Meyers   Their reply brief due.
        Thompson

2-9   Williams   Kingsley, *Amer. Productions* v. Industrial Ins. (90134-098)
        Allen   Our motion for rehearing due.
        Connors

2-11   Fields   Arthur v. *Ridgeway*, Jamison (Keep track only)
                         Their brief due.

2-14   Anderson*   *Powell* v. United States (43256-998)
        Gilbert   Their brief in opposition due.
        Friedson

2-21   Williams   *Carson* v. Pima County (98765-432)
                         Our filing fee due.

2-23   Fields   Randolph v. IC, *Lee Foods, U.S. Insurance* (11222-022)
        Johnson   Oral argument, 1:30 p.m., Dept. C, Johnson to argue.

2-24   Williams   Yaeger v. Sun City Schools (*Mutual Insurance*) (09877-257)
        Hill   Their record due (40 days up).

Notes
*   Denotes Appellate Lawyer
        Firm's client
( )   File number may be included with entry for reference
        (Keep track only) entries are listed per lawyer's instructions.
N.B.   Case may appear on calendar more than once, depending on due dates.

Form 13:5 — Appeals Status Report.
Text — § 13.4.3.

Appeals Status Report

Briefing Not Yet Complete:

CBA*	*Carson* v. Pima County (9th)	Our filing fee due 2-21-__
ASW	*Andrews* v. United States (USSC)	Their brief in opposition to Petition for Cert. due 2-28-__
RMF	*Roy* v. IC, Baker, Portland Insurance (CA)	Our reply brief due 2-14-__
ASW	*Ellison* v. Harcourt (CA)	Their cross-appellants reply brief due 2-7-__

Awaiting Oral Argument: To Be Argued By:

ASW	*Van Dyke* v. Walter (9th)	Williams
CBA	*Charles* v. Crandall (SC) (set for 2-26)	Hill
ASW	*Crawford* v. General Laboratories (CA)	Connors
RMF	*Smith* v. IC, Red Rock, Minnesota Ins. (CA)	Fields
CBA	*ALA Construction* v. Dwyer, Murphy (9th)	Anderson

Awaiting Decision: Date Argued:

CBA	*Powell* v. United States (USSC)	Their brief in opposition filed 12-30-__
RMF	*Harrison* v. Vista, Campbell (9th)	Oral argument waived.
ASW	*Bailey* v. State (CA)	12-15-__
CBA	*U.S. Insurance, Wiseman* v. IC, Peters (CA)	1-7-__

Awaiting Motion For Rehearing, Petition For Review, Or Certiorari Or Decision Thereon, Or Mandate:

ASW	*Riley* v. Buck County (9th)	Petition for Certiorari due in Washington 2-20__
ASW	*Stevens* v. Hallmark (CA)	Their Petition for Review granted 12-22__

Notes

*   Denotes Appellate Lawyer

( ) Appeal court involved

N.B. If appellate practice is large, total number of active appeals in each category may be included in report.

INDEX

SUBJECT MATTER INDEX

Subject	Section
Accident reconstruction expert, information required from	5.6.3
Accounting of assets, bankruptcy	10.4.4
Administrative assistant	2.8, 12.13
small firm	2.8.1
income production	2.8.3
medium to large firm	2.8.2
Adversary proceedings, bankruptcy	10.4.7
Affordability of legal services, assistants' effect on	2.2.1
Agencies, information source in skip-tracing	5.5
Allocation of personnel positions, federal	3.3
Answers to interrogatories, summarizing	6.3.1.4
preparation of by litigation assistant	8.10
Antitrust litigation, corporate assistant duties in	12.11
Appeal briefs and documents, preparation of	13.3.3, 13.3.5
Appeal docket file card	13.4.3
	Form 13:3
Appeal, management of trial record prior to	13.2
Appeal status report, quarterly inventory	13.4.3
	Form 13:5
Appeal status sheet	13.4.3
	Form 13:2
Appellate assistant, generally	13.1, 13.3, 13.4.5
responsibilities	13.3, 13.4.2
skills required	13.3.6
Appellate calendar	13.4.3
	Form 13:4
Appellate practice	1.2.1, 13.2
management of	13.2, 13.4, 13.4.6
use of assistants in	13.4
Appellate management system	13.4, 13.4.6
elements of	13.4.3
lawyer/assistant roles in	13.4.1
Assertiveness	4.6.1
Assigning lawyer	1.6

Working With Legal Assistants

Subject	Section
Assistants, selection of	1.3, 2.2.5, 9.2
Attorneys' fees, public view of	2.2.1
Audiovisual aids, medical-legal practice	9.6.3.2
Authorities, use of in trial	7.7.3
Authorization for release of medical information	9.4.1, 9.6.2.5 Form 9:10
Bankruptcy assistant's responsibilities	10.2
Bankruptcy information form	10.3.2.1 10.3.2.2 Form 10:1
Bankruptcy petition	10.3.2 10.3.2.5
Bankruptcy practice, assistant's role in	10.1, 10.2, 10.6,
Chapter 13 statement	10.3.2
trustee's duties	10.1, 10.4
Benefits in employment of assistants, generally	2.9
Bibliographies	
appeals	13.5
legal assistant program managers	1.10
medical-legal assistant	9.9
Billing rates for assistants	1.5
increases in	1.5
Bookkeepers/accountants, relationship with assistants	2.4.3
Briefs on appeal, preparation of	13.3.3
"Broker" of assignments	4.6.2
Budget, income and expense of assistants	1.5
Business cards, use of in seeking assistant position	4.4.3
Business entities, research of	6.2.2.3
Calendar of assignments, assistant's	4.6.2
Calendar monitoring and follow-up	8.6, 9.6.1.5, 13.4.4
Case background, investigation	5.3.2
Case decisions in trial practice	7.7
Case status report, insurance litigation	8.15, Form 8:5
Certification procedures	4.5.2
Chapter 13 statement, bankruptcy	10.3.2, 10.3.6
Checklists, generally	1.2.1
insurance litigation	8.4, 8.5
initial defense	8.4, Form 8:1
discovery	8.4, Form 8:2
trial	8.4, Form 8:3
investigations	5.3.4
master trial	7.2, Form 7:5
medical litigation	9.5, 9.6.7.1

Index

Subject	Section
Civil appeal time sequence, Arizona	13.4.3 Form 13:1
Claims, corporate assistant's responsibilities	12.3.1, 12.3.3
Client acceptance of assistants	2.2.5.1
Client/assistant relationship, family law	11.2, 11.4, 11.8, 11.11
Client conference, initial	
bankruptcy matter	10.3.1
by insurance litigation assistant	8.10
investigative techniques in	5.3.1
Client data, personal injury case	9.6.2.1 Form 9:7
Client information form, family law	11.4 Form 11:2
Client interview	
by investigation assistant	5.3.1
initial telephone interview form	11.4 Form 11:1
Client interview sheet	5.3.1 Form 5:1
Client questionnaire, bankruptcy	10.3.2.1 10.3.4 Form 10:1
completeness of information in	10.3.2.2
Code of Professional Responsibility	5.1
Competitive service positions, federal	3.3
Computers, use of in litigation	3A3.6, 6.4
Conclusions of law, preparation of	13.3.1
Consultation with lawyer, initial (family law)	11.4
Consumer Product Safety Commission	12.9
Contested matters, bankruptcy	10.4.7
Continuing education of assistants	1.6, 2.3, 2.5.3, 9.2.4, 9.6.7
on-the-job education	1.3, 1.6
Control of assistant assignments	2.2.3
Convincing lawyer of need for an assistant	4.5
Cooperation among assistants	1.6, 2.4.1
Copying of documents	2.6.2
Corporate legal department, use of assistants in	12.1, 12.2
duties of corporate assistant	12.1, 12.3, 12.13
Corporate law department practice, characteristics of	12.2
Corporate reference books, employment information source	4.3.2.2

Subject	Section
Correspondence, preparation by litigation assistant	8.9
Cost statement on appeal	13.4.5
County recorder's office, in investigation	5.5.1
Court personnel, assistant's relationship with	7.10
bailiff	7.10.3
clerk of court	7.10.1
process servers	7.10.4
sheriff and others	7.10.4
Court reporter	6.4.1.1
	7.10.2
Court records, use in investigation	5.5.1
Creating a position as legal assistant	4.1, 4.6
Credit bureau check, for locating witness	5.4.5
Creditor's claims, payment of	10.4.5
preparation of	10.5.1
Creditor contacts	10.3.3
Creditor's meeting, first	10.3.4
Creditor representation	10.1, 10.5
Creditor's rights matters, corporate legal department	12.5
Custody issues, family law	11.9
Damaging evidence	5.6.1
Deadlines for assistant	2.7.1
Debtor relief under Bankruptcy Code	10.3
Debtor representation	10.1, 10.3.3
Debt reaffirmation agreement	10.3.8
Dedication to success of assistant program, lawyers'	2.3.1
Delegation of lawyer's responsibilities	1.2.1, 1.2.3.2
Department of Interior, use of paralegals in	3.6
Depositions	
analysis of	7.5.1
	Forms 7:7, 7:9
arrangements for taking	7.5, 11:6
	Form 7:9
assistant feedback on	12.3.6
cross-examination in trial, use of	7.5.4.1
	7.5.4.2
conflicting testimony in	6.3.2.4
digest of	6.3.2, 6.3.2.1
chronological form	6.3.2.1, 6.3.2.3
colloquy in	6.3.2.4
format for	6.3.2.3

Subject	Section
index	6.3.2.1
information to include in	6.3.2.4
language techniques	6.3.2.2
narrative form	6.3.2.1
sequential form	6.3.2.3, Form 6:3
subject matter form	6.3.2.3, Form 6:4
effective use of	7.5
expert witness (corporate law department)	12.3.6
index of	6.4.1.2, Form 6:5 7.5.1, Form 7:7
lawyer's use of	7.5.2
on written interrogatories	7.5, Form 7:9
responsibilities of litigation assistant	8.11
summary of	6.3.3
system for filing	6.4.1
transcript collection in corporate file	12.3.6
trial use of	7.5.4, 7.5.4.3
witness's use of	7.5.3
Development of assistant's capabilities	1.7
Dictation by assistant	1.4.1
Dictation equipment, expense of	2.2.2.6
Digest of depositions—see Depositions, digest of	
Director of Administration, job description	2.5.1, Form 2:4
Directories, use of in investigation	5.4.1
Disability cases	12.4.3
Discharge hearing in bankruptcy	10.3.8
Discharge of debtor	10.3.7
opposition by trustee	10.4.6
Discovery, generally	6.1, Form 7:9
complex litigation	6.1
checklist for	8.4, Form 8:2
coordination of	6.3.1, 6.3.1.3
family law cases	11.6
insurance litigation cases	8.10
research and analysis based on	6.3
specialist, in corporate law	12.3
systems for coordinating	6.3.1
Diversity of assignments	2.7.6
Diversity of knowledge, corporate assistant	12.3.5
Divorce case—see Family law practice	

Subject	Section
Docket control entries	7.2, Form 7:2
Docket search, in investigation	5.5.1
Docket system for appeals	13.4.4
Documenting pain, suffering and disability	9.6.2.2 Form 9:8
Document control in corporate legal department	12.3.2, 12.3.3
Documents—see also specific legal subject	
assistant's role in	6.6
corporate assistant's review and analysis of	12.9
organization of in complex litigation	6.1
Document management in complex litigation and discovery	6.4
Document preparation by assistant—see specific legal subject	
Documents produced	6.4.2.2
filing	6.5.2.4
indexing	6.4.2.2 Form 6:6 Form 6:7
Document retrieval in complex litigation	6.5
assistant's role in	6.5.1
guidelines for	6.5.2
legal pleadings	6.5.2.2
research, filing of	6.5.2.3
simplicity of system	6.5.2.1
support personnel's role in	6.5.1
Driver's license search, in investigation	5.4.4
Duplication cost of medical records	9.6.1.4
Duties of assistant—see specific legal subject	
Economic need for assistants	2.2.1
Education of assistant by firm	9.2.3 Form 9:2
Educational programs for assistants	1.3, 1.9
Educational requirements, generally	1.3
for medical-legal assistant	9.2.1, 9.2.2
Emotional problems of client, family law	11.1
Employment claims, labor relations assistant	12.4.1
Employment discrimination cases	12.4.2
Ethical considerations in use of assistants	5.1, 7.11, 8.6
Evaluation of assistants	2.5.4, Form 2:5
Evaluation of law practice, need for assistants	1.2, 1.4.1
Evaluation of property, family law	11.7
Exempt property, claims for in bankruptcy	10.3.2.4

Index

Subject	Section
Exhibits	7.4
filing system for	6.4.1
index of	7.4.1.1
list of	7.4.3, Form 7:6
numbering of	7.4.3
offering in court	7.4.4
preparation of	7.4.2
system for control of	7.4
cross-references in	7.4.1.2
maintenance of during trial	7.4.5
reconstruction of	7.4.1.3
requirements	7.4.1
use of during trial	7.4.4
Expense account, assistant's	9.6.1.4
Expense factors in employment of assistants—see also specific expense items (office, furniture, etc.)	2.2.2, Form 2:1
Expert witness	5.6.3, 8.12, 12.3.6
ABA Journal advertisements	5.6.3
Fact-gathering by assistant, generally	5.1, 5.7
Fair employment practices, labor relations assistant	12.4.2
Family law practice	11.1, 11.11
assistant's qualifications for	11.2, 11.10
assistant's role in	11.3
document preparation	11.4, Form 11:2
fee arrangements	11.4
financial information from client, completeness of	11.5, 11.6
stages in case development	11.3
conclusion	11.8
decision	11.4
discovery	11.6
evaluation	11.7
maintaining status quo	11.5
unique problems in	11.1
Federal paralegal classification standards	3.4
Fee income, assistants' contribution to	2.2.4, Form 2:1
File control sheet	5.3.5, Form 5:4
File index, complex litigation	6.5.2.4, Forms 6:8, 6:9
File maintenance and control, corporate legal department	12.3.7
File organization	5.3.5, Form 5:4
File summary by litigation assistant	8.7
Financial contribution of assistants to firm	1.2.3.2, 1.5
Financial Disclosure Reports, Ethics Act	3.6

Subject	Section
Financial information form, family law	11.5, Form 11:3
Financial spread sheets, checking account information	11.5, Form 11:4
Findings of fact, preparation of	13.3.1
Firm administration, assistant's role in	2.8
small firms	2.8.1
income production	2.8.3
medium to large firms	2.8.2
Firm administrator, job description	2.5.1, Form 2:3, 2:4
Forms, generally—see also specific legal subject	1.2.1
client interview form	1.2.1
Form books, use of	4.6.1, Form 7:9
Forwarding address (postal check) for locating witness	5.4.2
Fraud, land and securities—research of	6.2.2.3
Fringe benefits for assistants	2.2.2.4
Furniture, assistant's office	2.2.2.7
Further review of appeal	13.3.5
Government agencies,	
assistant's contact with employees of	6.2.2.2
as employment source	4.3.2.3
jurisdiction, research of	6.2.2.2
Government litigation assistant—see Litigation, federal	
Group interview of assistant	2.5.2
Hearings and trials, assistant's responsibilities	7.2, 9.6.6
"Hierarchy of needs," Maslow	1.4.1
Historical background, format for	6.2.2.1
Historical report based on interviews (oral history)	6.2.2.1
Historical research and analysis	6.2.2
Hospital records, administrator of	9.4.3
ethical considerations	9.4.3, 9.4.4
Income production by assistants	2.2.4, Form 2:1
Incorporation checklist	5.3.4, Form 5:3
Index of exhibits to depositions	6.4.1.2
Indexing file information, corporate legal department	12.3.4
Index of major cases for use in trial	7.7.2
Information retrieval system	9.6.1.6, 13.3.3, 13.4.5
Initial defense checklist, insurance litigation	8.4, Form 8:1

Index

Subject	Section
Insurance defense litigation, generally	8.1, 8.16
assistant's duties in	8.3
instruction manual for	8.4
use of assistants in	8.1, 8.2, 8.16
Interrogatories	
corporate assistant's duties	12.3.5
drafting and wording of	6.3.1.1
form for	6.3.1.1, Forms 6:1, 6:2
personal injury cases	9.6.5
preparation of, generally	6.3.1.1, Form 7:9
preparation of by litigation assistant	8.10
Interview arrangements, for employment as assistant	4.4
Interview of assistant by office administrator	2.5.2
Interviewing techniques, generally	5.6.1
in personal injury cases	9.6.2
Introduction letter from lawyer	4.3.1.2
Investigation by assistants	5.1, 5.7
by litigation assistant	8.12
initial stages of	5.3
objectives of	5.3.3
other sources of information	5.4.6
Judges' recognition of assistant's fees	2.2.5.2
Judgment, preparation of form of	13.3.1
Jurisdictional disputes in firm	1.4.1
Jury information in trial book	7.3
Jury instructions	7.8
preparation of	7.8.1
presentation of	7.8.3
use of, in preparation for trial	7.8.2
Labor case flow chart	9.5.1, Form 9:4
Labor relations assistant	12.4
Language techniques in deposition digest	6.3.2.2
Law firm, definition of	1.1
Lawyer/assistant relationship—see also specific legal subject	2.7.2
in bankruptcy practice	10.2
in investigation by assistant	5.2
Lawyers, as source of potential employment as assistant	4.3.1.2
Lawyer supervision of assistant	1.4.1, 2.3.1, 9.4
Legal administrator, job description	2.5.1, Forms 2:3, 2:4
Legal assistant committee	1.6

Subject	Section
Legal authorities, use in trial	7.7
Legal clerk/technician series (federal agencies)	3.4
Legal practice, government vs. private	3.1
Legal secretaries as assistants	1.3
Legislative assistant, duties of	12.12
Legislative history and analysis	12.12
Letter of application for employment as assistant	4.4.1
Liquidations, in bankruptcy	
of assets	10.3.5, 10.3.8
of property	10.4.3
Litigation, federal government	3.8, 3A3.1, Form 3:3
computers in	3A3.6
discovery in	3A3.4
duties of paralegal	3A3.3.2
exhibits	3A3.8
exhibit books	3A3.9
legal clerk's role	3A3.3.4
legal technician's role	3A3.3.3
paralegal's role	3A3.3.1
review of documents	3A3.5
team approach	3A3.2
testimony	3A3.12
trial brief	3A3.7
trial record	3A3.11
witness folders	3A3.10
Litigation legal assistant, generally	7.1, 7.12
corporate legal department	12.3
job description	2.8.2, Form 2:2
responsibilities in insurance litigation	8.6
correspondence preparation	8.9
file summary	8.7
pleading preparation	8.8
suspense cards (tickler)	8.6
Local counsel/corporate assistant relationship	12.3.2
Loss of wages and profits summary	9.6.1.2
	Form 9:5
Magnuson-Moss Act	12.9
Managing clerk/litigation assistant, job description	2.8.2, Form 2:2
Management by exception	1.2.2
Management by objectives	1.2.2, 1.2.3.1
Management program, legal assistants	1.2.3.2
bibliography for program managers	1.10
Medical expenses, itemized statement of	9.6.1.2.1

Index

Subject	Section
Medical-legal assistant	9.1
bibliography	9.9
forms for	9.8
job description	9.1, Form 9:1
Medical library maintenance	9.6.1.6
Medical records	
ownership of	9.4.2
release form for	9.4.1, 9.6.2.5
	Form 9:10
subpoena for	9.4.2, 9.4.3
Medical reports, interpretation of	9.6.3
Medical research by medical-legal assistant	9.6.3.1, 9.6.4
Meeting of creditors, bankruptcy	10.3.4
Mineral rights, research of	6.2.2.1
Monthly status report, by litigation assistant	8.15, Form 8:5
"Moot court" argument of appeal	13.3.4
Motivation of assistants	1.4
Motor vehicle department, use in skip-tracing	5.4.4, Form 5:7
Newspapers, use in seeking employment as assistant	4.3.4
Notebook and index of assets, family law	11.6
Office administrator, generally	2.5
education of assistants	2.5.3
evaluation of assistants	2.5.4
interviewing and hiring assistants	2.5.2
role of	2.5.1
Office manager/administrative assistant	12.13
Office of Personnel Management, federal	3.3
Office policies and procedure	2.3.2
Office rent, assistant's	2.2.2.5
On-the-job training of assistants	1.3, 1.6, 4.2
Opposing counsel's acceptance of assistant	2.2.5.3
Oral argument of appeal, assistant's participation in	13.3.4
Orientation of assistants	1.2.3.2
Outline of procedural steps and time limits, Arizona civil appeal	13.4.3
	Form 13:1
Pain, suffering and disability, documentation of	9.6.2.2
	Form 9:8
Paralegals (legal assistants in federal government)	3.1, Form 3.3
advantages in hiring	3.2
delegation of work to	3.7
effective use of	3.6
hiring of	3.3, 3.5
job description	3.5, Forms 3:1, 3:2

Subject	Section
Paralegal series—GS-950, federal employee	3.4
Part Time Act	3.3
Patents, in corporate legal department	12.10
Patient information release form	9.4.1, Form 9:10
Personal injury investigation checklist	5.3.4, Form 5:2
Personal injury flow chart	9.5.1, Form 9:3
Personal injury practice, generally	9.1, 9.7
assistants in	9.1
interviewing in	9.6.2
medical agencies	9.6.2.4 Form 9:9
preliminary information	9.6.2.1 Form 9:7
witness interviews	5.6, 9.6.2.3
Personality requirements for assistants	1.3
Personal preference, type of assistant employment sought	4.2
Physicians, information from	9.4.4
Physician form letter	9.6.2.4 Form 9:9
Pleadings, preparation by litigation assistant	8.8
Portfolio, documents previously prepared by job applicant	4.5.1
Post-filing matters, bankruptcy	10.3.5
Post-office check, for locating witness	5.4.2
Production of documents, system for handling	6.4.2
court reporter's assistance in	6.4.2.1
Product requirements, corporate assistant's duties	12.9
Professional and Administrative Career Examination (federal)	3.4
Profitability considerations concerning assistants	1.5, 2.2.2
Projected income, assistants'	2.2.2, Form 2:1
Project manager, responsibilities of	1.2.3.1
Project teams (task groups)	1.2.3.1
Promises, unkept	2.7.5
Promotion to assistant position in present firm	4.3.1.1
Proof of claim forms, bankruptcy	10.5.1
Property, liquidation of in bankruptcy	10.4.3
Property pathfinder form, family law cases	11.6, Form 11:5
Property records in investigation	5.5.1
Property taxes, corporate assistant's duties	12.7
Publicity, adverse	6.2.1
Publicity research, possible change of venue	6.2.1

Index

Subject	Section
Questionnaire, witness—use in interview	5.6.2
	Form 5:8
Quotas, for assistants	2.2.3
Real estate transaction, aid by corporation to employee	12.6
Record of case, trial level	
appeal considerations	13.2
organization for appeal	13.3.2
Record on appeal	13.3.2
Records department, relationship with assistants	2.4.4
Recordkeeping, in personal injury litigation	9.6.1
file organization	9.6.1.1
financial information	9.6.1.2
Recruiting assistants	1.3
Reference books, as source of employment	4.3.2
bar directories	4.3.2.1
corporate reference books	4.3.2.2
legal association directories	4.3.2.2
Martindale-Hubbell	4.3.2.1
Reference directions for litigation assistant	8.5, Form 8:4
"Registers" of eligible government personnel	3.3
Registrar of voters, use in skip-tracing	5.4.3
Relationships of assistants in trial practice	
with court personnel	7.10
with lawyers	7.11
Report to client, by litigation assistant	8.6, 8.16
Reporting results of investigation, by memorandum	5.3.3
Reproduction of cases, for use in court	7.7.2
Requests for admission	6.3.1
drafting of	6.3.1.2
preparation of	6.3.1.2, Form 7:9
Request for oral argument of appeal	13.4.5
Request for production of documents	6.3.1
by corporate assistant	12.3.5
drafting of	6.3.1.3
Research, various substantive law areas	6.2.4
Responsibilities of assistant—see also specific legal area	
defining in early stages of employment	4.6.1
family law practice	11.10
generally	1.7
Resume	4.4.1
Retaining paralegals, guidelines for	3.6, Form 3:4
Retreat for assistants	2.3.4

Subject	Section
Retrieval system	9.6.1.6 13.3.3, 13.4.5
Review and evaluation of assistants	1.6
Review conferences, format for	1.6
Review process	1.2.3.2, 1.6
Routing system, for appeal documents	13.4.4
Rules of Bankruptcy Procedure, forms in	10.3.2
Salaries for assistants	1.5, 2.2.2.1
Satisfaction of judgment, insurance litigation	8.14
Schedule of assets and liabilities, bankruptcy	10.3.2 10.3.2.5
Schedule of liabilities, preparation of	10.3.2.3
Secretarial and clerical support for assistants	1.4.1, 2.2.2.2, 2.4.2, 2.6.1
Secretarial expense, for assistants	2.2.2.2 Form 2:1
Secretary, promotion to assistant position	1.3
Section meeting, assistant participation in	1.6
Secured creditors, collateral involved (bankruptcy)	10.5.2
Settlement decisions in family law, assistant's duties	11.6
Settlement negotiations, family law	11.8
Settlement of insurance defense litigation	8.14
Skip-tracing, locating witness	5.4
Skip-trace worksheet	5.4, Form 5:5
Social Security Administration, use in skip-tracing	5.4.6
Sources of assistants	1.3
Sources of investigative information	5.5.2
Special damages summary, personal injury litigation	9.6.1.2 9.6.1.2.2 Form 9:6
Special issue number, request for	7.8.1, Form 7:8
Specialization, of federal employees	3.6
Statement of affairs, bankruptcy	10.3.2
Statement of witness	5.6.2
Statistical research summary, checklist for	6.2.3
Status quo stage, family law case	11.5
Statutory stay order, bankruptcy	10.3.3
Stress, generally	2.7, 2.9
Sub-interrogatories, form of	6.3.1.1 Form 6:1
Substantive training of assistants	2.3.3

Index

Subject	Section
Summary	
of depositions	6.3.3
of medical expenses	9.6.1.3
of special damages and wage loss	9.6.1.2, Form 9:6
Supervising lawyer, responsibilities	1.2.3.2, 1.4.1
Support of assistants, from other personnel	2.4, 2.6
Support staff ratio, federal vs. private	3.3
Suspense card, maintenance by litigation assistant	8.6
Systems approach, generally	1.2.1
application to assistants	1.2.3.1
family law practice	11.4
for handling assignments	4.7
medical-legal assistant	9.5, 9.6.7
paralegals in federal government	3.6
Systems management techniques	1.2.1, 1.2.3.1
Task analysis, medical-legal assistant	9.6
Taxes, payroll and unemployment	2.2.2.3
Taxes, corporate assistant's responsibilities	12.7
Tax indebtedness, bankruptcy	10.3.2.3
Team approach, in federal agencies	3.8, Form 3:3
Telephone directories, in investigation	5.4.1
Telephone interview arrangements, for employment	4.4.2
Telephone interview form, family law	11.4, Form 11:1
Temporary hearing, family law	11.5
Territorial rights, research of	6.2.2.1
Time records, assistant in family law	11.10
Time sequence summaries, appeals	13.4.3
Time use/task analysis, medical-legal assistant	9.3
Title and registration search	5.4.4, Form 5:7
Transcription, errors in	6.3.2.2
Transfers of property	10.4.2
Transportation of goods, corporate assistant's duties	12.8
Transportation legislation, corporate record of	12.8
Trial, generally	7.1
participation of assistant	7.3
responsibilities of assistant, family law	11.8
Trial book	7.2
argument section of	7.3
organization of	7.2
procedures for	7.2, Forms 7:1, 7:2, 7:3, 7:4
Trial brief, timing and use of	7.7.1

Subject	Section
Trial checklist	7.2, Form 7:5
insurance defense litigation	8.4, Form 8:3
Trial coordination, by litigation assistant	8.13
Trial manual, discovery section	7.4.3, Form 7:9
Trial notes, generally	7.9
date and time taken	7.9.1
exhibits in	7.9.3
objections and rulings in	7.9.4
stylistic considerations	7.9.5, 6.3.2.2
use of by appellate assistant	13.3.1
witness and lawyer names in	7.9.2
Trial practice, use of assistants in	7.1
Trial transcript, digest of	6.3.4
use of in appeal	13.3.1
Trustee's responsibilities, in bankruptcy	10.4.1
Turnover costs, in hiring new assistants	2.2.2
Unavailability of lawyers	2.7.2
Uniform Commercial Code filings	10.3.2.3
"Unsuccessful" interview	4.5.3
Voir dire examination, in trial book	7.3
Voter registration information, in investigation	5.4.3, Form 5:6
Water rights, research of	6.2.2.1
Witness	
expert	5.6.3, 8.12, 12.3.6
location by investigation, skip-tracing	5.4
reluctant	5.6.2
Witness information, in corporate legal department	12.3.3
Witness interviews, generally	5.6, 5.6.1
Witness list	7.6
Witness statement, generally	5.6.1
exhibit information in	7.6.1
Witness questionnaire	5.6.2, Form 5:8
Word processing	
assistant access to	1.4.1, 2.6.1, 2.7.3
assistant/staff relationship	2.4.5
use of by medical-legal assistant	9.5.1
Worker's disability cases	12.4.3
Working relationships, generally	2.1
with other assistants	2.4.1
with support staff	2.4

Index

Subject	Section
Workmen's compensation	
corporate assistant's duties	12.4.3
medical-legal assistant's duties	9.7
Writing sample, in application for employment	4.5.1
Work area, conditions	2.2.2.5, 2.2.2.7, 2.7.4

TABLE OF CITATIONS

Articles	Section
S. Abrahamson, *Some Thoughts About Appellate Argument,* Wis. Bar. Bull., Feb., 1979, at 41.	13.5
"Adoption of Employee Selection Procedures," 43 Fed. Reg. 38,290 (Aug. 25, 1978)	3.5
J. Brill, *How Planning Your Practice Will Produce Pleasure and Profitability!,* Legal Economics, Spring, 1978, at 11	1.10
M. Closen and M. Ginsberg, *Preparation and Presentation of the Oral Argument in a Court of Review,* 13 New Eng. L. Rev. 265 (1977)	13.5
J. Davis, *The Argument of an Appeal* (delivered to the Association of the Bar of the City of New York, October 22, 1940)	13.5
E. Devitt, *The Search for Improved Advocacy in the Federal Courts,* 13 Gonz. L. Rev. 897 (1978)	13.5
W. Erickson, *Effective Appellate Advocacy,* Colo. Law., September, 1978, at 1548	13.5
C. Essrick, *Managing Litigation for the Federal Government* (1980)	Form 3:3
H. Feder, *How to Get a Case Ready for Trial,* in Manual for Managing the Law Office ¶7075 (Prentice-Hall, Inc., 1970)	7.2
J. Gardner, *How to Prevent Organizational Dry Rot,* Harper's Magazine, Oct. 1965, at 21	1.10
G. Gilhool, *Working Together: Professional and Paraprofessional,* Trial, Feb. 1978, at 54	1.10
J. Godbold, *Twenty Pages and Twenty Minutes — Effective Advocacy on Appeal,* 30 Sw. L. J. 801 (1976)	13.5

Articles	Section
L. Haire and P. Ulrich, *Writing an Appellate Practice Handbook: A Team Approach to Preparing Continuing Legal Education Texts*, Ariz. B. J., Dec. 1977, at 60, reprinted in ALI-ABA CLE Review, Nos. 1-3, Jan. 1978	Intro.
J. Harlan, *What Part Does the Oral Argument Play in the Conduct of an Appeal?*, 41 Cornell L. Q. 6 (1955)	13.5
F. Herzberg, *One More Time: How Do You Motivate Employees?*, Harv. Bus. Rev., Jan.-Feb. 1968, at 53	1.10
R. Jackson, *Advocacy Before the Supreme Court: Suggestions For Effective Case Presentations*, 37 A.B.A.J. 801 (1951)	13.5
I. Kaufman, *Appellate Advocacy in the Federal Courts*, 79 F.R.D. 165 (1978)	13.5
Litigation, Winter, 1978 (appellate topics generally)	13.5
G. Miller, *On Legal Style*, 43 Ky. L. J. 235 (1955)	13.5
J. Napoli, *Forceful Brief Writing and Oral Argument*, 12 Trial Law. Q. 82 (1977)	13.5
W. Oncken, Jr. and D. Wass, *Management Time: Who's Got the Monkey?*, Harv. Bus. Rev., Oct.-Nov. 1974, at 95	1.10
A. Reilly, *Courtroom Advocacy*, 8 Cap. U. L. Rev. 185 (1978)	13.5
Resolutions, 54 A.B.A.J. 1017, 1021-22 (1968)	Intro.
R. Simons, *Effective Appellate Advocacy*, N.Y. St. B.J., January, 1976, at 18	13.5
W. Statsky, *The Education of Legal Paraprofessionals: Myths, Realities and Opportunities*, 24 Vand. L. Rev. 1083 (1971)	1.10
W. Statsky, *Techniques for Supervising Paralegals*, 22 Practical Lawyer No. 4, at 81 (1976)	1.10
D. Thomas, *Strategy Is Different in Service Businesses*, Harv. Bus. Rev., July-Aug. 1978, at 158	1.10
L. Tracy, *Postscript to the Peter Principle*, Harv. Bus. Rev., July-Aug., 1972, at 65	1.10
B. Turner, *Finding People to Help Us*, in People in the Law Office (A.B.A. 1978)	2.5.2
L. Turner, *Effective Use of Lay Personnel*, in Proceedings of the Third National Conference on Law Office Economics and Management 27 (A.B.A. 1969)	Intro.
P. Ulrich and S. Clarke, *Building Your Firm's Legal Assistant Program*, Ariz. B. J., Oct. 1976, at 20, reprinted in 19 LOEM 117 (1978)	1.10

Index

Articles	Section
P. Ulrich and C. Multhauf, *Law Firm Working Relationships: Developing a Long-Term Legal Assistant Program,* 20 LOEM 289 (1979)	1.2.2, 1.10
P. Ulrich, *Managing an Effective Legal Assistant Program,* Ariz. B. J., Aug. 1978, at 42, *reprinted in* Legal Economics, Jan.-Feb. 1979, at 35	1.10
P. Ulrich, *Managing a Law Practice "By Objectives and Self-Control,"* 20 LOEM 183 (1979)	1.2.2, 1.10
P. Ulrich, *Organizing and Preserving Our Work Product,* 21 LOEM 215 (1980)	13.3.3
U. S. Civil Service Commission Standards Bulletin 930-17, Aug. 11, 1976	3.4
J. Wallace, *Wanted: Advocates Who Can Argue in Writing,* 67 Ky. L. J. 375 (1978-79)	13.5
M. Wallace, *Designing a Manual System for Legal Research Memoranda,* Legal Economics, Mar.-Apr. 1980, at 27	13.3.3
R. Wydick, *Plain English for Lawyers,* 66 Calif. L. Rev. 727 (1978)	13.5

Books	Section
A.B.A., People in the Law Office, Eighth National Conference on Law Office Economics and Management (1978)	1.10
M. Altman and R. Weil, How to Manage Your Law Office (Matthew Bender 1976)	1.10
AMA Guide to the Evaluation of Permanent Impairment (A.M.A., 1971)	9.9
Anatomy and Physiology (Health Education Aids 1972)	9.9
Appellate Procedure in Texas (Texas Bar Foundation, 2d ed. 1979)	13.4.2
J. Appleman, Approved Appellate Briefs (1958)	13.5
Arizona Appellate Handbook (State Bar of Arizona 1978)	13.4.2
E. Berne, The Structure and Dynamics of Organizations and Groups (J.B. Lippincott Co. 1963)	1.10
R. Blanchard, Litigation and Trial Practice for the Legal Paraprofessional (West Publishing Co., Paralegal Series 1978)	5.5.2, 9.9
R. Bolton, People Skills (Prentice-Hall, Inc. 1979)	1.10
C. Bruno, Paralegal's Litigation Handbook (Institute for Business Planning, Inc., 1980)	1.10, 4.3.2.2, 4.3.2.3, 4.4, 4.4.2, 6.2.3

Books	Section
W. Cobb, Planning Workbook for Law Firm Management (A.B.A. 1978)	1.10
F. Cole, Guide to Medical Reports (Med. Exam. Pub. Co. 1973)	9.9
W. Curran, Law and Medicine (Little, Brown & Co., 1960)	9.9
E. Dale, Management Theory and Practice (McGraw-Hill, 2d ed. 1969)	1.10
Dorland's Medical Dictionary (W.B. Saunders Co., 25th ed., 1974)	9.9
P. Drucker, The Effective Executive (Harper & Row 1966)	1.10
P. Drucker, The Practice of Management (Harper & Row 1954)	1.10
A. Frenay, Understanding Medical Terminology (Catholic Hospital Foundation, 1973)	9.9
J. Gardner, Self-Renewal (Perennial Lib. Ed. 1971)	1.10
H. Gray, Gray's Anatomy of the Human Body (Lea & Fiberger 1973)	9.9
F. Herzberg, Work and the Nature of Man (World Pub. Co. 1966)	1.10
S. Hornwood, Systematic Settlements (Bancroft-Whitney 1979)	9.6.7.1, 9.9
M. Houts and L. Marmor, Proving Medical Diagnosis and Prognosis (Matthew Bender Co. 1977)	9.9
A. Lakein, How to Get Control of Your Time and Your Life (Signet 1973)	1.10
D. Larbalestrier, Paralegal Practice and Procedure (Prentice-Hall, Inc. 1977)	1.10
Law Office Economics and Management Manual (Callaghan & Co. 1970)	1.10
R. Mackenzie, The Time Trap (McGraw-Hill 1972)	1.10
D. Mackintosh, Management by Exception: A Handbook With Forms, (Prentice-Hall, Inc. 1978)	1.10
P. Mali, Management by Objectives (Wiley-Interscience 1972)	1.10
Manual for Managing the Law Office (Prentice-Hall, Inc. 1970)	1.10
C. Marwick, ed., Litigation Under the Amended Federal Freedom of Information Act (Center for National Security Studies, 4th ed. 1978)	6.2.2.2
A. Maslow, Motivation and Personality (Harper & Row, 2d ed. 1970)	1.10
H. McCormick, Social Security Claims and Procedures (West Publishing Co., 2d ed. 1978)	9.9

Index

Books	Section
D. McGregor, The Human Side Of Enterprise (McGraw-Hill 1960)	1.10
D. McGregor, The Professional Manager (McGraw-Hill 1967)	1.10
Medical Terminology, an Individualized Approach (Westinghouse Learning Press 1975)	9.9
A. Mosier, Medical Records Technology (Bobbs-Merrill 1975)	9.9
R. Murdick and J. Ross, Information Systems for Modern Management (Prentice-Hall, Inc., 2d ed. 1975)	1.10
J. Newman, Release Your Brakes! (Charles B. Stack, Inc. 1977)	1.10
L. Peter, The Peter Prescription (Morrow 1972)	1.10
Physician's Desk Reference (Medical Economics Co., 34th ed., 1980)	9.9
M. Pittoni, Brief Writing and Argumentation (3d ed. 1967)	13.5
R. Ramo, ed., How to Create-A-System for the Law Office (A.B.A. 1975)	1.2.1, 1.10, 3.7, 4.7
J. Ross, Managing Productivity (Reston Publishing Co., Inc. 1977)	1.10
J. Ross, Modern Management and Information Systems (Reston Publishing Co., Inc. 1977)	1.10
G. Rossman, Advocacy and the King's English (1960)	13.5
G. Smith and P. Davis, Medical Terminology, a Programmed Text (John Wiley 1976)	9.9
A. Soukhanov and J. Haverty, Webster's Medical Office Handbook (G. & C. Merriam Co. 1979)	9.9
W. Statsky, Introduction to Paralegalism (West Publishing Co. 1974)	1.10, 5.5.1
G. Steiner, ed., The Creative Organization (University of Chicago 1965)	1.10
R. Stern and E. Gressman, Supreme Court Practice §§ 13.6-13.13 (5th ed. 1978)	13.5
W. Strunk, Jr. and E. B. White, The Elements of Style (2d ed. 1972)	13.5
Survey of Law Firm Economics (Altman & Weil, Inc. 1980)	3.3
J. Thomas and W. Bennis, eds., Management of Change and Conflict (Penguin Books 1972)	1.10
R. Townsend, Up the Organization (Fawcett Crest Book 1970)	1.10
Use of Computers in Litigation (A.B.A. 1979)	6.4

Books   **Section**

J. VanFleet, How to Use the Dynamics of Motivation (Parker Publishing Co. 1967)	1.10
Washington Appellate Practice Handbook (Washington State Bar Association 1979)	13.4.2
H. Weihofen, Legal Writing Style (1961	13.5
V. Watenmaker and S. Faber, Fundamentals of Civil Procedure (Charing Cross Publishing Co., Inc., 1976)	6.3.2
F. Wiener, Briefing and Arguing Federal Appeals (1967)	13.5
G. Zaltman and R. Duncan, Strategies for Planned Change (Wiley-Interscience 1977)	1.10

Statutes and Rules	Section	Statutes and Rules	Section
5 U.S.C. § 552 (Freedom of Information Act)	6.2.2.2	11 U.S.C. § 545	10.4.2
		11 U.S.C. § 547	10.4.2
5 U.S.C. § 552A (Privacy Act of 1974)	6.2.2.2	11 U.S.C. § 548	10.4.2
		11 U.S.C. § 704	10.4.5
5 U.S.C. § 3304 (1967)	3.3	11 U.S.C. § 727	10.3.7, 10.4.6
5 U.S.C. § 3321 (1967)	3.3		
11 U.S.C. §§ 101 *et seq.* (1978) (Bankruptcy Code)	10.1	11 U.S.C. § 1322	10.3.6
		11 U.S.C. §§ 1322 (a) (1) and (2)	10.3.6
11 U.S.C. § 327	10.4.7	11 U.S.C. § 1322 (c)	10.3.6
11 U.S.C. § 342	10.3.3	11 U.S.C. § 1325 (4)	10.3.6
11 U.S.C. § 343	10.3.4		
11 U.S.C. § 362	10.5.2		
11 U.S.C. § 363	10.5.2		
11 U.S.C. § 507	10.3.6, 10.3.8, 10.5.1	5 C.F.R § 315.801 *et seq.* (1977)	3.3
		5 C.F.R. § 7.1 (1977)	3.3
11 U.S.C. § 521	10.3.5	5 C.F.R. § 213.3102(d)	3.3
11 U.S.C. §§ 521 (2), (3)	10.3.5	Civil Service Reform Act of 1978, § 311	3.3
11 U.S.C. § 524 (a)	10.3.8		
11 U.S.C. §§ 524 (c), (d)	10.3.8	Rules of Bankruptcy Procedure, Rule 701	10.4.7
11 U.S.C. § 542	10.4.1		
11 U.S.C. § 543	10.4.1	Suggested Interim Bankruptcy Rule 2003	10.3.3
11 U.S.C. § 544	10.4.2		